Door County's
Emerald Treasure

Publication of this volume has been made possible with the support of John C. Brogan; Robert and Nancy Davis; the Door County Historical Society; the Herlache Foundation; the William and Myrna Kubly Family Foundation; John K. Notz Jr.; the Fred J. Peterson Foundation; William and Jean Quinlan; the Raibrook Foundation; and the Wisconsin Chapter of the American Society of Landscape Architects.

Door County's Emerald Treasure

A History of
Peninsula State Park

William H. Tishler

THE UNIVERSITY OF WISCONSIN PRESS

The University of Wisconsin Press
1930 Monroe Street
Madison, Wisconsin 53711

www.wisc.edu/wisconsinpress/

3 Henrietta Street
London WC2E 8LU, England

Library of Congress Cataloging-in-Publication Data
Tishler, William H.
Door County's emerald treasure : a history of Peninsula State Park /
William H. Tishler.
p. cm. — (Wisconsin land and life)
Includes bibliographical references and index.
ISBN 0-299-22074-5 (pbk. : alk. paper)
1. Peninsula State Park (Wis.)—History. I. Title. II. Series.
F587.D7T57   2006
977.5′63—dc22   2006006992

Dedicated to my family

AND THE MANY GENERATIONS OF

MY DOOR COUNTY ANCESTORS

Contents

Illustrations

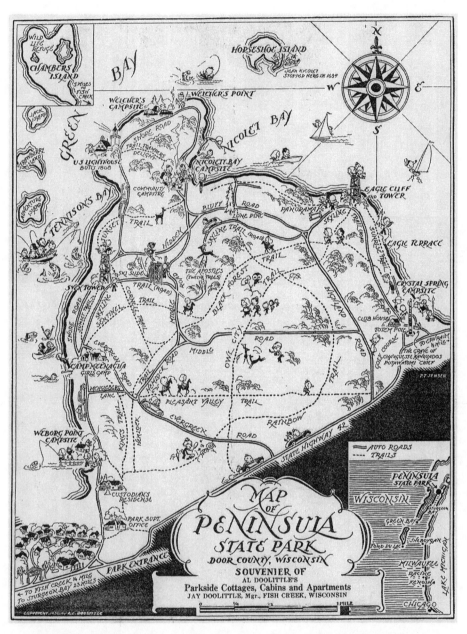

Whimsical souvenir map of the park provided by Al Doolittle's Cottages, Cabins, and Apartments situated at the Fish Creek entrance. The 1930s map portrays the park's principal natural and cultural features. (Courtesy Peninsula State Park office)

Preface

At the beginning of this century Wisconsin celebrated the one hundredth anniversary of its first state park. The purchase of land for Interstate State Park in 1900 marked the beginning of a system of magnificent state parks that would become the envy of the nation. This visionary system was conceived by the brilliant landscape architect John Nolen, who planned numerous parks and civic projects throughout the nation and in many Wisconsin communities. Nolen later described his 1909 report of the system as "one of the first systematic studies of state parks" in the nation.[1] Wisconsin's progressive action to establish state parks served as a model that many states would follow.

Nolen's landmark state park plan proposed setting aside four large tracts of remarkable scenic beauty. The first of these to be acquired was an elbow of land jutting into the waters of Green Bay on the Door County Peninsula. This landscape of more than thirty-seven hundred acres of magnificent forests, bluffs, shoreline, and breathtaking views became Peninsula State Park.

During the centennial celebration of Wisconsin's state parks, the *Milwaukee Journal Sentinel* polled its readers regarding their favorite park. It came as no surprise that Peninsula was chosen by an overwhelming margin.

As a native of northern Door County who went to Gibraltar High School on the very edge of the park at Fish Creek, I was always intrigued by this vast tract of scenic beauty. While a student at the University of Wisconsin in Madison, I spent two delightful summers working in the park while living at Nicolet Bay, the park's most popular destination. That proved to be an unforgettable experience. It shaped my decision to become a landscape architect—a career encouraged by then park superintendent Lowell G. Hansen, who had studied landscape architecture at both the university and The Clearing, under Jens Jensen. These experiences resulted in a lifelong interest in the park and all of the fascinating activities that occurred there during its colorful history.

This book is about that history. It is a story of the people, politics, dreams, and experiences of millions of persons who have fallen under the spell of Peninsula State Park, Door County's emerald treasure.

Acknowledgments

This book was a labor of love, but writing it was a daunting task that would not have reached fruition without the help of many people. I am especially appreciative for the vital support provided by the foundations and individuals listed on the donor page. Each saw the potential of this book and had a deep appreciation of the inestimable value that Peninsula State Park and Wisconsin's premier state park system have brought to countless individuals. Thanks to George Evenson, Mike Madden, and Maggie Weir for their advice in this regard.

I am also deeply indebted to Tom Blackburn, Steve Salemson, Jeff Weir, and Arnold Alanen for their help and encouragement.

I want to thank former students Linda Schmidt for her research on the park for an honors paper and Judith Borke and Carol Ahlgren, who wrote excellent masters theses that provided important aspects of the park's history.

I give special thanks to Laurence C. Day, who kindly loaned me a treasure trove of material, including back issues of *Pack and Padle,* about Camp Meenahga, which was started by his grandmother.

Several people were kind enough to review the manuscript and make important suggestions. These were Professor Margaret Bogue, Dr. Robert Dott, Bonnie Gruber, Kathleen Harris, and Professor Bill Laatsch. Diana Cook, Adam Mehring, and Carla Aspelmeier provided invaluable assistance in producing the book at the University of Wisconsin Press.

I was also fortunate to have Matt Baumgarten, Albert R. Czlapinski, and Jesse Ray—all excellent students in landscape architecture—help me with my research.

Thanks to Bruce A. Chevis, Signe Holtz, Sonja Slemrod, and Jim Treichel in the Wisconsin Department of Natural Resources for providing essential advice and information.

From Wisconsin's outstanding Historical Society, where I obtained much of the material for this book, I thank Rick Pifer, Harry Miller, James Hansen, and Geraldine Strey, as well as other staff members in Archives and Manuscripts and in the Microforms Reading Room.

I was fortunate to know people from northern Door County who shared precious memories and other important information about the park: Wilma Bettinger, Dick Boyd, Charles F. Calkins, Tim Cooke, Steve Grutzmacher, Dorothy Halvorsen, Ann and Fred Hansen, Paer Hansen, Kathleen Harris, Coggin Heeringa, Alvin Krause, Lucia Woods Lindley, Lynn Edmunds Mattke, Paula McCutcheon, Dianne Peil, Charles "Pat" Tishler, Elsie Krause Tishler, and Hank Whipple.

I am also extremely grateful for having grown up near the park and for a very special family and the values they instilled in me. They, along with my memories of the people I met and experiences I had while employed for two delightful summers at Peninsula, were the real inspiration for this book.

Finally, I want to acknowledge the love and patience of my wife, Betsy; my children, Bill and Robin, and their spouses; and my special grandson, James. Without their love and support this book could not have been written.

Door County's
Emerald Treasure

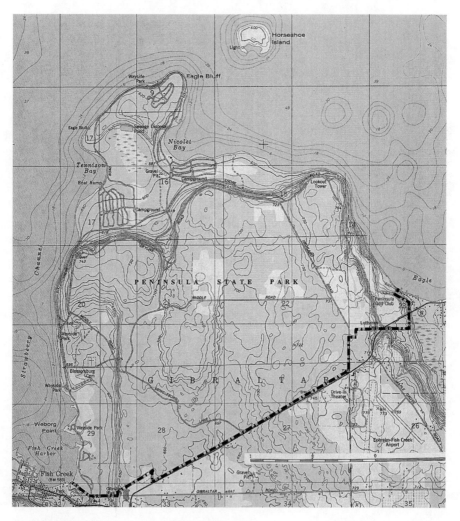

U.S. Geological Survey map of the park.

༄

CHAPTER I

Patterns of the Park's Landscape

Jutting into the shimmering waters of Green Bay between Fish Creek and Ephraim lies Peninsula State Park, one of Wisconsin's most scenic and popular vacation areas. This 3,776-acre emerald treasure has more than eight miles of shoreline, with sandy beaches and wave-washed rocks, plus a rich mixture of timber, wildlife, colorful undergrowth, and abrupt cliffs. These majestic dolomite outcrops almost attain the quiet dignity of mountains forming an indented arc that runs through the park and parallels the shoreline. Bathed in the golden hue of countless sunsets, the bluffs are the result of momentous events dating back five hundred million years or more.

Then, North America lay in the tropics. Over time it has moved slowly northward and rotated ninety degrees counterclockwise to its present location. The continent gradually sank beneath a vast tropical ocean—a large prehistoric extension of the Atlantic Ocean. A broad, bowl-shaped basin centered under present central Michigan subsided more rapidly than surrounding areas, and eastern Wisconsin formed the western rim of that Michigan basin. The first deposits in the ocean were sandstones, followed by shale and limestone from about 500 to 400 million years (Cambrian and Ordovician periods). Later, from 440 to 420 million years (Silurian period), dolomitic limestone was deposited.

Countless aquatic shelled animals and corals lived in this warm, Silurian saltwater sea, removing calcium carbonate from the seawater to create their shells and skeletal parts. Farther south, reefs grew on the sea floor. Over the centuries the animals lived, multiplied, and died, creating sediment on the ocean floor. The layers of this buildup of whitish lime, hardened by pressure, heat, and time, slowly formed limestone at the rate of an inch per several thousand years. Eventually this sedimentary rock reached hundreds of feet in thickness. Being more resistant than both under- and overlying strata, it has been eroded to form the prominent Niagara Escarpment—a major landscape feature in eastern Wisconsin.

The massive bluffs of Peninsula State Park are part of this dolostone outcropping. The huge Niagara Escarpment bowl forms a gigantic, 650-mile sickle-shaped cuesta extending along the northern shore of Lake Michigan, through Canada's Bruce Peninsula between Lake Huron and the Georgian Bay, and then jutting across Ontario to Niagara Falls, New York, where it was named.

Most of the marine deposition stopped after the Devonian period, around 350 million years ago, and the area started changing to dry land. Eventually, it was subjected to constant erosion, which removed younger layers to expose the Silurian dolostones of the Door Peninsula.

Then, about one million years ago, during the Ice Age, massive glaciers began to form in Canada and expand into the region. The last of the several glaciers to move over this area—the Wisconsin stage—came some fifty thousand years ago. This enormous ice sheet, estimated to be a few thousand feet thick in places, had an important role in shaping eastern Wisconsin. Its tremendous weight caused the land to sag and, as the ice reached the northern tip of Door County, it was split by the hard dolostone cuesta. One glacial lobe advanced in a southwesterly direction, forming the Green Bay–Lake

The bluffs of Peninsula State Park, along with its more than eight miles of shoreline, are the park's most distinctive features. (Author's collection)

Winnebago–Rock River lowlands. The other lobe continued southward down the Lake Michigan valley.

Beginning about fifteen thousand years ago, a change in climate caused the glacier to gradually recede and melt. As its weight diminished, the landmass of what is now Door County was lifted up and tilted gently to the east. The glacier also helped shape the peninsula, but as the ice sheet retreated northward, ancestral Lake Michigan sculpted the shoreline by forming terraces, wave-cut cliffs, sea caves, graveled beach ridges, and sand beaches. The general configuration of the park evolved into a series of bedrock highlands interspersed with bays of varied depositional material at Fish Creek, Tennison Bay, Nicolet Bay, and Eagle Harbor. As the landmass continued to rise with the reduced weight of the ice, caves cut by lake waves became elevated tens of feet above the present lake level where they can be seen in many of the lakeshore cliffs.

Today, evidence of primeval organisms from the Silurian ocean that once covered the peninsula can be found as fossils in the bedrock of the park. The most common and striking in appearance is the honeycomb coral, consisting of hexagonal-shaped tubes clustered together. Stromatopoids, extinct ancestors of sponges, can also be found. One of the most attractive is a robust brachiopod, which resembles a clam. Other fossils in the area include *Halysites* "chain corals," several forms of horn coral, and gastropods with their spiral, limy shells.

Eventually most of the region became densely forested. During the last half of the nineteenth century, however, much of the area's timber was harvested. On February 2, 1876, advertisements in the *Door County Advocate* said that A. Anderson of Ephraim wanted to buy cord wood, cedar posts, railroad ties, telegraph poles, posts, and bark (which was used for tanning), and P. Peterson of Ephraim wanted timber. Considering their proximity to the park area, some of the wood they purchased undoubtedly came from locations in what is now the park. In addition, on January 16, 1879, the *Advocate* noted that large quantities of firewood were being cut at Fish Creek. A variety of second-growth mixed coniferous and deciduous trees then sprang up in these cutover areas. Now, portions of the park's forest approach near-virgin maturity complete with spectacular pineries.

In fact, two of Wisconsin's now more than four hundred State Natural Areas (SNAs) are in Peninsula State Park. The State Natural Areas Program, in the Bureau of Endangered Resources of the Wisconsin Department of Natural Resources, was created by the legislature in 1951. An SNA is defined as "a tract of land in its natural state set aside and permanently protected or managed for the purpose of preservation of native plant or animal communities or of rare or valuable individual members of such communities."[1] The two park sites were recommended by the eminent plant ecologist John T. Curtis in 1952 and were among the first to be established.

Peninsula Park Beech Forest, SNA number 12, contains eighty acres. It can be reached via Shore Road, Highland Road, or the Sentinel Hiking Trail, which forms its northern boundary. The site features a continuum of forest types, from the dry edge of the Niagara Escarpment to rolling uplands forested with mesic species. The northern mesic forest is old second-growth timber with American beech, sugar maple, hemlock, yellow birch, white birch, and ironwood. The trunks of some trees in it are nearly two feet in diameter. The understory contains a variety of orchids and other wildflowers. Relict red oak and white pine are scattered through the area. To the east, between Shore Road and the bluff edge, is a young northern dry-mesic forest dominated by red oak and white pine. The bluff drops 150 feet to several terraces, which are forested with white cedar and hardwoods. The base of the bluff supports many ferns, while the beach is composed of dolomite cobblestones and little vegetation. Curtis used this site as a representative northern mesic forest study site.[2]

Peninsula Park White Cedar Forest, SNA number 13, is a forty-acre tract with access from Shore Road via the Sunset Trail, or Middle Road via Hemlock Trail. The area contains five distinct plant communities that change with elevation away from Green Bay. On the western side of the tract is a marsh and immediately east of it is an open calcareous meadow on a lake dune. A wet-mesic conifer swamp dominated by white cedar and black and white spruce is located in the transition between the lower and upper beach zones. Steep bluffs of Niagara dolomite, vegetated with ferns and other cliff-dwelling plants, are found on the western side. A mixed upland forest of mostly white cedar, white birch, and sugar maple is found at the top of the escarpment. Exceptional concentrations of lady's slippers and other orchids grow in the area. The bird life is characteristic of areas much farther north and includes winter wrens; red-breasted nuthatches; Nashville, black-throated green, and Blackburnian warblers; ovenbirds; and veeries.[3]

Mammals found in Peninsula State Park include deer, coyotes, raccoons, squirrels, chipmunks, possum, and foxes. Smaller creatures, including amphibians, invertebrates, and snails, are also prevalent. Some of the snails, found in the shaded bluffs, are considered quite rare.

According to Curtis's classic book *The Vegetation of Wisconsin,* the park lies within the northern mesic forest community—the state's largest forest community.[4] Its predominant trees are sugar maple, hemlock, beech, and birch.

Lesser numbers of other species include ironwood, red oak, American elm, red maple, white birch, white ash, and balsam fir. Additional northern mesic forest trees in the park include red oak, basswood, hawthorn, black cherry, white pine, red pine, jack pine, and trembling aspen. The ubiquitous white cedar (*Thuja occidentalis*) is abundant throughout much of the park, and it has established an amazing foothold along the steep Niagara Escarpment bluffs. Some of these trees are likely to be several hundred years old, and growing among them are rare ferns, sedges, and lichens. In wet areas of the park, such as the marsh near Weborg Point, black spruce and tamarack grow with white cedar and balsam fir.

The park understory vegetation includes Juneberry, buffalo berry, serviceberry, mountain maple, moosewood, sugarplum, and shadblow. Closer to ground level can be found grapevines, raspberry bushes, bittersweet, wintergreen, and poison ivy. Various stages of plant succession exist on disturbed areas, such as former cultivated fields, orchards, pastures, farmstead and building locations, burned over sites, and other areas of human activity. Here grow staghorn sumac, wild apple, juniper, lavender knapweed, mullein, butter-and-eggs, sow thistle, common St.-John's-wort, chicory, fleabane, fly campion, evening lichen, quack grass, crabgrass, bluegrass, brown eyed susan, strawberry, sweet everlasting, British soldier, pixie lichen, bracken fern, and an array of mosses. Shrubs include thimbleberry, raspberry, hazelnut, red-twigged dogwood, pussy willow, elderberry, mountain maple, Canada buffaloberry, and bunchberry.

Abundant stands of attractive wildflowers also grow in the park. These include trillium, hepatica, lady's slipper, fringed gentian, English violet, white baneberry, aster, trailing arbutus, bloodroot, trout lily, wood anemone, Dutchman's-breeches, bellwort, marsh marigold, jack-in-the-pulpit, goldenrod, squirrel corn, columbine, Queen Anne's lace, and rare lake iris. Unfortunately, with the deer population explosion in the park, some of these wildflowers have all but disappeared. Several invasive alien plants have also gained a foothold, especially honeysuckle and garlic mustard. They present a serious threat to native wildflowers, shrubs, and even the park's bird population.

Explorers, missionaries, fur traders, military expeditions, and travelers provided interesting early descriptions of the area. They traversed the shoreline of the park as they moved along the peninsula toward Fort Howard (now the city of Green Bay). Coming from the east through the Straits of Mackinac they paddled down the shore of northern Michigan until they came to the archipelago of islands lying across the mouth of Green Bay. Then they hugged the western side of the Door Peninsula. Some undoubtedly stopped at the protective bays at Eagle Harbor and Eagle Island to rest, fish, and hunt.

Early in the nineteenth century Samuel Storrow, a judge advocate in the U.S. Army, described Indian cultivation on what was probably Eagle Island after landing there in his birchbark canoe. Several years later, in 1830, James McCall noted the peninsula's bluffs that were "perhaps 150 feet [high] and almost perpendicular."[5] Traveling at the request of President Andrew Jackson, McCall was steaming toward Green Bay to settle differences and reservation disputes between the Menominees, Winnebagos, and other Indians.

By far, the best early accounts of the Door Peninsula landscape, including useful details of the area that would become the park, are found in notes and maps from the original land survey done during the spring of 1834 and 1835. Following standard government survey procedures, surveyors John Mullett and John Bruck established township and range lines first. The land encompassing the park fell within Township 31 North and Range 27 East—what later became the north half of Gibraltar Township. In May of 1834, they ran a survey line from the southeast corner of Section 36 in this township, due west to the waters edge of Green Bay. From the southeast corner of Section 36, they also ran a survey line north to the shoreline at Eagle Bluff. In his field notes, Mullett described the land as "rolling second and third rate" and "stony." The vegetation he recorded included "birch, beech, sugar [maple], hemlock, aspen, ironwood, and black oak." Curiously, his field notes also refer to measurements taken "on the ice" to Chambers Island—a distance he recorded as "4 miles and 32 links."[6]

Beginning March 18, 1834, Sylvester Sibley, a native of New York State, spent a year surveying the township's interior lines to establish the corners of its thirty-six sections. Summarizing the terrain in the "General Remarks" section of his field notes he wrote, "The country generally throughout in this town to the exception of the vicinity of Green Bay is rather rolling soil taken together is poor, second rate timber, birch, sugar [maple], hemlock, ironwood, cedar, birch, and tamarach, with some oak in places. Undergrowth beech, ironwood, hemlock. Stony banks mostly and high along Green Bay."[7] Measurements were also taken to Island No. 1 (Eagle Island) and Islands 2, 3, and 4 (the Strawberry Islands).

Maps created from the field measurements portray the shoreline and indicate the respective section lines and numbers. Two maps encompassed the area of the park. The uneven shoreline they portray was divided into numbered lots ranging from about fourteen to sixty-eight acres in size. The maps also include the four nearby islands (although the south-facing harbor of Eagle Island is not portrayed). Also shown is a long, narrow wetland beginning near the intersection of what is now Hemlock Road and Middle Road and extending south (through what is now Weborg Marsh), to well beyond the present location of the village of Fish Creek. Robert Lyth, surveyor general at the Surveyor General's Office in Cincinnati, signed his approval of the two maps on April 26, 1836.[8]

Early letters, diaries, and newspaper accounts also document the park landscape. Admiring the peninsula from Green Bay in a steamboat, one traveler from the East wrote this account of the park area in the *Milwaukee Sentinel:*

> No more lovely expanse of water can be found anywhere than here. . . . If there are no piles of blue mountains to make the distance complete, there are numerous islands that look like tufts of verdure in the distance, and expand as you approach into long stretches of forest, silent and wild. At times the shores come down abruptly to the water; and here and there miles of limestone cliff rise perpendicularly, among the trees, indented with beautiful harbors. In the middle of which there is frequently planted one of these verdant islands. . . . I cannot imagine any pleasanter summer trip than up or down this bay.[9]

Another traveler noted signs of early waterfront settlement as he sailed along the coast of the Door Peninsula in 1865: "The shore . . . is in many places high, bold, and rocky, and uniformly covered with a dense pine forest. All along the shore are occasional notches, cut back into the woods, in which could be seen the single house, or the mill, where the hardy lumberman, the fisherman, or the farmer, had taken up his residence."[10]

Writing from her hillside home in Ephraim in the fall of 1884, Anna Petterson admired her "very splendid" view looking across the "very, very blue" water of Eagle Harbor to the shore beyond where "a forest is now displaying its wonderful colors." The wife of a Moravian minister, she also described the ordeal of a journey home from the Blossomburg settlement in the park, where her husband had given a mission talk. The couple, traveling in a horse-drawn cart, took the "post road" home at the end of the day. Soon, she noted, darkness set in and they came to a dense forest "where the road is almost never dry—on the contrary, there were big holes," including what she referred to as "a lake, for you could hardly call it a ditch." Then, she added, "we had another fear—we weren't sure we were on the right road. There was not a house to be seen, not even a light." Finally, their shouting caught the attention of a local farmer who told them they were still two miles from Ephraim. Reaching home late that night, she wrote later that "it seemed impossible to us that we had not had a misfortune, and we thanked God."[11]

Even before the park was formally established, glowing reports about the potential of using the location for a park were being circulated. Advocating preservation of the site, Milwaukee's *Evening News* noted, "The agricultural possibilities on this rocky projection are meager, but the timber, and eventually the stone, may tempt commercial operations that would rob it of natural beauty."[12]

As a landscape architect with an astute eye for "reading the landscape," John Nolen wrote the following description of the park site in his 1909 report, *State Parks for Wisconsin:*

> It is wild and as yet unspoiled, with alternating interests of woodland and cliff, bay and land. Reminding one constantly of the coast of Maine, the shore with its many graceful indentations is a never-ending delight. It sweeps from point to point, here a beach of fine sand, there of gravel, then, in contrast, precipitous limestone bluffs, rising to a height of a hundred feet or more and covered with a heavy growth of native trees and shrubs, mostly evergreen. The vegetation is rich and varied. Extensive forests of pine, cedar, balsam, maple, basswood and birch, covering large tracts, with every now and then a pleasant opening in the more fertile, level land. Birds are numerous, as might be expected, and wild flowers abound. It is no exaggeration to say that the broad beauty of the scenery of this section is not surpassed in Wisconsin. Indeed . . . this type of scenery does not exist elsewhere in the State.[13]

In 1913 a writer on a large sailboat traveling north along the peninsula described the majestic bluffs in the park. He referred to "the Indian Head cliff in the park" on the west side of Eagle Harbor where they saw "the cave in the rocks."[14]

What was probably the first reasonably comprehensive map of the park was prepared by the Wisconsin Conservation Commission and dated July/August 1916. It names the park's six categories of natural areas as "open land, planted land, orchard, marsh, bluff and spring." Built features noted in the legend are "house, lighthouse, barn, tower, dock, cemetery, road, trail, telephone line and camp site.[15]

An excellent early map of Door County portraying important details about the park is in the 1918 *Soil Survey of Door County, Wisconsin,* a report prepared from field observations made in 1916 by the U.S. Department of Agriculture. Its large, colorful, foldout map designates ten soil types in the park, with Miami loam being the most prevalent. This soil type, derived from glacial material, predominates in Door County. The real value of this map, however, is that it also portrays important cultural features. These include each farm or dwelling, as well as roads and two cemeteries existing at that time.

Eagle Cave.

The park's fame as a veritable "Garden of Eden" began receiving more publicity. Even the 1923 *Wisconsin Blue Book* touted the glories of Peninsula Park:

> The park is well timbered. The flora is not extensive, but the forests (some of
> which are of virgin growth) of white and red pine, hemlock, balsam and hard-
> woods are beautiful. Several stands of white cedar are found along the shore
> and on the well moistened ledges, while in some of the fields, juniper and more
> rarely the shrubby yew (*Taxus canadensis*) give the effect of formal planting.
> The trails and pathways, which have been constructed through the fields and
> woods to the points of chief interest in the park are always delightful to the
> nature lover.
>   With the exception of three distinct bluffs, the land over the entire park is
> gently rolling. Svens Bluff. . . Norway Bluff. . . and Eagle Bluff. . . [rise] grad-
> ually from the south side, but on the side facing the water they drop abruptly,
> leaving precipitous cliffs of limestone, which vary from 10 to 200 feet above the
> water's level.[16]

In 1929, the Wisconsin Legislature appropriated money for a survey of land
use in the state. Called the Wisconsin Land Economic Inventory, the program
was directed by John S. Bordner, and later it was sometimes referred to as the
Bordner Survey because of his unflagging dedication to the project.[17] Over-
expansion of agricultural land during World War I and the decline of farming at the end of the war had resulted in abandoned lands, cutover areas, and
ill-conceived drainage projects. This idle land resulted in tax shortfall and tax
delinquency, and, consequently, the reversion of large tracts of land to public
ownership. The inventory assessed the land's current use, economic status, and
relative potential for farms, forests, and recreation areas. Using this information, counties could then develop appropriate zoning and plan reforestation
programs, watershed improvements, and recreation areas, while promoting
more intensive agriculture on better soils.

Field workers inventoried seventy counties, crossing the land at half-mile
intervals, reaching each forty-acre tract, while mapping an array of land char-
acterisics. Works Progress Administration (WPA) workers, in conjunction
with the Wisconsin State Planning Board, undertook the survey in Peninsula
State Park. Many of the field workers were local residents. The resulting map
for Township 31 North, Range 27 East, covers most of the Town of Gibraltar,
including the park. The maps classify most of the land in the park as "upland forest." The maps also indicate scattered patches of "cleared crop land,"
mostly along the west side of the park, along Middle Road and at the north

end of Highland Road. A "lowland forest/grass marsh" at the narrow stretch of land between Nicolet Bay and Tennison Bay also was portrayed.

Roving reporter Richard S. Davis gave a more poetic description of the park's delights in the *Milwaukee Journal:*

> Once again this stuttering pen is taken in hand to proclaim the glories of Door county, this time particularly the refuge known as Peninsula state park. You may travel the length and breadth of this great commonwealth . . . and you'll never find a spot superior to this haven of the hemlock and the pine. . . .
>
> There's a drive that fairly takes your breath away. There are places to park and to look out from over the water, at pine created islands with alluring names like Strawberry and Horseshoe. You can see the Michigan shore here. If you're lucky you can see wild deer and eagles and even, perhaps, a bear. They say one got away from the little zoo of the park and is roaming around waiting to scare some dear old lady from Boston.
>
> The prize attraction, however, in an artificial way, is the Eagle observation tower, which strangers are invited to climb. It isn't so high, as heights go, but ladies with weak hearts are affected with violent palpitation only half way up and are forced to cling tightly to their swains. . . . When you get up you can see twice as much as when you were down. You immediately feel, if your legs don't ache, an ode coming on. You murmur, tentatively, something about the soul in its relation to God and nature. . . . There's much else to see and feel and smell. But this should be enough of a teaser.[18]

Other newspapers continued to proclaim the wonders of the park. In a 1932 editorial, the *Green Bay Press-Gazette* stated:

> This state park is one exhibit to prove what may be done by government direction when it is fortunate enough to function capably.
>
> Even the originators who carried the burden of selling the idea, and the land, to the legislature many years ago, could not, taking their colors from the rainbow, have overdone, either in beauty or utility, this prize possession of the people of the state today. . . .
>
> A relatively new roadway, skirting the broad expanse of the Bay, passing on from Eagle Light to Nicolet Bay, for years known by the less euphonious title of Shanty Bay, runs into a camp at which may be found any evening in the summer something like two hundred lovers of the outdoors.
>
> The park is a vast and splendid center of beauty and of health than which nothing finer or more picturesque may be found in the state—or many states.[19]

A quite comprehensive map of existing features of the park was prepared by the Wisconsin Conservation Department in December 1934. It indicated park roads and general masses of vegetation with hardwoods as the predominant tree group. It also noted that some of the hardwood areas were interspersed with aspen, hemlock, conifer, and pine. It showed three clusters of Scotch pine along the north edge of Highway 42, several pine plantings just northwest of the former CCC campsite, and two stands of conifers near the center of the park. Two swamp areas were shown: one near Weborg Point, the other to the north on the narrow neck of land between Nicolet Bay and Tennison Bay. Cedar and cedar with balsam were located along the bluff on the west side of Eagle Harbor, running to just beyond the lookout tower. Very little open space appeared, most of it in areas running inland from the south end of Shore Road, immediately north of Gibraltar High School. Finally, orchards were indicated above the bluffs west of the golf course clubhouse, and further north at the end of Highland Road. This map is useful for locating early features and places in the park that have disappeared or been virtually forgotten, such as the game farm, Camp Meenahga, Sven's Tower, numerous cottages, farm buildings, and what was called Devil's Pulpit.[20]

Four years later, the *Green Bay Press-Gazette* devoted a special sixteen-page supplement to the charms of Door County—"Door County 'tis of Thee!"— and its magnetic attractions for tourists. It featured seven photographs of Peninsula Park, with such captions as "scenes of beauty are everywhere" and "there is nothing more beautiful than a drive at sunset through the [park]."

Shortly after World War II, the park began to suffer from both heavy demands on its facilities and limited funding. A 1957 article in the *Wisconsin Conservation Bulletin* highlighted this dilemma. It pointed out the park's tremendous value to the public and described many of its appealing features. The shoreline, it noted, had "a half-dozen beguiling little bays where there are protected beaches." It went on to say:

> Across the northern part of the park the gently-rising hills suddenly rise to a series of sharp, dramatic limestone bluffs, giving a quite unexpected and different character to the landscape. From Eagle Bluff . . . the visitor looks off across the water to Chamber's island and Eagle island; or down upon the sparkling white town of Ephraim. There are those who compare the little towns of northern Door county to New England, others are reminded of certain parts of France, along the Mediterranean coast. Whatever the validity of these comparisons, everyone feels that the Door county area is quite unlike any other part of the state.[21]

Many articles extolling the park's breathtaking beauty appeared in newspapers during later decades. In 1967, for example, Bill Hibbard, the *Milwaukee Journal's* travel editor, described it in a long article entitled "Beauty on the Bluffs." He began with the following glowing description: "Take a 3,640-acre slab of limestone and erode its edges to produce bluffs, bays and sandy beaches. Top it with a rich mixture of timber, wildlife and colorful undergrowth. Decorate it with a lighthouse, a nature museum, a golf course, picnic areas, campgrounds. Garnish it with legends of Indians, explorers, loggers, lake sailors. Place it in Green bay, three-quarters of the way up Wisconsin's "thumb" and call it Peninsula state park."[22] The article went on to note that it "is one of Wisconsin's most popular state parks," and "offers the widest variety of activities of all Wisconsin's state parks." Further, the park's "beauty is, perhaps, equaled, but probably unsurpassed in the state. And the view from Eagle bluff . . . is one of the most photographed vistas in Wisconsin."

Thus, for centuries the glorious features of the park's setting have been praised. They represent a unique natural treasure for millions of past and future visitors.

᷎

CHAPTER 2

The Native Americans

Long before settlers of European ancestry arrived, Native Americans camped within what became Peninsula State Park. The surrounding waters provided excellent fishing, and flocks of geese and ducks frequented its marshes and bays. Deer, bear, turkeys, and pigeons were plentiful. The abundant maple trees provided sugar.

Over the years, several tribes battled for control of the area. Initially, some of the Algonquin groups, including the Ottawas, Sacs, Fox, Menominees, and Potawatomis, fought the Sioux and then the Iroquois. The Iroquois pushed their enemies westward, only to be opposed by the Winnebagos who came from the southwest. The Potawatomis, however, maintained a presence in Door, Kewaunee, and Manitowoc counties for many centuries. This group was present when La Salle traversed the peninsula in the seventeenth century.

Campsites, mounds, burial sites, flint quarries, petroglyphs, and pictographs in Door County have yielded a rich array of archaeological data. Many objects found on the peninsula are in museums or private collections. Some of the county's antiquities were described as early as 1869. S. A. Storrow mentioned planting grounds and graves on Detroit Island and indications of early cultivation on Plum Island. Another early report, in 1906, noted findings from two burial mounds on Chambers Island. In 1935 archaeologists wrote that "there are no Indian mounds in Peninsula Park." An article in 1950 mentioned Indian pictographs at Porte des Morts, but it is likely that these no longer exist.[1]

In "Indian Remains in Door County," J. P. Schumacher tried to describe all of the major archaeological sites of the peninsula and locations in or near the park where he found artifacts. They included the Shanty Bay Site (Nicolet Bay), which had "indications of a camp site" where he found "two flint arrow points, a scraper, perforator and potsherds"; a site at Fish Creek with "indications of a small camp site and four refuse pits" where he found a "copper spear point about five inches in length, a bone awl and several flint arrow points"; and other sites with Indian remains at Ellison Bay, Newport, Mink River, Mud Bay (now known as Moonlight Bay), Heins Creek, Jacksonport, and White-fish Bay.[2] Schumacher's collection of Indian artifacts is now at the Neville Public Museum in Green Bay.

Native Americans had special names for various locations and features on the peninsula. In fact, one article in the *Wisconsin Archaeologist* stated, "Wisconsin is probably as rich in Indian place-names as any other state." The Menominee referred to the Door County Peninsula as Kenatao. In the imme-diate vicinity of the park, a village at the present site of Fish Creek was called Ma-Go-She-Kah-ning, meaning "trout fishing." Chambers Island was Ke-Che Mab-Ne-Do, or "the Great Spirit," and its lake was Mac-Kay-See. Other place-names included Wah-Sa-Ke-Ta-Ta-Wong ("burning island") for North Bay; Wah-ya-qua-kah-me-kong ("lands end") for Gills Rock, Ah-Quah-o-me-ning ("fish to shore") for Baileys Harbor, and Ah-Quas-He-Ma-Ganing ("save our lives") for Whitefish Bay.[3]

Additional insights into the park's early inhabitants have been obtained from more recent surveys. In 1990, Victoria Dirst, an archaeologist with the Wiscon-sin Department of Natural Resources (DNR), investigated Weborg Point to determine if a new septic system would affect significant archaeological remains.

In 1994, proposed improvements at Nicolet Bay—modifying surface drain-age, installing a sprinkler system, creating sandpit volleyball courts, and in-stalling a buried cable to replace an overhead power line—prompted park superintendent Tom Blackwood to request funds for an archaeological survey before work began. Dirst directed the investigation, assisted by several DNR employees and numerous volunteers, and reported that the site had "great potential for future research."[4] The investigation yielded significant informa-tion about prehistoric settlement at the site and provided new insights into Native American activities elsewhere on the Door Peninsula.

Dirst confirmed four occupation periods. The earliest, found near the beach, appeared to be Early Woodland, dating to about 600–400 B.C. This period was established from her analysis of the thick, heavily tempered, stamped pot-tery which had been dated at other locations on the peninsula.

Another and more substantial habitation phase, the second North Bay com-ponent, suggested that the site once served as a village that was probably occupied from spring through late fall. Charred food from this period was radiocarbon dated to within fifty years of 195 B.C. Pottery (ceramic) vessels were associated with North Bay ware from other locations on the Door Peninsula.

A third period, the "Heins Creek occupation," was "tentatively dated to around A.D. 700–800, [and] was responsible for the majority of the artifacts and features found at Shanty Bay," including a human burial. At this time "the site was thought to have served as a three-season village," but there was "no way of knowing how many years the people returned here in the spring from their winter hunting camps." The fourth occupation, at Shanty Bay, was by the Oneota. However, their remains were scanty and "indicate a small short term campsite" with pottery from "a date sometime between A.D. 1300 and the beginning of the historic era."[5]

Many artifacts were recovered from the Shanty Bay site. They included a variety of ceramics, many scored with cord marks, which are useful to archaeologists for analyzing and dating the remnants. Also found were burial pits, projectile points, post molds, a knife, scrapers and wedges, two dolomite "stone balls" (probably used for games), a vast quantity of stone shards, and specimens of fire-cracked rock.[6] The rock was used to produce steam in sweat lodges and for domestic hearths and pit ovens. A few bone and antler tools were also discovered. Nearly ten thousand pieces of animal bone, antlers, and teeth provided clues to the park's early fauna. They included the remains of deer, beaver, black bear, fisher, elk, a variety of fish, and a few birds, including a bald eagle.

The most interesting discovery was an oval-shaped burial pit containing a single skeleton. It was located directly beneath an abandoned sewer pipe that ran close to the ground surface. The body was laid on its left side, with the head to the west and face to the north. The hands were near the chin and the arms and legs were tightly flexed. The pelvis was crushed. The evidence suggested that the skeleton was that of a woman at least forty-five years of age. The only item thought to have been interred with the deceased was a canine tooth from a black bear. Its root tip was faintly grooved for attaching a cord. The skeleton was mapped and photographed. Immediately before backfilling, a local woman said a prayer and sprinkled tobacco over the remains.

Indian myths have also been attributed to the park. In 1937, Charles E. Brown, then affiliated with the Wisconsin Folklore Society, wrote of one such legend in the *Door County Advocate*. Entitled "The Indian Lover's Leap at Eagle Cliff," his article gave the following account:

At Eagle Cliff in the beautiful Peninsula State Park is one of the many Lovers' Leaps in Wisconsin. From the top of this high cliff, according to an Indian legend, a Potawatomi girl from one of the Door County villages of this nation cast herself down to death rather than become the wife of a man whom she did not love and to whom her parents had promised her. This was long ago, before any white man landed on the shores of the Peninsula.

This man who wished to possess a young wife was the aged chief of a village near that of her parents. He had made many presents to her parents and obtained their consent to take the girl away to his wigwam. But before this could be accomplished, Mashigwa (Red Corn), who was being courted by a young warrior of another encampment, fled from her home. Had she run to her lover's wigwam all might have been well, but she was bewildered by her sorrow and fear and decided to end her life. Although pursued she managed to reach the top of the rock cliff and there met her death as noted. Her warrior lover sought to end his own life by joining a Potawatomi war party. He won distinction in several battles and was later killed in a fight with a party of the . . . raiding Iroquois. Thus two Indian lives, which might have been happy, ended in sorrow.[7]

Native Americans were the focus of what was probably the largest and most important public event ever held in the park. The occasion was the burial ceremony, in 1931, of the Potawatomi Chief Simon Onanguisse Kahquados, the last lineal descendant of a long line of Potawatomi chiefs. Born on May 18, 1851, near Mishicot in Manitowoc County, Kahquados inherited a title that had come down over a span of some six hundred years. His father was the longtime ruler of the tribe in Door, Kewaunee, and Manitowoc counties and was chief when Euro-Americans first came to Door County.[8]

The Potawatomis once had a long-standing presence in Door, Kewaunee, and Manitowoc counties. They had lived in villages at Kewaunee, Two Rivers, Algoma, Sturgeon Bay, and Washington Island and were united in repulsing the Sioux who had crossed the Mississippi in an attempt to take fishing lands along the Lake Michigan shore. Simon's father, Onenningahsong ("shimmering light"), died at Whitefish Bay when Simon was five years of age and he was raised at Mink River by his paternal grandfather, Kahquados ("try walking").[9] At the age of eighteen, he became a timber cruiser for lumber companies operating around Bark River and Escanaba, Michigan. Later Simon worked as a land surveyor. A man of great intelligence and an entertaining speaker, he was a popular guest at historical gatherings, and he made several trips to Washington, D.C., on behalf of his people. Chief Kahquados was intensely interested in Potawatomi history and genealogy, and he helped preserve extensive knowledge of Indian place-names, traditions, and legends. As Simon grew older, his passionate wish was to be buried in the sacred land of his ancestors.

The removal of the Potawatomis from their traditional lands in east central Wisconsin represented one of many low points in the history of our nation's relationship with Native Americans. In 1831, a blundering government agent established a treaty with the Menominee Indians ceding to the government all land bordered by Green Bay, Lake Winnebago, the Milwaukee River, and Lake Michigan. Had he investigated actual ownership of the land more carefully, he would have found that the Potawatomis had claimed most of this land for centuries. Unfortunately, they knew nothing of this transaction until many years later. Kahquados and his people were deprived of more than three million acres of land without any just compensation.

The idea of a memorial totem pole in Peninsula State Park to honor the Potawatomi originated with the flamboyant historian and founder of the Door County Historical Society, H. R. Holand.[10] At one time, Holand had lived in the park and employed Indians to work in his large orchards. He came to sympathize with them about the brazen swindle of their ancestors' land and their relegation to a desolate spot in Forest County. In April of 1926, Holand proposed the idea of a memorial pole to the Ephraim Men's Club. The group enthusiastically endorsed the project. Later that year he spearheaded the organization of the Door County Historical Society, whose several goals included placing markers at the county's major historic sites and erecting a totem pole in the park. At its first annual meeting, the society appropriated one hundred dollars for the project.

By early summer of 1927, work was well underway. Holand prepared the general design for the pole, a thirty-foot pine log from a huge tree located where the Owl City trail "comes out at Eagle terrace."[11] Robert Petschneider, a master carver of church furniture from Kewaunee, carved a small bear at the top. The prominent portrait artist Charles M. Lesaar from Belgium, who had lived in the park for several summers, sculpted the rest of the pole. It was then given two coats of brown paint as the base for the brighter colors. Holand had proposed the design: twenty-six different scenes interspersed with such Potawatomi symbols as the thunderbird, the northern lights, lightning, the fish and the serpent, and the dog. These were laid out in six horizontal bands representing important segments of the tribe's history. Potawatomi designs separated each band.

The six bands portrayed the following aspects of Native American history:

1. A hunting scene. Native Americans shooting a deer and living a happy life in a land of abundance.
2. The coming of the white man, who was received as a supernatural being.
3. Native Americans carrying furs in their canoes to Montreal where they met a New World.

4. The missionary comes to preach a new faith while holding out a cross to the Native Americans.

5. The Potawatomi fight valiantly for their French friends in the French and English Wars.

6. The coming of white settlers who drove the Native Americans from their ancient hunting grounds, and their departure for unknown regions toward the setting sun.

Vida Weborg, an artist who lived in the park, laid out the composition. Kurt Stenzel of Fish Creek assisted with painting. When finished, the pole was moved to the park's golf course and positioned so that the bear on top overlooked the bay to the village of Ephraim. Generous donors from the Ephraim Men's Club and the Peninsula State Park golf committee had covered nearly all of the total cost of fifteen hundred dollars.

Formal dedication took place on August 14, 1927. A large platform built around the pole seated those presenting the elaborate program and a delegation of Native Americans. Thirty-two Potawatomi, in their colorful ceremonial dress, were guests of honor. Holand had traveled 170 miles to their village in

The memorial pole situated on the golf course marks the grave of Simon Onanguisse Kahquados, the last lineal descendant of a long line of Potawatomi chiefs. The Potawatomi once had a long-standing presence in east central Wisconsin. (Author's collection)

Forest County to extend a personal invitation. In this barren, stony, cutover land he found appalling poverty—a problem exacerbated by federal policies. Seventy-six-year-old Chief Kahquados, one of the few Indians who spoke English, accepted the invitation with dignity and on behalf of his people.

The impressive two-day ceremony attracted thousands of people "from all parts of Middle West."[12] Frank Londo, a Sturgeon Bay fiddler, began the program with old-time melodies, and Congressman George J. Schneider gave a brief address on Indian legislation. The highlight of the ceremony followed when Chief Kahquados sang "America" in his native tongue and, speaking in English, recalled the days when his forebears ruled the Door County area peacefully. Then the chief proudly pulled a cord and the muslin wrappings of the monument rippled gently to the ground, revealing the totem pole in all its colorful glory. The ecstatic crowd applauded loudly and car horns clamored. Jens Jensen, the prominent landscape architect who had been spending summer vacations at Ellison Bay since 1919, spoke on the topic "When Door County Was Young and Beautiful." Vocal selections by the Sister Bay male chorus closed the day's program.[13]

The following afternoon the Indians formed a ring around the totem pole and danced to the beat of a large drum. In his proclamation to the Potawatomi tribe, Kahquados indicated that the "Green Corn, Shawano, Waubahne,

A group of Potawatomi who were guests of honor at the impressive two-day ceremony to dedicate the memorial pole on August 14 and 15, 1927. (Author's collection)

Fish, Partridge, Haw, Medicine, friendship and Harvest Dances would be performed."[14] When they finished Holand was invited to the center, where the chief conferred upon him the Indian name Kyagigesdonk, meaning "the sun in the fullness of its course," or "one who has a long and fulsome life."[15] That evening the Indians again danced around a campfire near the clubhouse. Holand gave a closing address, pointing out the symbolism of the bear on top of the pole. For Native Americans, the bear held the highest place among all animals because of its strength and courage.

Holand had arranged lodging in Ephraim for three nights for the Potawatomi. On their last night, he joined them for dinner at the Evergreen Beach Hotel. As the conversation drifted to the chief's old age, Holand asked the honored guest if he would like to be buried at the foot of that monument. With great eagerness the chief indicated that it would be an extraordinary honor. According to his will, "It is my wish and I hereby direct that I be buried in the Wisconsin State park at Ephraim, Wisconsin, according to my previous arrangements with the Door County Historical Society."[16]

On November 27, 1930, at the age of seventy-nine, Chief Kahquados died in poverty, near Blackwell, in the Indian community near Laona and Crandon in Forest County. The classic WPA book *Wisconsin: A Guide to the Badger State* described living conditions for many there as "tar-paper shacks, one-room huts with sagging frames and dirt floors."[17]

Automobiles parked on the golf course for the thousands of people who witnessed the burial ceremony for Chief Kahquados on Memorial Day 1931. (Courtesy Peninsula State Park office)

Of Kahquados's sad demise, the *Advocate* wrote: "Chief Kahquados did not have enough support from the Government during his declining years to keep body and soul together and died on a heap of rags in a cold and barren hut, penniless and practically deserted."[18] Fortunately, his friend Holand had already begun to carry out the chieftain's wish. The Wisconsin Conservation Commission had approved his burial in the park and designated C. E. Broughton, editor of the *Sheboygan Press,* to direct the ceremony. A member of the commission's advisory council and a curator of the State Historical Society, Broughton had been concerned for the chief's welfare. He and other admirers of the chief had arranged for the body to be placed in a vault in Wabeno until appropriate services could be held the next year. Working through Congressman George J. Schneider, the Door County Historical Society tried to obtain one thousand dollars from the Bureau of Indian Affairs for the burial, but the agency granted only one hundred dollars. To mark the grave, a massive boulder weighing several tons was selected and transported to the burial site from Potawatomi State Park. Affixed to it was a bronze tablet with an inscription paying tribute to the chief and his nation's legacy.

On Memorial Day 1931, Chief Kahquados's remains were laid to rest in an impressive ceremony. Twenty Potawatomi from Blackwell, Laona, and Wabeno had accompanied his body to the site. Thousands of people gathered to witness the last rites. The Sturgeon Bay High School Band played "America." Six Potawatomi pallbearers carried the casket from the hearse to the grave. A missionary to the Potawatomi read the burial prayer, and the tribe's secondary chief unveiled the huge boulder marking the grave. Lengthy speeches by Joseph Schafer, superintendent of the State Historical Society, and Holand followed. The chief's friend stated eloquently the great debt the nation owed to the American Indian, particularly the Potawatomi. The event ended with a colorful Potawatomi ceremonial tribute.

Accounts of the chief's burial were sent out in United Press and Associated Press news releases that were published throughout the country. In addition, pictures of the ceremony appeared in newspaper feature sections and in newsreels at movie theaters.[19]

The original memorial pole stood until the 1960s when two Ephraim friends, J. Spencer Gould and sculptor Adlai Hardin, discovered that large areas of it had rotted. With help from the Ephraim Foundation and Gould, funds were raised to reconstruct the pole from a laminated pine column. Hardin donated his carving expertise. An additional band designed by Chief Roy Oshkosh to honor the Menominee tribe was added at the bottom. The new nine-hundred-pound memorial pole was installed on July 14, 1970. As it was raised

to its upright position, the small crowd in attendance, including park superintendent Ralph Halvorsen, broke into applause. This time, a more intricate
base held the long column, a ten-inch steel pole that extended seven feet into
the wood and was welded into a steel plate bolted to the concrete foundation.

Excavations in 2002, in connection with the Highway 57 expansion between
Green Bay and Sturgeon Bay, provided further information about early Native
Americans in Door County. They revealed that nomadic tribes roamed across
the peninsula as long ago as eight thousand years. These travelers, hunters,
and fishers left a virtually untouched work area containing thousands of stone
flakes from spearheads and hunting points. No human remains were found.
More excavations will undoubtedly occur in the future.[20]

It is evident that Peninsula State Park and all of Door County played a
significant role in the lives of Wisconsin's earliest inhabitants. Yet, just a hand-
ful of articles, Holand's *Old Peninsula Days,* and several recent archaeological
studies give us only a limited overview of the area's Native American culture. Much remains to be discovered of their rich legacy both in the park and
throughout the entire Door Peninsula.

❧

CHAPTER 3

Early Residents

THE PARK'S PIONEERS

Euro-American settlement in the park began several years after the United States land survey of the area was completed. In 1844, Increase and Mary Claflin, credited with being the first permanent settlers in Door County, moved to the park after having lived for a time at Little Sturgeon Bay. According to Holand's *Old Peninsula Days,* they "settled on a promontory one-half mile north of the present site of Fish Creek," which placed it near present-day Weborg Point.[1] The point was one of a series of numbered irregular lots the survey had platted along the water's edge; however, the inland area was divided into standard one-mile square, numbered sections.

In 1850 a patent for this lot—thirty-three-acre parcel number two in Section 2—was granted to John Fitzgerald.[2] Two years later, Fitzgerald sold it to John L. Reynolds and in 1855 Reynolds sold it to Increase and Mary Claflin.[3] There they raised a family and lived out their lives.

Between 1847 and 1849 Claflin's son-in-law, William Marshall, built a log house just to the south, near what is now the Fish Creek park entrance. As late as the 1960s, the Marshall cabin, still in its original condition, survived as probably the oldest standing dwelling in Door County.[4]

The Claflin family cemetery, now known as the Thorp or Claflin-Thorp cemetery, can be found in the woods directly east of the Weborg Point Campground. Surrounded by a low concrete border, this tiny (about twenty-two-feet square) burial plot contains over a dozen discernible markers. Three members of the Thorp family are buried there.[5]

Another of the first inhabitants of what became Peninsula State Park was Ole Larson. Born in a village near Oslo, Norway, on April 6, 1806, Larson immigrated to Buffalo, New York, where he ran a boardinghouse, then followed the Great Lakes water route westward to Fort Howard, where he operated a store and trading post. There Indians told him of a beautiful island with a protected harbor lying further north in the waters of Green Bay. The Eagle Island (now called Horseshoe Island) location appealed to Larson and he moved his family to this isolated outpost in 1850. There he fished and supplied wood for steamers from Buffalo on their long run to Fort Howard. Three years later, having exhausted the island's supply of timber, Larson dismantled the logs of his small house, floated them across the bay, and erected them at the end of a grassy lane leading down to the water on his new property west of Eagle Bluff (the present-day Nicolet Bay Campground).

Larson helped establish the large Scandinavian settlement in the area and he helped Pastor Andrew Iverson establish the Norwegian colony at Ephraim. In February of 1853, Iverson and three of his Moravian brethren walked north from Fort Howard to stay for a time with the Larson family while seeking land for their settlement. Under Larson's guidance, Iverson selected a 423¾-acre site on the east shore of Eagle Harbor. Larson then accompanied him on a pony-drawn sled to the new Menasha land office to buy the large tract for five hundred dollars. In May, Iverson left Fort Howard for Eagle Island on the *Dove*, a small three-masted schooner he had built the previous year, while his wife and baby son left on the steamer *Columbia* to join him. During the following weeks more members of the Moravian congregation moved to Eagle Island. There they occupied temporary shanties while they fished and rowed each day to the mainland to lay out building lots, clear land, and begin building houses. By November, they had moved to their new settlement, which they called Ephraim (from the Hebrew meaning "to be fruitful"). As a tribute to their friend and guide, the Moravians took up a collection for Larson. Iverson later wrote in his diary, "Larson declined at first to receive the contribution, but after my presentation of the matter he accepted it with great gratitude, for he too was in poor circumstances."[6]

Larson's house stood for a century before the park burned it down. In 1958, a stone monument was erected to mark its location. Its bronze plaque reads: "The home of Ole Larson, first farmer in Door County, stood here. . . . In 1957 the house, oldest in Door County, was removed."[7]

In the 1850s several more shoreline lots platted by the original land survey had been sold by the government. By the early 1860s, more of the lots and most of the interior land were sold. Most of the other buyers had Norwegian, Swedish, and Yankee surnames. None except Ole Larson show up in the 1860 federal census.[8] Thus, many of these initial buyers were probably nonresident speculators who hoped to profit from reselling the land. However, there were at least two exceptions. Tobias Morbek, a friend of Pastor Iverson's, built one of the Ephraim area's first houses. Martin Johnson, another member of the Ephraim Moravian congregation, married Ole Larson's daughter Pauline and built a small house near Eagle Bluff. Pauline became the teacher at Ephraim's first school.[9]

Others, mostly of Norwegian descent, settled in the park, including Peter Wiborg (later known as Weborg), who arrived in 1853 and settled at the point that was named for his family. Several of Weborg's relatives followed, acquiring land at the west shore of the park where they engaged primarily in fishing.

Little is known about these early settlers, since it was not until the 1870s that occasional news columns for individual communities began appearing in the *Advocate*. These sometimes reported interesting insights regarding the park's early settlers, but usually they were gossip-like tidbits about visits to nearby friends, accidents, illnesses, and other mostly insignificant happenings.

A prominent feature of the park's landscape, Sven's Bluff, also attests to the early presence of Norwegian immigrants. According to an article in the *Democrat*, this precipitous cliff was named after "Swen" Anderson, a Norwegian

The Hans B. Olson farmstead at Shanty Bay in 1876. Note the rocky soil, which made farming in the park a burdensome task. Olson was later hired as a warden and became the park's first employee while he continued to reside on his farm. (Courtesy Peninsula State Park office)

sailor. In the 1850s, Anderson bought forty acres of government land that included the bluff. For many years, he sailed as a watchman on the *Queen of the West*, the biggest and most handsome passenger boat on the lakes, which ran between Chicago and Buffalo. When the steamer went out of commission, Anderson built a cozy cottage near the edge of the cliff. A confirmed bachelor, he lived a simple life for thirty years, clearing roughly fifteen acres to the edge of the precipice without a horse or plow. He also built two roads leading up to his farm. Well liked by those who lived in the area, Anderson had many visitors. His ready humor and common sense made him a respected acquaintance. During his final illness, he refused doctors and medicines, saying, like a true philosopher, "I am an old man and have lived my allotted days; let me go." Confident of going to heaven, he insisted, "Raise no stone to my memory."[10]

Over the years, the bluff has been called Lone Pine Bluff, Schoolhouse Bluff, Sunset Cliff, and other names, but its original name, Sven's Bluff, is common to those knowledgeable about the park. The name does justice to the good man who lived there. Although the tract book record of sales from the government land office at Green Bay does not indicate any land sale to a Swen Anderson, his name appears in the 1875 and 1880 censuses. The 1880 census indicates that he lived alone and lists him as a fisherman.[11] Thus, there may be some truth in the above account.

View to the southwest from Sven's Tower. Note the cleared fields used for crops and pastures. In the distance is Fish Creek Bay. (Courtesy Peninsula State Park office)

Early atlases provide useful information about nineteenth-century settlement patterns in the park. The 1878 *Historical Atlas of Wisconsin* indicates that
no improved road had yet been built into the park. The road that is now
Highway 42 is shown, but it does not run in the straight southwest-northeast
direction across what is now the south boundary of the park. Instead, it makes
a graceful curve extending about one mile to the north into the park, before
swinging down near its present location just south of Ephraim. The *Illustrated
Atlas of Door County, Wisconsin,* published in 1899, contains the first actual
map of land ownership and, to some extent, land use at the park site. It shows
not only roads but the locations of the District School No. 8 and Blossomburg
Cemetery. The one-room log school had been built by Charles Gustafson near
Tennison Bay about 1895 or 1896.[12] By this time, many of the original lots
on the west shore of the park had been subdivided into smaller parcels. Most
of the interior land holdings were forty or eighty acres in size. With only a
few exceptions, the owners were Scandinavian, primarily Norwegian. The atlas
also indicates that thirty-one dwellings and/or farmsteads had been built.

State and federal census records provide important information about
Gibraltar Township's early population, including the area that later became

Children and their teacher from Blossomburg's District School No. 8. Access to the
adjacent shoreline provided an adventuresome play area for the young students.
(Courtesy Peninsula State Park office)

the park. The majority of its nineteenth-century residents were American born, most coming from New York State. However, many others were born abroad. Before the turn of the century, immigrants from Norway remained the largest foreign-born group. The 1860 federal census recorded ninety-seven household heads in the township.[13] Over half were born in America, and one-fourth came from Norway. The others, in order of their numbers, came from Germany, Ireland, England, Canada, Scotland, Denmark, France, and Sweden. The 1870 census recorded not just household heads but all family members, totaling 454 persons.[14] At that time, Gibraltar's 174 American-born residents represented nearly 40 percent of its population, while the 106 people from Norway again represented by far the largest ethnic group from abroad. In later years, the number of foreign-born residents declined steadily. By 1880, the census indicated that only one-third of the residents of Gibraltar Township's came from a foreign country with nearly one-third of these from Norway.[15] Population numbers were not available from the 1890 census, since a fire destroyed many of these records.

By 1900, the township's population had grown to 1,285 residents.[16] More than three-quarters (976) were American born. Now, however, the residents

The Blossomburg school located just off Shore Road south of the Tennison Bay campground. The school closed when residents began moving from the park after their land was purchased by the State of Wisconsin. (Courtesy Peninsula State Park office)

from Norway were elderly and represented only 10 percent (130) of Gibraltar's population. Yet, the area, including the village of Ephraim, continued as a distinctive Norwegian-American enclave.

In fact, the community was so proud of its Nordic culture that in 1913 the Ephraim Men's Club, no doubt with Holand's blessing, sent a resolution to the governor protesting Columbus Day. It stated, "It is erroneously claimed that he [Columbus] discovered America. . . . Whereas, it is a recognized historical fact that the Northmen discovered and settled on the continent of America in the year 1000," and "Scandinavian explorers penetrated to the very heart of the American continent a century before Columbus was born."[17]

Vestiges of Ephraim's Scandinavian culture remain strong to this day, and are evident in family names as well as festivals, log buildings, food preferences, and other Old World characteristics.

Since only about 4 percent of Norway's rugged land was arable, many Norwegians who came to America dreamed of having their own plot of land and prospering from farming. Indeed, many of the early residents of the park hoped for just such a future. Those who farmed often supplemented their income by logging, fishing, and general "handyman" work that included carpentry and other odd jobs. However, the park's wetlands, steep terrain, and shallow rocky soil presented a tremendous challenge for growing crops. Hence,

Steamboats and sailboats docked at Peter Weborg's brother Henry's pier at Weborg Point. (Courtesy Peninsula State Park office)

only part of the acreage on most farms in the park could be cultivated, and tilling this land still required backbreaking work. Wheat, oats, barley, rye, corn, and hay were important crops, and many farms had orchards and large gardens where vegetables, especially potatoes, were grown for consumption.

Coming from a nation with extensive coniferous forests, Norwegians from rural areas were skilled at working with wood. They were adept at elaborate woodcarving, building handsome wooden stave churches, and especially at crafting impressive log structures with the North European method of corner timbering.[18] Typical early dwellings built in the park, as well as in the village of Ephraim, were log structures. The abundant white cedar of the area was ideal for log construction since it was relatively light in weight, durable, and easily shaped with basic carpentry tools. Later, when lumber became plentiful, many of the early dwellings were covered with board siding to protect the logs and portray a more modern appearance.

Today it is difficult to imagine that many hundreds of people once resided in the park. Several families moved away when whitefish and trout catches

Lunchtime for the threshing crew at Olaf Hanson's farm, located at what is now the park's golf course. Left to right: Mrs. Bart (with coffee pot), Olaf Hanson's daughter; Albert Hanson, Olaf's brother and owner of the threshing machine; Olaf Hanson; Simon Hanson, in white shirt; Albert Jarman, next to end in front row; T. Goodletson at end of front row. Others remain unidentified. (Author's collection)

declined. Others grew tired of the grueling work required to farm their rugged land. Some simply found opportunities for a better livelihood elsewhere. Several descendants of the park's early settlers still reside on the Door Peninsula, but most are scattered throughout the United States. All of their dwellings, some of which had important historical value, have been removed. Such obliteration may seem drastic, but at the time it seemed the solution to vandalism concerns and the desire to enhance the natural character of the park. Today, however, the National Park Service and park officials throughout the nation emphasize parks' historic and cultural features, including the preservation of early buildings and other evidence of prior human habitation.[19]

At Peninsula State Park, unfortunately, the only evidence of its former inhabitants is an occasional forest clearing, several ancient apple trees, scattered remnants of stone fences, and barely discernible foundation fragments. To the sharp-eyed park visitor, these vestiges of its thriving settlement still serve as reminders of a fascinating aspect of the American pioneer experience in this once-remote corner of Wisconsin.

CHAPTER 4

❧

Weborg Point

Just inside the Fish Creek entrance to the park is Weborg Point, a small elbow of land jutting into Green Bay that is now used as a campground. Adjoining it, to the south and east, is a shallow bay and wetland—the Peninsula White Forest Natural Area. The land here was once covered with mixed coniferous and deciduous forest, but early Euro-Americans cleared the forests for cordwood and barrel production for ships traveling to Green Bay. Second-growth forest eventually grew up, but the campground remains relatively open with a fringe of trees and shrubs bordering each campsite.

Eventually settlers, mostly of Norwegian ancestry, came to the park led by Peter Weborg and Evan Nelson. Born in the town of Lom in Gudbrandsdalen, Norway, in 1823, Weborg married Oluffa Wilg in 1848, and three years later the couple set out for America. After living briefly at Green Bay, the Weborgs settled at the point in 1853 where they purchased a twenty-five-acre parcel of land from Increase Claflin in the north half of lot two.[1] There, up the rocky slope overlooking the waters of Green Bay, Weborg built a one-and-a-half-story log house. Like most Norwegian immigrants, he would have been familiar with the North European method of log construction and he probably built his cabin in this manner.

According to Weborg's obituary, when he came to the point "the country north of Sturgeon Bay was a wilderness, and he found only one family near Fish Creek and another on Eagle Island."[2] After erecting his log dwelling, Weborg walked to Sturgeon Bay, the nearest trading place, for provisions, which he carried home on his back. He worked as a cooper and fished with a sailboat kept at their pier. In 1854–55, he built a frame addition to the log cabin to which he added a one-story wing or ell with porches on each side, one facing west with a majestic view of the bay and distant islands. The rambling building was clad with horizontal clapboards while numerous windows admitted natural light to the interior. His daughter Vida later wrote, "The log part of this house is the oldest building . . . north of Sturgeon Bay."[3]

In 1859 two of Peter's brothers, Henry and Andrew, also settled near the point. Andrew and his wife moved to Gills Rock in the 1870s, where he established a successful fishing enterprise that is still operated by Weborg descendants. Today the Weborg name remains synonymous with commercial fishing in Wisconsin. Henry sold his seventy-two-acre property near the park's Fish Creek entrance to the State of Wisconsin when land acquisition for the park began.

Peter Weborg and his wife had nine children, four of whom, Johanna, Ella, Vida, and Alfred, survived into adulthood. After nearly forty years of marriage, Peter's wife died in 1888. Alfred, who served as town clerk, eventually moved to Texas after selling his sixty-acre farm north of the point to the state. His house was later moved to become the park superintendent's residence. None of Weborg's resourceful daughters married. Two of them, Johanna and Vida, became teachers, while Ella remained at home to care for their father. An adept and dedicated teacher, Vida was also a talented artist. Hjalmar Holand's

The Weborg home sometime after the turn of the nineteenth century. Originally a log dwelling, the structure was later modified with clapboards and additions. The two women in the foreground are probably Vida and Ella Weborg. (Courtesy Peninsula State Park office)

classic *Old Peninsula Days,* first published in 1925, is illustrated with her delightful pencil sketches of places and people described in the book. Working with C. M. Lesaar, she also helped implement Holand's design for the memorial totem pole at the entrance to the park.[4]

Because the Weborg property was within the proposed park boundaries and occupied a prime area of shoreline, the State of Wisconsin needed to acquire it. How this occurred is an interesting aspect of the park's history, a fascinating human interest story, and a tribute to the courage of this pioneering family and their steadfast love for the home they had carved from what was once a veritable wilderness.

In 1907, after Assemblyman Charles Reynolds had proposed a bill to examine lands in the county for a state park, there was considerable interest in locating it between Fish Creek and Ephraim and options to acquire land there were being explored. Governor James O. Davidson, a native of Norway, had contacted the Weborgs to determine, as Johanna Weborg noted in a letter to the governor, "if there were any difficulty when the time came to option our land for state park purposes," after it was appraised by a state park board. Apparently landowners in the proposed park were given notice that "those who do not within a few days option their lands for what they are worth will have them appraised by a state board." She also stated that they were told that their father "Peter Weborg who is eighty-five years of age will get a permit to live in his home till his death."[5] Johanna noted that the family was deeply concerned about their sister Ella, who had stayed at home to care for their father and wanted to live out her years in their home, which she "idolized." Because Ella had "no trade or profession," said Johanna, and had been "sick and very nervous for some years," leaving home would render Ella "homeless" and "kill her or drive her insane." Ella's tenure in the family home "would only be for a few years more or less and eventually the state could do with it as it saw fit," she said. The house had been "kept neat and in good repair" and "summer visitors all look upon it as an interesting relic and declare it ought to be left standing." Finally, and tactfully, Johanna requested a lifelong tenancy for her father, herself, and her sister Ella.

The following month, the good-natured Davidson wrote back: "There is really nothing to fear at present. The state cannot establish a park at Fish Creek, or anywhere else, until the legislature have decided to do so and have made a proposition to purchase the land. . . . Do not allow any one to scare you about condemnation proceedings." He further stated that "if this legislature of 1909 should decide to purchase the property, I will be here as governor of this state, and will render you all the assistance in my power." He added:

I must beg you to keep this letter to yourself and show it to no one, but when the proper time comes, if you do not get a square deal, you call on me, and I will see to it that you either get what pay you are entitled to, or that you keep the property as long as you live, even though the state should purchase it for a park. Of course, you understand that the Commission does not wish to make any deals of this kind for fear there will be too many people in the park area who will want the same privilege, but your case, in my opinion, is different from a great many. . . . I will see that no injustice is done to any of you while I am in authority here.[6]

Eventually the Weborg family became vociferous opponents of the park. According to the September 10, 1909, minutes of the State Park Board, the attorney general was ordered to begin condemnation proceedings against the remaining landowners in the park, which included Peter Weborg.[7] The following month park board members visited the Weborg property and appraised it at fifteen hundred dollars. According to Miss Weborg's correspondence with Governor Davidson, the board did not reveal this figure to the Weborgs, who learned of it only after the thirty-day period for appealing had passed. Like many other landowners within the proposed park, the Weborgs believed their land was worth more. Johanna retained attorney Thomas Sanderson from Sturgeon Bay to represent their case. Later she submitted the following appraisal of their property to Governor Davidson: "Main building, log cabin and barn valued at $1700; 14 acres of clover and timothy $350; 6 acres of woodland $100; and 4½ acres of wooded hillside sloping to the beach that included "an orchard of 16 apple trees, a good well, and ½ forty length of beach $350." The amounts totaled twenty-five hundred dollars. A footnote to this figure said, "Father offered to accept only $2000 if a written permit were given for us to live in the house and use [the] orchard as long as his youngest daughter Elenora age 37 wished to retain this privilege. If not, he asked $2500."[8] Sanderson filed for an injunction to restrain the State Park Board from taking possession of the land. He stated in his complaint that the park board did not comply with the requirements of the law in making its appraisal, and instead of meeting on the day established to make the appraisal, it met the next day when only two board members were present. County Court Commissioner Jacob Dehos granted the request.

By the end of 1910, after considerable legal sparring, the State Park Board upped its offer to twenty-five hundred dollars and provided Peter Weborg with a lifelong lease to his home and one acre of land.[9] In subsequent correspondence, both Johanna and Vida Weborg maintained that Thomas Brittingham, head of the State Park Board, made a verbal promise that they could live there rent free after Peter's death but that the attorney general's staff refused to furnish written documentation for this provision.

With their neighbors gone and roads blocked with snow, the family moved to Fish Creek for the winter during Peter Weborg's final three years.[10] In 1913 the staunch old pioneer passed away at the age of eighty-nine. "The end was peaceful and painless," the *Sturgeon Bay Advocate* reported, "the sands of life running and he falling quietly to sleep."[11] He was buried at Ephraim's Moravian cemetery.

The following year bids were ordered to move the Weborg house to the Andrew Johnson property for the park superintendent's use. No such action occurred, however, and the daughters were permitted to reside there for forty-eight dollars per year. It was also agreed that they could rent rooms and one of their small buildings to tourists.

Johanna died in 1930. She had taught school for more than forty years, most recently near Chicago, but returned to the park for summer vacations. During the depths of the Great Depression, Vida again asked the Wisconsin Conservation Commission to allow Ella to live in the park rent free. Forced to retire from teaching, Vida had only her Illinois teacher's pension of four hundred dollars per year and their meager rental income, hardly enough for the two women to live on. Nearing the age of seventy, she was concerned that her death would leave Ella destitute and unable to pay the rent. Without written provision for future use of the dwelling, conservation officials insisted that the sisters pay rent, despite their frequent appeals to subsequent governors. Peter Weborg's daughters continued to reside at their home during summers as late as the 1940s. They were the last of the original residents to live in the park.

In the 1930s, another controversy involving Weborg Point erupted at the park. Influenced by its president, H. R. Holand, the Door County Historical Society proposed erecting a monument to honor Increase Claflin, the settler who had built northern Door County's first house, at Weborg Point. Such a monument was in keeping with one of the society's objectives of memorializing, preserving, and marking historic sites on the peninsula. As initially proposed, the memorial would be "in the form of a replica of Claflin's first house" and "about eight feet in its dimensions . . . reproduced on an elevation with a suitable marker" and located "on or near the original site of the Claflin house."[12] At the time, the society had access to a tiny replica of Claflin's house that a nephew who was familiar with its details had made.

After the project was proposed at the society's September 1930 meeting, William J. Gilson, the organization's secretary (and then county superintendent of schools), wrote to Conservation Commission director Paul D. Kelleter for permission to proceed. Kelleter consulted with Conservation Department director C. L. Harrington, who visited the park to discuss the proposal with the park supervisor, A. E. Doolittle. Foreseeing problems with the suitability of such a monument, they suggested that, instead of a miniature building, "a suitable bronze tablet, using the native rock for a base . . . would much more appropriately and permanently mark the spot."[13] The determined Holand traveled to Madison to discuss the matter with Kelleter, who then, according to Holand, granted Gilson permission to proceed with the original project. He also urged that the society communicate this matter to Doolittle.

Two months later, Holand wrote to Kelleter that when he "presented the matter to Mr. Doolittle, we found to our surprise that he was violently opposed. While he favored the erection of a monument he did not like our particular plan and declared with vehemence that he 'would not stand for it for a minute'" and would "stop any work which he did not approve of." He added that Doolittle was vehemently opposed to constructing a miniature log house and insisted that it instead be built of concrete. After discussing the use of concrete, which they concluded would not result in a "true replica of the original house," the society stuck to its original proposal, which Doolittle doggedly continued to oppose. In conclusion, wrote Holand, proceeding with the project would not be "worth all this disturbance of peace of mind," and the society "has therefore dropped the entire project."[14]

Several days later Doolittle explained his position in a letter to Kelleter. Holand failed to provide him with Kelleter's written permission, he said, and Doolittle "would not consider a memorial unless same was put up of material that would last." Since the society had agreed to pay for the memorial, he was concerned when Holand insisted that the state pay for its foundation and the fence set in concrete around it. "Personally," said Doolittle, "I think it is all junk to fence a place already used as the main camping ground and for a memorial built of poles, unprotected from the sun, snow, sleet, rain, cold and heat, that in a few years will have to be rebuilt, and of course state money to do it." Those concerned with memorializing Claflin, he added, might consider taking care of the "abandoned . . . cemetery where Mr. Claflin is buried . . . located just across the road . . . but hid . . . with brush etc."[15]

In the last correspondence about the project, Kelleter told Doolittle that because the historical society had dropped the project, Doolittle was "not to permit any construction work on the park which might have a bearing on this proposed monument." His letter also clarified the commission's policy regarding other projects, such as the airport and toboggan slide that were being discussed locally. To avoid further misunderstandings, he said, any such project should be submitted to the commissioner's office along with Doolittle's recommendation. "By submitting such tentative projects to this department," he noted, "you are keeping us currently informed and we are in a much better position to back up your recommendations if we know of the project in advance rather than letting it come to us later on from the individual who may have discussed it with you." This official clarification was certainly in keeping with appropriate management of the park. Kelleter concluded with the important policy statement that "it is the intention of this department to give you every possible support in maintaining the integrity of the park and guarding against onslaughts due to personal hobbies or projects in themselves probably very satisfactory but out of place when they come in connection with the location on the state park."[16] Eventually, a memorial plaque commemorated Increase Claflin. It is attached to the fireplace in the rustic shelter house at Weborg Point.

Today, Weborg Point is a small but heavily used camping area. Campers, hikers, bicyclists, and others enjoy sweeping views of the community of Fish Creek and the same dramatic sunsets the Weborg family observed from their cabin. Most are probably unaware of the pioneer saga and love for this setting that took place here over a century and a half ago. With its ties to one of northern Door County's earliest Euro-American settlements, it is one of the most historically significant locations in the park.

Early campers at Weborg Point.

Eagle Bluff Lighthouse in the 1950s. The porch was added to the original structure. (Author's collection)

CHAPTER 5

❧

Eagle Bluff Lighthouse

GUARDIAN OF THE GREEN BAY PASSAGE

The premier cultural icon in Peninsula Park is the picturesque lighthouse that has graced its high bluff-top setting since 1868. In 1867 the United States Lighthouse Board proposed several additional lighthouses on Lake Michigan in northeast Wisconsin. At the time, northern Door County was essentially a wilderness, with just a few fledgling hamlets situated at its sheltered harbors. When travel was necessary, people walked, rode on horseback, or used horse-drawn sleighs or buggies to maneuver over rough, muddy, rock-and-stump-clad trails, since roads were virtually nonexistent. On one occasion in 1902, for example, the keeper at Eagle Bluff Lighthouse sustained a fractured collarbone when his cutter hit a stone and overturned.[1] Thus, access to and within the county was often by boat. With 250 miles of shoreline, the peninsula became the center of extensive maritime traffic. Navigation along its shores could be difficult, however, because of the many islands, treacherous shoals and reefs, strong winds, dense fogs, and dangerous currents, especially the passage at its tip, Port des Morts. Early sailing ships and steamers were often forced from their designated routes to spend considerable time running to seek refuge in harbors or, where possible, on the protected lee side of land. If they were fortunate enough to make it, they could spend days at anchor waiting for favorable sailing conditions when the storm subsided. It was not uncommon for ships to be lost during ferocious storms that swept across the lake. Hence, waters of the peninsula and adjacent islands are littered with shipwrecks. Between 1878 and 1898, six thousand vessels were wrecked on the Great Lakes. Shipowners who suffered huge financial losses deluged Washington with petitions for more navigational aids.[2]

Light beacons or beams reaching far out over the water have guided maritime traffic since ancient times. Bonfires on top of hills near the shore assisted early navigators on the Mediterranean. As early as 311 B.C. the Egyptians used fires at the mouth of the Nile to signal the area's bustling ship traffic. The first actual lighthouse was the Lighthouse of Alexandria, designed about 280 B.C. One of the Seven Wonders of the World, it stood nearly three hundred feet high and used reflectors to concentrate light from wood fires.[3] The first lighthouse in the continental United States was built by the Province of Massachusetts in 1715–16 at the entrance to Boston Harbor. One of President George Washington's first official acts was to order that the Sandy Hook Light, built at the entrance of New York Bay in 1764, be kept burning until Congress could provide for its maintenance. Because of the importance of lighthouses, in 1789 Congress authorized maintaining them at the expense of the United States and established the federal Lighthouse Service.

In 1818 a survey was taken of the Great Lakes to determine potential lighthouse locations. In Wisconsin considerable lighthouse building followed that lasted until the end of the century. The first lighthouse on Lake Michigan was the Chicago River Light in 1832. Five years later, Wisconsin's first lighthouse was constructed on the north shore of Rock Island. In 1852 Congress established the Lighthouse Board, which organized the nation into districts, each with an inspector. The Great Lakes became the tenth and eleventh districts. Lighthouse construction on the Great Lakes flourished with the growing maritime commerce. Soon lighthouses extended along Wisconsin's Lake Michigan shore as far south as Kenosha. Door County eventually had more lighthouses and lifesaving stations than any other county in the United States. While most lighthouses were situated on critical mainland sites, some were built on islands or reefs. Basically they consisted of a small house attached to a tapered, cylindrical tower topped with a huge magnifying lens that encased an oil lamp.

One of the earliest references to Eagle Bluff Lighthouse appeared in the *Milwaukee Sentinel* on August 12, 1867. The brief account indicated that three lighthouses were to be built at "Baileys Harbor, another at Fish Creek, in Green Bay, and the third at Escanaba." It noted that "The schooner *Toledo,* of this city, has been chartered to carry all of the material to be used in the construction of these new buildings." Work was progressing, said the *Sentinel,* on three other Lake Michigan lighthouses: at Big Point Sauble (Grand Point au Sable), Point Waugashance (Waugoshance), and Skillagalee (Skilligallee). After arriving at Fish Creek, the crew unloaded the supplies at nearby Lighthouse Bay since it was too difficult to deliver them up the abrupt cliff at the actual lighthouse location.

The following year, the *Sentinel* reported that "working parties who are to build the lighthouses at Chambers' Island and Fish Creek, Green Bay, have arrived," by schooner, "and commenced operations."[4] Tons of cream-colored "Cream City" (Milwaukee) brick, boards, roofing, and hardware were carried to the building site, which had been cleared of vegetation. A hole was blasted for the basement, and masons proceeded to erect the handsome one-and-a-half-story structure. Eventually a small landing with wood steps leading up the steep bluff was added. Construction was completed by November, at a cost of twelve thousand dollars.

Situated on a twelve-acre federal reservation of land, the lighthouse measured twenty-six-by-thirty feet. It had a gabled roof with flared eaves and decorative trusses at its peak; vertical ornamental posts extended through the roof, terminating in spires above the ridge. The sturdy structure had a kitchen, dining/living room, formal parlor, and master bedroom, along with a hallway and formal front entrance facing the bay. Its spacious basement had three rooms. A twelve-by-twenty-foot kitchen wing was attached to the east side, and a brick outhouse stood on the north edge of the property. The square light tower was forty-four-feet high and built diagonally into the northwest corner of the dwelling. It enclosed a gracefully winding cast-iron spiral staircase that extended from the basement to the cupola, with landings at each floor level of the house. Throughout its many years of occupancy, the building never had electricity or indoor plumbing.

When the tower was completed, sections of the ten-sided, cast-iron lantern were hoisted into place. Constructed by the Detroit Locomotive Works, an iron foundry and machine shop, it measured seven feet in diameter. It was topped with a cast-iron roof with a ventilator ball and lightning rod.[5] The light had a three-and-one-half-order Fresnel lens (replaced in 1918 with a fifth order Fresnel lens) and stood seventy-six feet above lake level. Its fixed white beam had a range of sixteen miles over the east passage of Green Bay. Invented by a French physicist, the Fresnel lens consisted of a series of separate concentric rings with highly polished glass prisms, forming a large lens. It revolutionized lighthouse construction by reducing the bulk and weight of the light while increasing its brilliance.

The Eagle Bluff Lighthouse strongly resembled the nearby Chambers Island Lighthouse, which was built the same year, but their towers were different. Eagle Bluff's was square and Chambers's was hexagonal so each would be a distinctive marker for sailors. Unlike many other lighthouses in the United States, neither structure was painted with various patterns or colors to make them stand out from their surroundings.

The Eagle Bluff Light was lit for the first time on the night of October 15, 1868.[6] Initially, it was fueled with lard-oil; on March 14, 1882, the Coast Guard finished installing fixtures for burning mineral oil; later, kerosene was used. As a precaution against fire and lightning, the kerosene was stored in a building specially constructed at a safe distance from the dwelling. On July 23, 1899, the steamer *Arcadia* delivered the brick and iron for this new structure. It was erected the following year "with an iron roof and shelving."[7]

Located at the highest point on Eagle Bluff, the lighthouse was often struck by lightning. The keepers' descendants have reported that sometimes lightning traveled down the circular iron staircase, damaging walls and furnishings along its path. The keeper's log often noted heavy squalls, strong winds, or gales that damaged the light. On August 8, 1892, for example, "at ten at night there was a very heavy squall. It blew the top off the stone fence in front of the station." Two weeks later "the assistant engineer arrived to assess the damage and see what repairs were needed at the light."[8] The chimney also required frequent repairs.

Henry Stanley was the first keeper at Eagle Bluff Light. Born in Norway, Stanley came to America in 1844 at the age of twenty-one. After an unsuccessful attempt to find gold in California he moved to New York where a young immigrant from Germany, Katherine Hesh, caught his eye. They married and moved west where Stanley sailed the Great Lakes, eventually becoming co-owner of several ships. When Stanley received his appointment as a light keeper, he sold his shipping interests and the family (the Stanleys had two children, ten-year-old John and eight-year-old Elizabeth) moved to Eagle Bluff Lighthouse in the fall of 1868.[9] There Henry assumed the routine duties of a light keeper, including keeping a log of his activities. In the first several years he made only a few entries in the station log. After the annual inspection in August 1876, however, Stanley began recording many more activities at the lighthouse. The log indicates that the family had many friends and visitors and did not lead the isolated existence of many lighthouse keepers in more remote locations. Stanley served at the light until September 30, 1883, when he was transferred to the Sherwood Point Light at Sturgeon Bay.

William Henry Duclon became the next keeper at Eagle Bluff Light. A native of Alexander Bay, in Jefferson County, New York, Duclon began sailing on the Great Lakes at the age of sixteen. When the Civil War broke out, he served as a volunteer in New York's Fourteenth Heavy Artillery Regiment. Wounded in the Battle of Gettysburg, he was hospitalized for several months and was honorably discharged shortly before Christmas in 1864. Three years later he married Julia Davenport and engaged in fishing until 1873 when he took an examination for the lighthouse service. He was appointed second assistant at the Waugoshance Lighthouse near the Straits of Mackinac, with an annual salary of $390. When eligible for promotion, he was given the choice of going to Lake Michigan or Lake Superior. When he chose Lake Michigan he was transferred to the lighthouse at the southern end of Beaver Island, near the Straits of Mackinac, on December 6, 1875, with an increase in salary of $170. Transferred again, Duclon took charge of the Eagle Bluff Light on September 20, 1883.[10] He would spend the next thirty-five years of his career there.

The Duclons raised seven sons at Eagle Bluff Lighthouse: Ambrose, William Jr., James, Charles, Frank, Walter, and Joseph. From early spring when the ice broke up in Green Bay, until the lake froze over again in winter, Duclon lighted the light each day. It shone across the water every night from sundown to sunup. Before the conversion to kerosene, his work involved cleaning the light of carbon that formed on its prisms from the burning lard and mineral oil.

Keeping the lighthouse and its grounds neat and orderly was another strict requirement of the Lighthouse Service. Periodically, inspectors came by boat, often on the steamer *Dahlia,* to inspect the lighthouse. The Duclon boys always kept a sharp lookout for the boat. When they sighted it, there was a flurry of activity—last minute cleaning, polishing, and tidying up the grounds. The inspectors' visits were important events and were always recorded in the logbook. For example, an 1898 entry stated that Mr. Jas. Adams "came ashore and inspected the light." Sometimes their visits became a social event, as on

Early view of Eagle Bluff Lighthouse and several members of the Duclon family. (Author's collection)

September 8, 1902, when "Commander L. Young, inspector of the lighthouse district and Cap Hurbord of the supply steamer *Dahlia* came over from Baileys Harbor . . . with a team and had their ladyes [*sic*] with them."[11]

The keeper's supplies were delivered by the Coast Guard, which hauled the cargo up the steps and stored it in the cellar—sacks of salt, barrels of flour, sugar, cornmeal, and other staples—alongside the potatoes, corned beef, summer sausage, and other items. Other important cargo items were household goods, such as linens, kerosene, supplies for maintaining and cleaning the light, and huge quantities of paint for the buildings. As on all United States Navy and Coast Guard ships, painting was a constant task whether needed or not. Before leaving, the crew of the tender would also put out or take up the buoys at Frying Pan Shoals off the front of the lighthouse.

As at most Great Lakes lighthouses, the family depended on their large garden for fruit, vegetables, and herbs. It was fenced to keep out the wild animals, some of which—deer, squirrels, and rabbits—formed an important part of their diet. The family also kept pigs and chickens. Wild fruits and berries were brought home for Mrs. Duclon's delicious jams, jellies, and pies. In addition to cooking and baking, she had the important household tasks of laundry and sewing for her family.

Over the years, changes and improvements were made at the lighthouse. To help keep the residence cool during the warm summer months, a summer kitchen for cooking and eating was built south of the house. An addition to the south side of the kitchen wing was attached later. In the fall of 1876, a stone wall was built along the bluff (the foreman for the project boarded at the lighthouse for three weeks while he worked). A white wood fence was built around the clearing. In 1893, "a barn was built 16′ × 24′ 1½ stories high" for the horses and a cow, and three years later, a tall "flag staff was erected" south of the dwelling.[12] The buildings and other features formed a tidy complex in their spacious clearing in the woods.

To keep active during the long winter months, the growing Duclon boys made sleighs, skated, and spent considerable time fishing through the ice. Sometimes they stayed out on the frozen bay until darkness set in. Then, since the lighthouse beacon was extinguished for the winter, their thoughtful mother placed a lamp in the window of the upstairs music room so the boys could find their way home. Winter was the prime time for social activities since responsibilities for keeping the light were fewer and travel was easier with the bay frozen. To help pass the time, the Duclon boys learned to play a variety of musical instruments. Walter Duclon later recalled the grand piano that his father, an accomplished pianist, had purchased for fifty dollars. When it arrived by steamer, friends strained to hoist it up and over the bluff only to discover that it was too large to move through the dwelling's doors or windows. It was shipped back by schooner for a smaller, less bulky piano.[13] Eventually, the men of the family formed the Duclon Band. Frank played the violin, and the others played piano, guitar, accordion, and cello. During the winter the group loaded their instruments, including the piano, on a sleigh to revel in an evening of fun mingled with musical interludes. The popular group played at dances and weddings in nearby communities. On June 12, 1884, the *Advocate* reported that "William Duclon, keeper of the Eagle Bluff light, with his two sons has organized a string band and the music is equal to any to be found in this region. Whenever there is a dance or an entertainment of that character . . . the Messrs. Duclon are sure to be called upon to furnish the music."

At first the Duclons walked to Fish Creek to get their mail and provisions. Eventually, a road was built that provided access by wagon. Initially, they did not even have a well or pump. The boys used a yoke to carry two pails of water at a time from the bay up the steep steps of the bluff to the house, where it was used for cooking, laundering, and bathing. A well was finally drilled in the late 1880s with a horse-powered treadmill.

The beacon from Eagle Bluff Lighthouse saved an untold number of ships and sailors from death and disaster. The most dangerous time for shipping along the Door Peninsula's western shore was during summer storms, the gales

Eagle Bluff Lighthouse as seen from the water. Note the steps to the pier at the base of the bluff and the accessory buildings, including the barn, on the right. (Author's collection)

of November and early December, or early spring when the ice began breaking up. In the pitch-black darkness of night or in the thick fog that sometimes
enveloped the eastern passage of Green Bay, sailors unfamiliar with the area
faced the possibility of running aground or even colliding with other ships.
Such was the case of the *Alvin Clark,* which, in 1864, while traveling under full
sail, capsized when struck by a summer squall. More than a century later, in
the summer of 1969, divers raised the historic ship from its resting place not
far from Chambers Island.[14]

The lighthouse keepers typically recorded noteworthy events in their log:
detailed weather conditions, visitors, personal insights about their families,
and dates of lighting the beacon in the spring and extinguishing it at the end
of the sailing season. The log provides a rare glimpse into what life was like at
this remote location.

Sometimes the lighthouse keeper risked his life to come to the aid of sailors
or stranded fishermen. On one cold January day in 1909, Captain Duclon made
a gallant rescue of nine fishermen from what could have been a watery grave,
after they were stranded on an ice floe. The men, who were from Ephraim,
were hook and line fishing for trout through the ice just east of Chambers
Island.[15] Ice fishing was a common seasonal activity for residents of the shoreline villages on Green Bay, since it provided food and some income during the
winter months when they could not farm or do other outdoor work. A heavy
prevailing "south wester" wind suddenly parted the ice, stranding the group.
The dangerous crack extended from Horseshoe Shoal to the Strawberry group,
cutting the men off from land on the moving ice floe.

Duclon, who had a commanding view of the bay from his station, was the
first to notice their plight. With the assistance of several volunteers, he maneu-
vered a small boat to the scene. The stranded men were then transported to
solid ice after several trips across the open water. By the time the last fishermen were removed, the perilous crack had widened to a distance of two and
a half miles. Had Duclon not acted swiftly, wind and wave action would soon
have broken up the ice. The fishermen lost five of their six fish sleighs and the
ice carried out their gill nets and a lifting shanty owned by Anton Amundson,
a local fisherman. By the time the wind subsided, the ice had gone out of
Green Bay as far as the Strawberry Islands.

The following month, the Fish Creek news section of the *Advocate* noted
that Captain Duclon suggested that enough timber be cut "to render the light
visible from this village." It would be a great aid to navigation, he maintained,
and would "prevent any possible mistake on the part of masters navigating
these waters in the dark."[16] The Lighthouse Board approved the proposition,

but nothing could be done without the consent of the owners of the standing trees, which apparently was never given.

One can only wonder about the deep concerns Duclon and other area lighthouse keepers had about the fate of mariners during the horrendous storms that sometimes raged across the lake. With winter setting in and temperatures dropping dangerously low, November was a particularly perilous time for ships. Little did Duclon know that the "Big Blow" of 1913 would go down in record books as one of the worst storms in Great Lakes history. Less than twenty miles to the northeast, the bulk carrier *Louisiana* was experiencing serious trouble as it headed for Escanaba, Michigan, after leaving Milwaukee with a load of iron ore. Around midnight on November 8, 1913, it passed through Death's Door Channel and into a howling storm with winds exceeding seventy miles per hour. The captain sought shelter near the northwest corner of Washington Island but its anchors could not hold in the heavy seas. The ship was driven aground at nearby Schoolhouse Beach and its crew barely made it to shore in a lifeboat. Subsequent salvage attempts and the ravages of ice broke up the hull.[17] Its remains have become a popular diving spot, and in 1992 the *Louisiana* was listed in the National Register of Historic Places as an underwater archeological site.

Eagle Bluff Lighthouse has been a popular attraction for park visitors virtually since the park began. The girls at Camp Meenahga in Fish Creek made frequent treks there, one of which was recorded in *Pack and Paddle* in 1925:

One Monday the girls and councilors decided it was too cold to go in swimming in the morning, so they decided to go on a hike. It was finally decided that we go over to the Government Lighthouse Tower, a place where the new girls had never been.

We arrived there and in a few minutes the lighthouse keeper took us up. We climbed to the top of the winding staircase. It was lots of fun and a little scary, too. When we reached the top the keeper opened another door and took us out on a balcony. From this point we had the view of the bay. It was a beautiful sight. One of the girls took a Kodak picture of it.

We soon went back into the little room and the keeper took off the cloth, which kept the dust from getting on the light. The light is a wonderful instrument. It is of French make and of such powerful glass that although only a small light put inside of it is reflected and made so large that it can be seen for thirteen miles.

We hiked back to camp and agreed that we had had one of the most interesting trips of the year.[18]

That same year, another camper expressed her lighthouse sentiments:

> Have you ever seen a lighthouse, a lighthouse by the sea?
> If you care to hear my story, just listen now to me.
> In a little white cottage sitting beside the lighthouse tower
> The rugged lighthouse keeper smokes his old pipe by the hour
> Sometimes when we go visiting, he tells us strange sea tales
> Of what becomes of the great steamships when the lighthouse lantern fails,
> He tells of cries and shipwreck, and of many a sorry sight,
> When the wind comes up and the moon goes down and the storm blows
>   through the night.
> So if ever you chance to visit the lighthouse by the sea,
> You will likely hear the stories that the keeper told to me.[19]

Captain Duclon remained in charge of the Eagle Bluff light until 1918, when he was retired on a pension to spend more time at the house he had built in Fish Creek. During his long career, the service awarded him many merit stars, and he always enjoyed relating stories of his exciting adventures and thrilling experiences. In 1926, after a brief illness, Duclon died at the age of eighty-one at the home of his son in Green Bay. Six of his sons served as pallbearers at his funeral in Fish Creek, which was attended by many from his large circle of friends. Duclon's obituary referred to him as "one of the pioneer lightkeepers of the Great Lakes."[20] He had been in the Lighthouse Service for forty-three years, thirty-five of them at Eagle Bluff. He was interred at Blossomburg Cemetery in the park, as was his wife when she died, four years earlier.

In 1919, after Duclon's retirement, Superintendent Peter Coughlin became keeper of the light. Previously, he had been at the Beaver Island Lighthouse and was the first lighthouse keeper at St. James Harbor. Coughlin served at Eagle Bluff until the Lighthouse Bureau installed an unmanned automated acetylene gaslight in 1926. In 1930 at the age of seventy, he retired from the Lighthouse Service and died at Green Bay that same year after being struck by a car.

In 1929, with the government no longer maintaining the light, the *Advocate* reported, "The property is becoming run down, making a bad appearance within the well-kept park." The Conservation Commission asked Congressman George Schneider to look into the matter and requested that "if the property cannot be turned over to the state, . . . some arrangements . . . be entered into to keep the appearance of the property up."[21]

In February 10, 1933, the *Advocate* announced on its front page that "the state of Wisconsin may acquire a portion of the Eagle Bluff Lighthouse reservation for state park purposes." Congressman Schneider and Senator Hiram Johnson, chairman of the Committee on Commerce, had introduced bills for this action, and in 1936 the lighthouse was deeded to the State of Wisconsin. The Coast Guard, however, would maintain the light. Since the State Park Commission had been leasing vacant buildings in the park for many years, requests to rent the living quarters of the lighthouse started during the summer of that year.[22]

After the light was automated, the dwelling remained vacant for long periods of time. Sometimes it was rented to summer residents and, on occasion, the Boy Scouts used it. While park workers did their best to maintain the dwelling, it gradually deteriorated; visitors, vandalism, and the lack of interest took their toll. Tales that it was haunted circulated among students at nearby Gibraltar High School. One told of a mysterious blue light that appeared in the upper windows at night. Eventually, the accessory buildings were moved to nearby locations in the park. In 1936 Mrs. Theodore Peterson leased the summer kitchen, moved it into the woods north of the lighthouse, and remodeled it into "the little cottage."[23] She occupied it for many summers. Renters could have the barn and an old log stable on the south edge of the lighthouse grounds for fifty dollars a year and repairs, at their own expense.

In the 1960s the lighthouse was spared from what might have been an unfortunate end. At the instigation of Bert Sanderson of Sturgeon Bay, a group of dedicated volunteers restored the lighthouse to its original condition. A partner in the *Advocate,* Sanderson was concerned about the future of an important collection of artifacts owned by Mrs. D. E. Bay of Sturgeon Bay. He favored placing the collection in a historic Door County building and, with the help of Harry Dankoler of the Sturgeon Bay Museum and others, he helped reorganize the Door County Historical Society in 1957. When an initial plan to place it in the Cana Island Lighthouse near Baileys Harbor proved unworkable, the society considered Eagle Bluff Lighthouse. A series of antique and arts and crafts shows raised three thousand dollars to restore Eagle Bluff Lighthouse, which was furnished with many antiques from Mrs. Bay's collection.

In April of 1961 volunteers began the challenging task of restoring the historic treasure to its appearance back in the days of the Duclon family. Park superintendent Lowell Hansen obtained the original plans from the Coast Guard and gave generous support to the project. At times the group underwent heartbreaking setbacks and had to overcome serious obstacles. In winter, for example, the park roads were not plowed and it often took over two hours to reach the building. Vandals damaged the interior and broke windows almost as fast as they were replaced. Woodstoves were brought in to heat the dwelling for the workers during cold weather. Considerable effort went into removing additions and modifications to the structure, which had been partitioned into ten rooms over the years. The south-facing porch and small wing built onto the kitchen were removed. An attempt was made to bring back the barn, which had been moved elsewhere in the park. As many as eighty coats of paint were scraped from the pine woodwork—most of it Coast Guard gray. The government had sent so much paint that the Duclons sometimes painted twice each year. The wide plank floors were sanded, at first by hand because no electricity was available. The loan of a generator by Hansen greatly facilitated this task. He also furnished a generous supply of firewood during the winter months. Removing paint and layers of whitewash from the plaster walls proved so difficult that they were covered with wallpaper—one of the few aspects of the restoration that was not authentic. Four century-old stoves, including a black cookstove and a "cathedral-type" stove suitable for the formal parlor, were acquired from various sources. Upstairs, a sewing machine and spinning wheel were added to the furnishings, which included a blue sea chest with primitive painting inside. It was said to have survived the great Peshtigo Fire that swept through the southern reaches of Door County in 1871. A wooden sailing vessel carved by one of the Duclon boys while recuperating from a broken leg was placed in another room. It resembles a vessel the lad had watched while it sailed past on Green Bay.

As work progressed, various pieces of period furniture were donated to the project. Descendants of the Duclon family provided several important items, including a Victorian love seat and a black walnut dining table and chairs. Monetary contributions came from many parts of the United States. Walter Duclon Sr. of Green Bay, youngest of the family's seven sons and the only then-surviving member of the original family, provided valuable input. Then in his eighties, he managed to visit the project almost every Sunday during the summer.[24]

Two problems remained before the lighthouse could be opened to the public as a historic site operated by the Door County Historical Society. The original lease to the Wisconsin Conservation Department did not permit subleasing to the society, so a new lease was drawn up with the Coast Guard in May of 1963. Another problem related to the society's request to collect fees to help defray operating costs. The following year, with the assistance of U.S. Senator Gaylord Nelson, the lease was amended to grant "permission to charge a nominal admission fee to the general public."[25] By the summer of 1965, the lighthouse was open to the public. It became the focus of numerous newspaper articles and considerable interest among lighthouse enthusiasts and tourists. Several years later a large anchor was placed in front of the lighthouse. It came from the *Oak Leaf,* a three-masted schooner launched in 1866.[26]

The Eagle Bluff Lighthouse was listed in the National Register of Historic Places in 1970. The nomination for its designation stated that it was "a good example of functional design for efficient utilization of combined living and working quarters for a lighthouse keeper" and "of significance to commerce and transportation."[27]

On October 16, 2003, representatives of the U.S. Bureau of Land Management, the Wisconsin Department of Natural Resources, and the Door County Historical Society signed documents transferring ownership of the land to the state. The transaction placed the lighthouse in the custody of the society, which has managed the property as a museum within the park.[28]

The Eagle Bluff light still shines over the bay, but it now uses a solar-powered light in a 300 mm. plastic lens. It is one of some 340 lighthouses currently in use in the United States. Perhaps, in the future, the barn and summer kitchen will be reconstructed so that the full ensemble of buildings can more accurately portray what life was once like at this historic northern Door County outpost.

❧

CHAPTER 6

Thomas Reynolds, John Nolen, and Legislation to Establish the Park

Wisconsin was one of the first states to create a state park system. A national movement for state parks had begun in 1864, when the federal government ceded Yosemite Valley and the Mariposa Big Tree Grove to the State of California.

The indomitable Increase Lapham, sometimes referred to as the father of Wisconsin's conservation movement, fostered early interest in conservation in Wisconsin. Lapham, who arrived at Milwaukee from Ohio in 1836, studied portions of the state as an archaeologist, botanist, cartographer, geologist, and meteorologist. Alarmed at the rapid destruction of Wisconsin's vast forests, in 1867 he wrote a seminal report entitled *The Disastrous Effects of the Destruction of Forest Trees in Wisconsin*. His work resulted in legislation that established Wisconsin's first Forestry Commission.

In 1878, the Wisconsin Legislature set aside a fifty-thousand-acre tract of land in Iron and Vilas counties as the state park. In part, this initial interest in parks was spurred by the designation of Yellowstone National Park (our nation's first national park) six years earlier. Unfortunately, in 1897, due to powerful lobbying interests, the legislature placed the land on the market. Commenting on this travesty, the *Racine Daily Times* wrote, "Who are the lumbermen behind the scheme? [This] . . . territory known as park lands . . . contains the most valuable standing pine in the state." The editorial concluded with the charge that "the state school fund has been robbed of millions of dollars by the timber wolves who ought to be in the penitentiary, but are in other places of public trust. And what little pine land there is left should be carefully guarded from the lumber thieves."[1] Unfortunately, about thirty-two thousand acres were sold to lumber companies for approximately eight dollars per acre.[2] It is interesting to note that the state later repurchased the land for a forest reserve, paying about one-third of the original price, but with the timber cut.[3]

A milestone in establishing state reserves of public land occurred in 1885, when the State of New York acquired portions of Niagara Falls and the vast Adirondack Forest. Michigan obtained federally owned Mackinac Island that same year and, in 1891, Minnesota began purchasing lands that became Lake Itasca State Park. Four years later, in 1895, the Wisconsin Legislature authorized the acquisition of 250 acres in the St. Croix River area of Polk County, but the necessary funding was not appropriated.

By the end of the century, interest in state parks was growing throughout the United States. At its 1898 meeting in Minneapolis, the American Park and Outdoor Art Association passed a resolution urging that a forest reserve be established at the Dalles of the St. Croix River. It also recommended purchasing additional land "to preserve the reservation and its views from the introduction of inharmonious objects."[4] In 1900 initial funds were approved and by joint legislative action Wisconsin and Minnesota established Interstate State Park at the Dalles of the St. Croix River. This park sparked renewed action for a system of state parks in Wisconsin.

Shortly after the turn of the century, interest in creating a state park at Devils Lake was growing among Baraboo residents. In 1903, Sauk County Assemblyman Franklin Johnson introduced a bill authorizing the governor to appoint a three-member commission to consider the matter. It was to report to the governor on "the advisability of purchasing lands about, upon and surrounding Devil's Lake . . . for the purpose of establishing a state park thereon."[5] In the next session of the legislature, another bill relating to "establishing state parks about Devil's Lake . . . and the Dells of Wisconsin" was introduced.[6] This initiative received growing support in 1906, when William H. McFetridge, a prominent Baraboo industrialist, headed a group of citizens attempting to establish the Devils Lake area as a state park. To garner public support, McFetridge distributed two thousand copies of his pamphlet "An Appeal for the Preservation of the Devil's Lake Region."[7] Legislators and their friends took a special train to visit the area for a festive outing and examination of the area on May Day in 1907, but efforts to establish Devils Lake State Park floundered for two more years.

In response to increasing public awareness of the need to save places of great natural beauty for future generations, legislation was passed to set up the State Park Board.[8] The law went into effect on July 11, 1907. The assignment of the board was to investigate, and report to Governor James O. Davidson and the legislature, proposed parks and their acquisition. The board consisted of three prominent Wisconsinites: Madison attorney Thomas E. Brittingham, president; State Senator E. E. Brown from Waupaca; and McFetridge. Initially, the board's annual appropriation was a mere five hundred dollars. This was a modest beginning; yet, at this time twenty-nine states still had no state parks.

By now state park boosters were active in Door County, where a state park was seen as a way to preserve significant natural areas and as an economic boon for tourism. Assemblyman Thomas Reynolds of Jacksonport is credited with conceiving the idea of having a state park in the county and he became a vigorous proponent of legislation to establish it. A native of Longford, Ireland, Reynolds came to America in 1866. After working for one year in Dane County, he bought a large tract of land in the Jacksonport area where he worked for eight years at cutting cordwood and cedar posts for the Chicago market. He then began farming and served on the county board. In the fall of 1906, he was elected to the assembly where he served two terms.[9] The following year Reynolds introduced a bill amending the earlier State Park Board bill for an "examination of lands in Door county for a state park."[10] At this time another bill was also passed to create a state park in the vicinity of the territorial capital in Lafayette County.

Under the powers granted to it by the legislature, the State Park Board began discussing possible park sites, giving emphasis to the Door County location. It decided to visit the tract of land between Fish Creek and Ephraim and determined, "if no facts nor conditions be discovered that would alter their present opinion, that the Attorney General should be notified to commence proceedings for obtaining title" of the land "for the State."[11]

It was clear that the board would need professional expertise to evaluate proposed park sites, make land acquisition recommendations, and help avoid undue political influence in site selection. For this task the board contacted John Nolen, a brilliant young landscape architect from Cambridge, Massachusetts. Retaining Nolen came about largely through the efforts of John Olin, a prominent Madison attorney who, as president of the Madison Park and Pleasure Drive Association, had worked closely with Brittingham. Madison did not yet have a city parks department, but the Park and Pleasure Drive Association had made great strides in creating parks for the community. It was also responsible for hiring landscape architect Emil T. Mische as the city's park superintendent.[12]

In 1908, Mische resigned to take a higher-paying job in Portland, Oregon. Recognizing the importance of this position, Olin was determined to fill the vacancy with a landscape architect of national acclaim. Before his departure, Mische recommended several, including Nolen. Olin realized that the park superintendent position alone would not be adequate to lure a person with such high standing to Madison, and he sought to make the hiring arrangement more attractive. He first attempted to add a position as professor of landscape architecture and chair of a new department for this young profession at the university. Having taught there, Olin had close ties to its president, Charles R. Van Hise. Unfortunately, because of budget limitations, the proposed landscape architecture program did not become a reality and Nolen was reluctant to leave Cambridge.

Undeterred, Olin persisted. After a complex series of negotiations, he arranged for Nolen to work not only for the State Park Board but also for the Madison Park and Pleasure Drive Association, the City of Madison, and the State Board of Control (which oversaw the state's many institutions).

On March 11, 1908, Nolen wrote back to Olin that it would mean "breaking away from my established home and business connections," and not being able to "keep in touch . . . with the leaders in my profession and with that big civic movement that is now sweeping the country." He did, however, suggest maintaining his office in Cambridge and retaining Wisconsin as a "preferred client," giving its work priority over other jobs. He also proposed several extended visits to Wisconsin for a month or so at a time, and corresponding regularly when not in the state.[13] Nolen was hired under this arrangement. In his letter of acceptance, he stated, "I should enter this field with enthusiasm, looking upon the opportunity as one of the greatest that this country has yet offered to a landscape architect."[14]

A native of Philadelphia, John Nolen graduated first in his class from Girard College, a high school for poor, fatherless boys. After working to save enough money, he enrolled in the University of Pennsylvania's Wharton School and graduated with distinction. In 1905 he earned a master's degree from the new landscape architecture program at Harvard University. A career in this profession provided an outlet for his strong commitment to public service. By this time he had opened an office in Cambridge and started an array of landscape architecture and city planning projects in several states. A prolific writer, he began amassing a long list of professional publications. One of his earliest articles was about public open space, which he coauthored with Frederick Law Olmsted Jr.

As the first American to identify himself exclusively as a town and city planner, Nolen became the rising star of his profession. By 1908 his fame had spread to Wisconsin where he eventually worked on a variety of important commissions, in addition to his pioneering state park plan. These included several projects in the capital city, as well as at Milwaukee, Kenosha, Janesville, and Green Bay; a comprehensive park report for La Crosse; plans for state institution grounds at Wales, Chippewa Falls, and Sparta; designs for several private estates; and a land subdivision (Lakewood, now part of the Village of Maple Bluff) in Madison.[15]

A dynamic leader in his new profession, Nolen achieved many positions of prominence, including serving as president of the National Conference on City Planning (1925–27), the American City Planning Institute (1925–27), and the International Federation for Housing and Town Planning in London, England (1931–35).

During the Depression, he became a consultant to virtually every federal agency and program dealing with the physical planning of towns, cities, states, and regions, as well a member of President Franklin D. Roosevelt's National Resource Planning Board. Nolen's prodigious work spanned a nearly forty-year period while the Progressive movement and the New Deal were sweeping the nation with a variety of reforms. Working out of the Harvard Square office, he and his firm completed more than four hundred commissions in the United States, Canada, and Cuba. He died in 1937 at the age of sixty-eight. As a landscape architect and city planner, John Nolen was a lasting influence for better urban life in cities all across America. The citizens of Madison and communities throughout Wisconsin were fortunate to have inherited some of the highlights of his planning legacy.

Once Nolen was retained, Olin worked to ensure that he would receive a warm welcome on his first visit to Wisconsin. He arranged for Nolen to be the featured speaker at the annual meeting of the Madison Park and Pleasure Drive Association in April of 1908. He invited Governor Davidson to attend and meet Nolen, and urged State Park Board members to be there. The audience was impressed by Nolen's speaking powers, and Olin himself commented, "I expected that Mr. Nolen would do well from what I have heard of him, but he far surpassed my expectation."[16] Indeed, the standard Nolen set for himself during that speech was one he attained for all of his work for Wisconsin.

By this time speculation was growing in Door County regarding the location for the state park. Several areas were considered. In fact, the *Door County Democrat* suggested that "every town in the county should have a fair chance to secure this park," and it urged residents who knew of an available site to "call the attention of their town chairman to it or communicate with Assemblyman Thos. Reynolds."[17] Within a week, the paper reported that citizens from Baileys Harbor and Jacksonport (including Reynolds) had met and offered "the state a tract of land comprising over one thousand acres located between Kangaroo Lake and Lake Michigan . . . land bordering on both bodies of water." The newspaper added, "This is the kind of work that should be done in every town that wants a chance to secure this park and the people of other towns should 'get busy.'"[18]

Early in May of 1908, State Park Board members, accompanied by Nolen and Senator H. P. Bird of Wausaukee, arrived by train at Sturgeon Bay. There, joined by Reynolds, the group traveled by carriage to Clarks Lake, one of the proposed locations in Door County. The following day they left for Fish Creek where they were welcomed by local residents and escorted to two tracts of land, "one south of the village and including the Fish Creek bluffs, the highest point of land in Door County, and the other . . . on the point between Fish Creek and Ephraim, including Eagle Bluffs." They were also taken on F. P. Crunden's launch to view the area's high limestone bluffs from the water. The following Saturday was spent "investigating the county north of Ellison

Members of the State Park Board and other dignitaries on their May 1908 reconnaissance visit to northern Door County to inspect potential park sites. Left to right: Mrs. John Nolen, John Nolen, John M. Olin of Madison, Mrs. Olin, Mrs. Bird, Senator H. P. Bird of Wausaukee, unidentified woman, Mrs. Thomas Brittingham, Senator E. E. Brown of Waupaca, University of Wisconsin Dean Edward A. Birge, unidentified man, Senator Isaac Stephenson, unidentified man, Mrs. Stephenson, former Governor W. D. Hoard, unidentified man, Thomas Brittingham, Governor James O. Davidson, and state forester E. F. Griffith. (Courtesy of Rare and Manuscript Collections, Carl A. Kroch Library, Cornell University)

Bay, going to Newport, Garrett Bay, Gills Rock and Europe Lake." They spent the night of May 12 at Baileys Harbor, and the next day they examined the tract east of Kangaroo Lake, which was "not exactly what they were looking for." The group then left for Green Bay, where they took the train to Madison. While expressing delight over what they had seen, they made no official statement about their visit. The *Door County Democrat,* however, speculated that "the result will be the establishment of a state park in this county and that this will be the best possible advertisement of the attractiveness of this peninsula as a resort for summer tourists."[19]

By the end of June, Nolen and Olin were corresponding about tentative state park sites. Nolen suggested traveling by boat to traverse the tract between Fish Creek and Ephraim on his next visit to Wisconsin. Meanwhile, Brittingham had arranged to visit Door County accompanied by local citizens and interested officials. Olin wrote to Nolen detailing plans for the trip: "You undoubtedly have heard from Mr. Brittingham in regard to his plan to take a trip from Marinette on a yacht to the proposed park in Door County. . . . I wonder whether after taking that trip and looking over 'Thunder Mountain,' . . . it will be possible for you and me to return to Door County and spend a day or two looking over some ground Mr. Brittingham has talked to me about, with

Main Street in Fish Creek about two years after the park reconnaissance team's visit. At the end of their trip through the park site, the group gathered for a banquet at Dr. and Mrs. Welcker's inn, shown at the end of the street on the right. (Author's collection)

a view of my perhaps making a purchase and with becoming more familiar with the location."[20]

The purpose of that trip was to gather more information and support but more importantly, said Brittingham, "The sole object . . . was to get U.S. Senator 'Uncle Ike' Stephenson to give this park to the State, or at least fifty thousand dollars towards securing it."[21] At a time when legislative funding for the parks was a new and difficult undertaking, it was hoped that the wealthy Stephenson might donate additional funds.

The *Advocate* predicted that the arrival of the delegation "will go down in history as a red letter day in the annals of Fish Creek, through the presence within her portals of some of the most notable and distinguished citizens of Wisconsin."[22] Local residents who wanted the beauty of their area—which they fondly referred to, as Nolen later wrote, as the "paradise of Wisconsin"— to be shared with the rest of the state warmly welcomed the group.[23] Both county newspapers and the Marinette *Daily Eagle-Star* described the trip. Aboard Stephenson's yacht, *Bonita,* when it arrived at Fish Creek from Marinette was the group of distinguished citizens accompanying the State Park Board. According to the Marinette *Daily Eagle-Star,* it included "Governor J. O. Davidson, ex-Gov. Hoard, Mr. and Mrs. John Nolen, Mr. and Mrs. John

Early road in the park similar to the one visited by the park reconnaissance team. (Courtesy Brittingham Collection, Steenbock Library, University of Wisconsin–Madison)

M. Olin of Madison, Senator H. P. Bird and wife, Assemblyman C. E. Ester-brook of Milwaukee, author [of the] state park law, Dean Brigs [Birge] of the Wisconsin University . . . E. F. Griffith, State Forester, H. S. Eldred of Mil-waukee and F. E. Noyes of the *Daily Eagle-Star*."[24] Board member McFetridge, who wanted Wisconsin's first state park to be at Devils Lake, was absent.

At lunch at the Thorp Hotel were Reynolds, Dr. Eames, Henry Fetzer, Frank Long, Herb Peterson, Frank Wellever, John Bertschinger, and several other interested citizens. Afterward, the party went by carriages over the rocky roads to view the proposed park site. John J. Pinney of Sturgeon Bay, "who has been foremost in promoting the project," guided them.[25] Their first stops were at the Eagle Bluff Lighthouse and Shanty Bay. Next they traveled to the southern boundary of the site before returning to Fish Creek. Later, they set out again for "School House Bluff" (Svens Bluff), where they enjoyed "the glowing sunset from this great height, from where it seems one could leap right out onto the Strawberry Islands." After sunset, they returned to Dr. and Mrs. Welcker's Inn for a banquet and speeches, with Olin as toastmaster. Governor Davidson spoke first, expressing his appreciation for the beauty of the proposed park. "We live for future generations," he stated. "The beauti-ful spots should be preserved, and I take my stand now, and also before the next legislature, in favor of State Parks." Remarks followed by Hoard, Bird, Reynolds, and Nolen, all of whom praised the area and the day's events. Nolen remarked on his observations, stating that "the Eastern States would jump at the situation offered in Door County. I trust that the state will secure it." Olin had more comments, but the conclusion was the same: "The view offered at various points of the proposed site excels everything I have ever yet seen in Wisconsin. There is nothing to be done to the site; all the enjoyment is already there. I trust that it will be secured by this legislature." Speaking on behalf of Door County residents, Reynolds closed by stating: "We are glad that you gentlemen have honored us with your presence here and we are grateful for the good things you have said about our park site, and if when you are ready to go to Heaven you should need our endorsement, you shall have it."[26] All of the speakers praised the valuable services of Pinney, who had spent several weeks at Fish Creek securing "options on a majority of the pieces of land within the proposed park, to be presented to the legislature when it meets."[27]

Following dinner, the guests took a brief jaunt to the Welcker "casino" and then retired at the homes of "Messrs Eldred, Crunden, and Clark." The next day they boarded the *Bonita* for Marinette, where most of them took the train home.

Three days after the much-publicized visit, Door County residents were excited and enthusiastic about having a state park in their midst. They realized, however, that the main obstacle would be the landowners who would ask exorbitant prices, realizing the importance of their properties' value to the park.[28]

By the end of August, the *Madison Democrat* published several articles by John Nolen entitled "Wisconsin State Parks."[29] They included his impressions from the Door County visit and his hopes for the future of Wisconsin's state parks. Impressed with the Door County site, Nolen compared its beauty to the coasts of Maine, extolling its wild and unspoiled scenic quality. In his remarks, which appeared the following year in his milestone state park report, he spoke of

> the alternating beauty of woodland, cliff, bay, and land. The shore, with its many graceful indentations, is of unending beauty. It sweeps from point to point, here a beach of fine sand, there of gravel, and then in contrast the precipitous limestone bluffs, affording at each step or each boat's length a new composition, a new vista. To add even greater interest and beauty to this series of paintings upon the landscape with all the glorious color and marvelous form of nature herself, we have the little islands which stretch along the shore and which, it is hoped will form part of the state's possession. With a temperature always moderate, the purest of air laden with the fragrance of woods, with boating, sailing and fishing, with fine country roads and footpaths stretching over hills and valleys, this region might easily become a famous pleasure spot of the highest order.

While recommending the Door County state park, he cautioned Wisconsinites to think hard about their conservation priorities: "Has Wisconsin nothing further worthy of preservation, or is the state too poor or too indifferent to take timely action in a matter of such paramount importance? These are the questions which the people will soon ask their representatives in Madison and upon the answers will depend in no small measure the happiness and welfare of present and future generations."[30]

Upon leaving Door County, Nolen visited the Thunder River region near Marinette, another prospective state park site thought to be "the highest point of land in the state of Wisconsin."[31] (Senator Stephenson, who owned a resort there, had recommended this location.) Nolen then traveled to the junction of the Wisconsin and Mississippi rivers, an area that would later become Wyalusing State Park. As with other locations, Nolen took down his first impressions of its beauty: "The view of wooded bluff from river is superb. . . . Long views over and around the Mississippi River and up Wisconsin River."[32] The site was also important for its historic and legendary significance. Located in Grant

County, it was the easiest to establish as a state park and the least expensive. Purchasing it would be relatively easy because its owner was an active proponent for state parks and its cost, a mere thirty thousand dollars, could be paid over a three-year period. With funding and government approval, this park was established in 1917.

Nolen also visited Devils Lake, but land costs there had escalated quickly. The area had other problems. Many local people opposed selling land to the state for a park when they already enjoyed it free of charge—"We own this lake, why should we pay money to induce the state to buy it?" In addition, the board was having problems with an active stone quarry on part of the proposed parkland, and there was a question of legal boundaries, which would lead to even more complications. Nolen also visited the Dells, but his notes revealed his bleak outlook for the area—"Milwaukee people know Dells better than Devil's Lake. Why?"[33] He could see that the area was already being engulfed with tourism development. The public needed to be convinced that that area would be better off as a state park than a commercialized tourist center. Nolen was familiar with H. H. Bennett's extraordinary photographs of the Dells and would use some of them in his report to impress the public and legislators with the area's spectacular scenery.

Dealing with the citizens of Door County seemed easy compared to the State Park Board's trials in acquiring land for Devils Lake. Asking prices became so excessive that sometimes Brittingham and L. C. Colman, secretary of the State Park Board, fronted the money for land acquisitions from their personal accounts. Finally, in June of 1911 the assembly voted 69 to 9 to establish Devils Lake State Park.[34]

An avid photographer, Nolen kept a photographic log of his visits to the proposed park sites and used them when recommending park plans. He also took extensive notes on three-by-five cards, for example, in Door County: "8.3 miles shore line . . . picturesque bluffs of limestone—cave." In addition, he noted missing information: "Birds and wildflowers? Elevation of bluffs? Look up Coast Survey."[35] He was meticulous about acquiring adequate information to write his report.

Although Interstate Park already existed at St. Croix, apparently Nolen wanted to visit it to gain an understanding of a preservation success in Wisconsin. Thus, he spent an entire day there with a tour guide. He also might have stopped at St. Croix because it was not far from a meeting of the American Association of Park Superintendents in Minneapolis, which, said the *Madison Democrat,* "more then 150 park officials from nearly as many American cities are expected" to attend.[36]

The four sites Nolen would recommend were "not the only ones in Wisconsin suitable for State Parks. Other sites, such as Thunder Mountain, Blue Mounds, and Platte Mounds, are all worthy of future inspection," he said.[37] Thunder Mountain was too close to Door County and the money could be better spent acquiring land representing different landscapes of Wisconsin. Nolen did not have time to visit Rib Mountain in Marathon County and for the time being accepted state forester Griffith's opinion of it as undesirable.

Since state parks were relatively new, and their beauty not as refined as that of city parks, it was more difficult for the public to justify spending money for them. Not everyone was negative, however. From the very start of efforts to establish the state park system, some landowners made offers to sell that were quite reasonable. Nolen was quick to note these offers and have board members follow up on the proposals.

John Nolen's report *State Parks for Wisconsin,* submitted to the Park Board on January 9, 1909, was a clear and convincing document. Four days later, as directed by the legislature, the board submitted the report to the governor. Their accompanying letter gave Nolen's recommendations a hearty endorsement and urged that his recommendations be implemented quickly. "No question before the American people today is of greater importance than the conservation of our natural resources," Nolen began. It noted the importance of both national and city parks, but "between these two classes of parks . . . there is a gap, a field for profitable public action which until recently has been almost unoccupied." This great need could be fulfilled by state parks, "not of such character as to form National Parks, nor are they so situated as to serve the needs of a single city." He then referred to the actions, albeit limited, of other states, citing precedents in Massachusetts, New York, and California. His requirements for state parks followed. They should: (1) be large, because great numbers of people would destroy the amenities of a small area (2,000 to 3,000 acres at a minimum, 5,000 acres even better; (2) be accessible within a reasonable time and at reasonable expense; (3) have healthful air and climate; (4) be of reasonable cost, including construction and maintenance; and (5) have a "decidedly uncommon charm and beauty." Utilizing these criteria, he recommended four sites as especially suitable: the Dells of the Wisconsin River, Devils Lake, the Door County Peninsula between Ephraim and Fish Creek (including the "little islands—Strawberry, Horseshoe, etc."), and the Wyalusing area in Grant County.[38]

After describing each of the four proposed sites, Nolen gave the Door Peninsula site his highest recommendation:

A visit to Door County cannot fail to be memorable. Whether the belief of its residents that Door County is "the Paradise of Wisconsin" is true or not, there can be no question that the peninsula, whose shores are washed on one side by Lake Michigan and on the other by the waters of historical Green Bay, is pre-eminently qualified for selection as a State Park. . . . So far as I know, the opinion is unanimous that here at least, if nowhere else in Wisconsin, is a tract that can be selected with confidence. . . . Discriminating people, numbering now at least a thousand a year, have discovered its charms and become familiar with its attractions. But fortunately for the State and for the people at large, this movement to occupy Door County with private summer places has not yet assumed large proportions. . . . This Door County region under State control might easily become a famous pleasure resort of the highest order.[39]

Nolen also had the brilliant idea that the four parks should "ultimately be connected by great State roads or parkways." Such a road could run from "Green Bay to Prairie du Chien, following the historic route along the Fox and Wisconsin Rivers; [with] another diagonal connecting St. Paul and Minneapolis with Milwaukee and Chicago, and roads along the Wisconsin shores of Lake Michigan and Lake Superior."[40] Finally, the report set forth six important and highly persuasive reasons for establishing the park system. In an appendix were letters of support from such distinguished national leaders as Charles W. Eliot, president of Harvard University; J. Horace McFarland, president of the American Civic Association; reformer and photographer Jacob Riis; University of Wisconsin President Charles R. Van Hise; ex-Governor W. D. Hoard; and others. The report ended with a series of breathtaking photographs of the recommended sites. Nolen's state park report became a model for other states and, even today, continues to influence our state park system.

A spurt of park-related action occurred in the legislature immediately after Nolen's report was released. On the following day, Governor Davidson expressed his strong support for state parks in his annual address to the legislature:

> With the advance of civilization, one by one all the places of scenic beauty, and historical interest, are passing away. Before it is too late, it is well to pause and consider whether it is not befitting that some of them be preserved for all time as state parks. Coming generations will have just cause to regret the short-sighted selfishness of this generation if all such places within the state are destroyed, and no action taken to preserve at least a few of them. Once destroyed, they can never be restored. I therefore, recommend that action be taken, before it is too late, to the end that one or more places be set aside as state parks for the use

in common, of the people now living, and as a heritage from them to future generations.[41]

Three weeks later Senator Bird, who had accompanied the State Park Board to Door County in May, introduced a bill "to provide for the establishment of four state parks by the State Park Board, and to make an appropriation thereof."[42] The bill died, however, and legislation to appropriate funds to establish all four parks at one time would never reappear.

On February 3, Assemblyman Reynolds introduced a bill that authorized the board to acquire specific lands between Fish Creek and Ephraim for a new state park and requested seventy-five thousand dollars for that purpose.[43] The bill was referred to the Forestry Committee, which added an amendment that "no land shall be purchased . . . at a higher rate that the assessed valuation, plus fifty per cent."[44]

The next day, Assemblyman J. E. McConnell introduced a bill that asked for seventy-five thousand dollars per year in 1909 and 1910 "for the purchase and improvement of state parks."[45] It was referred to the Forestry Committee, which recommended passage. The Claims Committee, however, stubbornly postponed it indefinitely. Further action came on February 5, when Senator C. L. Pearson from the Sauk-Columbia district introduced a bill similar to McConnell's. It requested seventy-five thousand dollars annually for the next three years for "the acquisition by the state of Wisconsin of certain lands for use as state parks."[46] Early in June, the legislature reduced this amount to fifty thousand dollars per year for two years.[47]

Meanwhile Reynolds was working his bill through the legislature. After receiving favorable committee reports, it reached the assembly. There, he made a passionate plea for its passage. So eloquent was his speech that it was published in the *Assembly Journal* for 1909, under the title "Plea for the Door County Park," as follows:

> The park has more to it than a mere pleasure resort. Well directed pleasure is the best tonic ever used if taken in the open air. There is no place on God's footstool more appropriate for preserving good health and for those who are unfortunate enough to have their health impaired. In the proposed Door county park, such as these will find a Mecca. The state is bound by traditional training to care for the unfortunate of its citizens; the monotony of many people's existence has caused them to lose their minds. Two months of the year in the proposed Door county park, when it is made safe for people of all classes and sexes will teach people to forget the dreary, lonesome life circumstances compel

them to live. On account of the surroundings of this natural beauty spot, it is not only a healthful location for man's body, but will, with some artificial trimming become an educational center for the student of the state—not only of the state but of the nation, just as soon as its location becomes known. In one direction lies Lake Michigan with its brave blustering breezes filtering through the cedars, pines, hemlocks, and many others of different varieties. Those of the delicate portion of humanity who cannot stand Lake Michigan in July can turn their backs to the great lake and face Green Bay with its gentle breezes of invitation to all to go for a sail on its beautiful waters.

For all of those privileges and many more not enumerated, the state of Wisconsin is asked to contribute the small sum of $75,000. With that amount contributed by the state we can appeal to the lovers of humanity to contribute to put the park into respectable shape to be used for the good of humanity. There are many men in Wisconsin who would be glad to help financially if the state takes the lead.

The state of Wisconsin has before it the opportunity to give to the people of the state a public playground. A state park in Door county would be of an inestimable benefit to the people of this commonwealth for many reasons.

It is a spot that will afford breathing for the people crowded together in the more densely populated cities—people that cannot afford to go to the high priced summer resorts. A man with only a few weeks vacation can take his wife and children to this garden provided by nature, and away from the dust and filth of the city, they can breathe in the clear, pure, invigorating air fresh from the waters of Green Bay, or the breezes from Lake Michigan wafted through the forests and scented with the perfume of the balsam and the pine.

I recently had occasion to visit some of the cities in our state, and I noted in the boarding houses the evidences of consumption in the faces of many of the workingmen, and I thought how countless numbers of these men and the women working in the factories and the shops of the cities might be given a new lease of life if they could be given a few weeks, in the heat of summer, where they could fill their lungs with the cool, pure air, fresh from the lakes and the forests. Granting that the state of Wisconsin might see fit to provide tents or other accommodations for the poorer people, to accommodate them, would it not be better to do so, to keep them well and healthy and useful citizens, rather than to wait until they become helpless and then provide for them at sanitariums?

Many people are today in our sanitariums, hospitals and asylums, insane and feeble minded, and weak in bodies, as well in mind, because they could not endure the monotony of their existence. A place where they could have gone, if only a few weeks in the year, at a moderate cost, where mind could have met mind; where people of different ideas could congregate and converse, and go back to their homes refreshed by the change with the thoughts of others carried with them, we would possibly have a less number in our asylums and sanitariums, and the state would be the richer by so many more useful citizens, and richer in the knowledge that it had made an effort to help its people while they were well and to keep them so.

It is hardly necessary to dwell upon the beauties of the region. Suffice it is to say that any one who has driven over the picturesque drives, lined with nature's shrubbery; who has gazed upon the mighty balsams and pines in all their mighty majesty, and who has inhaled the perfume of their breath; one who has seen the flitting deer in the distance, those beauties of the forests, who has stood and gazed at the calm waters of Green bay, dotted with its islands, like gems in a sea, and who has been conscious of the abrupt and stately bluffs arising from the waters beneath; bluffs with their faces carved into fantastic shapes by the wash of waters and the knife of time; conscious of the rolling waters of Lake Michigan in the rear, and of the dim lines of the shores of Wisconsin and Michigan in the distance; one who has stood at any of the innumerable spots on this park site where he might enjoy and be conscious of these things, must indeed have thought, "Here truly, lies Nature, in all its beauty."

This effort to possess this region for the enjoyment of the people is not a new one. It is as old as the region itself. For if you have heard of the Indian traditions of that part of your state, you will have heard of how the inhabitants of the north and of the east, wishing to be the proud possessors of a home so grand, came in their canoes, hundreds of them, to conquer or to die. And the tradition relates how the inhabitants of this unsurpassed hunting ground, unsurpassed in beauty as well as game, meeting the enemy in their boats on the open waters, fought them to a finish, until by the deadly work of arrows, and the interference of the great spirit, who caused a storm to rise, and the waters to roughen, the attacking forces were annihilated. And these waters are called Death's Door—the door which is the passage between the waters of Lake Michigan and Green bay, and upon which now sail the peaceful ships of commerce.

Let the state of Wisconsin give to its children this vast playground, where the old, and tired, and worn may grow young in spirit and rested in body, nursed by the purity of Nature's medicine, and where the young may romp and their bodies grow strong among the wonders of scenic beauty.[48]

Early in June the assembly passed Reynolds's bill by a vote of 57 to 23. Two days later, the senate unanimously approved it, and on June 9, 1909, Governor Davidson signed it into law. It "did not specify," pointed out Senator Bird, "that the state park shall be in Door County because the contention for other localities was so sharp, that it could not be passed in that form; but it is well known that Door County will have the Park, provided the property holders treat the park commission fairly in the matter of prices."[49] The legal foundation for establishing the first park from John Nolen's plan—Peninsula—had finally become a reality.

Oddly enough, within a year of submitting his *State Parks for Wisconsin* report, Nolen did no more work for the State Park Board. Perhaps his main contribution to the park project was his expertise and ability to influence the state legislature on the matter. Olin expressed his desire for Nolen's continued involvement: "If you were here through the next session of our legislature, you could be very helpful in securing proper additional legislation with reference to state parks. The state is much interested, I think, in this subject, but it is comparatively new for the state and it is a work that very much needs proper guidance. There is a grand opportunity, I think, furnished at this point for some one to do an admirable service for the whole state."[50] Nolen's role became that of an evaluator and persuader—and he did a superb job with both tasks.

In 1911, Devils Lake became the next park to be established under the Nolen plan, followed by Wyalusing. Unfortunately, the Wisconsin Dells area was never acquired as a state park and the land reverted to the commercial tourist industry. Thus, a mere eight years after Nolen wrote *State Parks of Wisconsin,* three spectacular sites were designated as parks. Of the four areas he suggested, only the Wisconsin Dells was rejected by the legislature.

Two individuals—Thomas Reynolds and John Nolen—were the key figures in establishing Peninsula State Park. A progressive thinker, Reynolds was elected to the assembly in the fall of 1906 and reelected in the fall of 1908. After leaving the legislature he remained active in town and county politics. Reynolds died at his home in Jacksonport in 1919. His obituary in the *Door County News* referred to him as "an honored and highly respected citizen" and quoted from a resolution introduced by Assemblyman Frank Graass: "It was through the efforts of Mr. Reynolds that the State Peninsular Park was located in Door county. This park will always remain a monument to the efforts and public services of Mr. Reynolds."[51] Without Reynolds's efforts, the park might never have become a reality.

The people of Wisconsin can be grateful to Thomas Reynolds and John Nolen for their role in convincing others of the necessity for parks, prodding them to acquire them before it was too late, and establishing Peninsula as what is arguably the premier park in the entire system.

༃

CHAPTER 7

Naming the Park and Purchasing the Land

As legislation to establish the new park moved closer to passage, two serious complications arose: the name it would be given and acquisition of the land. Each would generate considerable controversy and have political implications both in northern Door County and at the state capitol.

Because the legislature had reduced the appropriation for the park to only fifty thousand dollars per year for two years, the State Park Board sought additional funds from other sources. Thomas Brittingham had discussed obtaining matching funds from U.S. Senator Isaac "Uncle Ike" Stephenson when the board and the second delegation of officials visited the park site in 1908. Now the board turned to Stephenson, who was eager to make a sizable donation.[1]

A wealthy lumber baron and industrialist from Marinette, Stephenson had old friends in Door County where he had worked many years earlier. He began building his fortune by acquiring valuable tracts of wooded land in Michigan and Wisconsin when the Northern Michigan Land Office opened in 1848. He later managed a vast financial empire with interests in mills, railroads, paper, sugar factories, and other industries, before serving three terms in Congress. He was elected to the United States Senate in 1907.

In a letter to the *Advocate* Thomas Reynolds, the park bill's sponsor, hinted that Door County's "old friend Stephenson" might provide funding for the park. He pointed out that in Stephenson's 1882 congressional election, Door County residents gave Stephenson an overwhelming majority of more than one thousand votes. "Door County elected him, and he is going to help the county now," Reynolds claimed.[2]

Soon the *Advocate* brought Senator Stephenson and his tentative donation back into the news noting that "when the subject was called to . . . [Stephenson's] attention . . . he is said to have denied that he had any intention" of making such a donation, "but offered a site for a park on the headwaters of the Escanaba River, in upper Michigan, at what is known as Thunder Mountain," near his home in Escanaba.[3]

Following up on his offer, Stephenson told Governor Davidson in August of 1909 that he would donate not the fifty thousand dollars Brittingham originally requested but twenty-five thousand dollars "if they wish to call it [the park] after me."[4] Davidson replied that he did not have the authority to choose the name of the park, but if it were called Stephenson Park, his name would be perpetuated for generations to come. The senator then sent his written offer of twenty-five thousand dollars to the board, under the condition that the park bear his name. Despite Reynolds's enthusiastic support, the board unanimously rejected Stephenson's offer. However, Stephenson again renewed his offer providing that the park be named after him. At their next meeting the board reconsidered and accepted the gift agreeing that the "park shall be named in perpetuity, 'Stephenson State Park.'"[5]

Many in Door County opposed naming the park after Stephenson, as did several state newspapers and legislators. Some of the latter were friends of Robert M. La Follette, who eventually became Stephenson's political adversary. Meanwhile, the *Democrat* claimed to have originated the name "Peninsula" for the park.[6] This name, it said, "would undoubtedly meet with approval by

Thomas Reynolds.

the people of the state to a far greater extent than naming it after any politician."[7] The *Algoma Herald* took a similar position, saying that the name of a state institution "should not be allowed to be purchased with money."[8] Even the *Milwaukee Daily News* commented, pointing out the desirability of "Peninsula Park" because the name described it "geographically as the park is located on the most prominent peninsula within the state."[9] Responding to the controversy and broad support for the name "Peninsula," Door County's new assemblyman, Lewis L. Johnson, introduced a bill to name the park accordingly and return Stephenson's twenty-five-thousand-dollar donation. The bill was passed.

The park has also been called a slightly different name, Peninsular. It appears incorrectly on the title of some old postcard scenes and, occasionally, in early literature about the park. This misnomer was revived in the 1930s when, curiously, the Civilian Conservation Corps camp in the park was called Camp Peninsular. Its newspaper was even called the *Peninsular Breeze.*

The second major difficulty in the park's early progress was purchasing the necessary land. Assuming that the park would soon become a reality, the State Park Board began securing options on parcels as early as July of 1908. Because of his knowledge of the area, John J. Pinney, editor and publisher of the *Democrat* and an ardent park booster, assisted them. However, some residents within the park were reluctant to move and give up their homes and farms.

By August, the board was becoming concerned about a price "hold-up" by some landowners. "There are a few men," the *Democrat* noted, "who are asking and insisting on a price from two to six times as much as the land is worth. Properties of little value a month ago are now almost priceless."[10] Yet, by the end of 1908 options were acquired from thirty-five willing sellers whose holdings ranged in size from 1.5 to 200 acres at prices ranging from $5 to $266 per acre. In general, options on larger tracts were purchased at lower per-acre cost. Smaller lots, many presumably situated along the shoreline, usually commanded the highest prices.

Twenty-four landowners refused to move, for various reasons. Some wanted higher prices. Others, like Peter Weborg, because of his advanced age, maintained that moving would be a severe hardship. Thus, considerable negotiating was necessary and, as a last resort, condemnation proceedings were used to obtain some parcels. Among these were all of Horseshoe Island, forty-seven acres owned by Andrew Johnson, and the 108-acre Simon Evenson farm.

By the beginning of 1909, resistance to establishing the new park was growing. A critical issue became the amount owners would receive for their property. The county's newspapers became embroiled in this dispute, each expressing somewhat different views. Pinney's *Democrat* remained a strong supporter of the park, and the *News* also favored the project. On the other hand, Frank Long, editor and proprietor of Pinney's competitor, the *Advocate,* had reservations. His newspaper often served as an outlet for H. R. Holand's sometimes vicious, antipark letters.

By now, the board was also turning its attention to acquiring land to establish Devils Lake State Park. With the addition of several additional parks, Wisconsin's efforts to create a state park system were reaching fruition. Meanwhile the conservation efforts of Governor Davidson, Thomas Brittingham, and the university's Charles R. Van Hise were being recognized throughout the nation. Brittingham and Van Hise were chosen to serve on the executive committee of the National Conservation Association. Gifford Pinchot, prominent conservationist and chief forester of the U.S. Forest Service, headed this prestigious group. The association was an outgrowth of the Conference of Governors at the White House called in 1908 by President Theodore Roosevelt to address state conservation efforts. By this time Van Hise had become familiar with attractions of the Ephraim area, since his wife, Alice, stayed at the Eagle Inn for much of the summer of 1910.[11]

The lack of funds to improve the park soon became a contentious issue for Ephraim and Fish Creek area residents—especially those who still resided on land the state had not yet acquired. "It does not appear that Peninsula Park . . . will get much in the way of improvements for a long time to come," wrote the *Democrat.*[12] Apparently, the park board was reluctant to do so until all the land had been purchased. This task was complicated by the need to secure property at Devils Lake, plus land at Wyalusing in Grant County, for which options had been obtained.

Leading the opposition to the park was H. R. Holand, who owned a large tract with a productive orchard near the park's eastern boundary. His letters started a salvo of correspondence, articles, and editorials for and against the park in the county newspapers. In a vitriolic letter to the *Advocate,* Holand wrote to "throw a little light on the subject . . . as a resident very closely concerned in the project and one who has personally sacrificed a few thousands to build up the county."[13] His lengthy epistle indicated that funds were available only to purchase the land, while nothing was set aside for "improving or beautifying the tract." He expressed six arguments against the park: (1) without funds to develop and maintain the new park, the tract, including the roads used by tourists for pleasure driving, would be "laid waste"; (2) without residents in the park, there "would be a grave danger of forest fires which might sweep far out over the neighboring county"; (3) the park would provide a dangerous hiding place for wolves, "which would sally out and destroy scattering flocks of sheep all over the northern part of the county"; (4) the park would take undeveloped land which, in the future, could be used for hotels and cottages with their commensurate economic benefits to the area; (5) taxes would rise since "residents of Gibraltar . . . can ill afford to shoulder the extra (tax) burden of one thousand dollars annually which the present owners of the park site bear"; and (6) "When this promising tract is laid to waste: when the woods will stand charred and blackened by frequent forest fires; when the untilled fields will be overgrown with weeds; when the houses where they [tourists] have stopped so many times will stand deserted, broken down and wrecked, the impression will be so dismal that hundreds of our present annual visitors will spend their vacation elsewhere . . . This will prove a most serious set back to our present summer hotels."

In the same issue, the *Advocate* ran an editorial that candidly asked Reynolds if he would be willing to sell his Jacksonport farm for a park at its assessed valuation. State agents could use those figures in their purchasing negotiations. While noting it was "most heartily in favor of a park," the newspaper did not "propose to sit by quietly and see the people bulldozed and coerced into the acceptance of such prices as these self-appointed . . . agents may see proper to fix on the property." It added, "These places are the only homes that these people have, and if they are crowded out by the state, as is proposed by these promoters, they will have to seek other locations, which are not so easily to be had as many seem to think. To refuse to indemnify these deserving people to a reasonable degree for the sacrifice that they will be called upon to make by a change of habitation would be a great wrong, which no amount of sympathy or mere empty words would ever condone."

Responding to the *Advocate*'s editorial, Reynolds said land values would be determined when purchased. He concluded by stating, "Please don't misrepresent me any more."[14] On the same page, editor Long noted that in previous correspondence Reynolds stated that "the state wants to buy the site . . . on a fair valuation from the owners. If that can't be done their property can be appraised . . . from the valuation the assessor and town board put on it." Long further charged, "If this is not an open and an avowed threat . . . the *Advocate* will publicly acknowledge that it has 'misrepresented' Mr. Reynolds, and will ask his humble pardon."

In a letter to the *Democrat,* Reynolds stated that "Holand attempts to mislead the people" and rebutted each of the Holand's six arguments: the intent of the park was to enable people to enjoy the tract's scenic beauty, and eventually better roads would give tourists greater opportunities for driving; forest fires would be prevented by "state fire wardens and forestry departments"; wolves would not be a problem since "in a few years the wolf will be practically exterminated"; the park would not drive tourists away but instead would "be the magnet that would draw them"; tax increases would be so small that they would "hardly be worth considering"; and Holand's point that present conditions in the park area are entirely satisfactory to visitors was "no argument at all," since eventually "thousands of tourists" would come to enjoy the site if it became a park! He concluded with eloquence: "Let us bury our personal whims and selfish interests and prejudices, in the larger and more public-spirited way and secure the greatest good to the greatest number, and have in Door County a park that will rival or excel the State's most beautiful spots."[15]

Holand's next letter appeared on the *Advocate*'s front page under the headline "More about the State Park."[16] This time he lambasted Reynolds as "dreadfully sleepy" when legislation came up regarding the county's interests. Holand reiterated his earlier concerns, noting "we would not get a park but a dreary wilderness" and alluding to an alleged quote from the park commissioners that "they do not for some time intend to put any money into improving the tract." He also implied that Reynolds received money from Senator Stephenson "for alleged services," and that the county's representative had "easy access" to Stephenson's "campaign barrel."

The following week Holand penned another scathing letter under the headline "A Public Scandal."[17] The park, he said, "will be of no greater benefit to us than the Ephraim swamp . . . or the North Bay wilderness." He added that since each of the forty families living in the park spent an average of two hundred dollars a year at local stores, Ephraim and Fish Creek merchants would lose about eight thousand dollars per year! The bill in the legislature provided only sixty-five thousand dollars to buy land for the Door County park. This, he added, came to an average of seventeen dollars per acre and was inadequate for the six square miles of "well timbered lands and fertile farms, including large orchards, with several farm houses costing from $2,000 to $4,000 apiece." He also charged that Reynolds had acted to lower the overall appropriation for the four state parks the legislature was considering to $150,000, which, if divided equally among them, averaged not quite ten dollars per acre.

Many of the landowners, said Holand, "came here fifty and sixty years ago, when the nearest railroad was three hundred miles away. They had [walked] seventy-five miles through a pathless wilderness to market and post office. They have suffered hardships of pioneer life unequaled almost anywhere. They have fought the wilderness, forest fires and starvation. They have seen their children die in helpless suffering because the nearest physician was three days journey away. Their own limbs have grown stiff and their backs bent with incessant stone picking and grubbing." Continuing his criticism of Reynolds, he added, "Shucks! Twaddle! Banish such niggardly behavior on the part of the state . . . banish the ingrate who would persuade his neighbors and constituents—the men who have worked and voted for him that he might protect their interests—to sell at such beggarly prices! His name is Judas?"

The Holand-Reynolds debate continued. Reynolds clarified a point in the *Democrat:* the bill he introduced called for seventy-five thousand dollars for a state park in Door County, not the sixty-five thousand dollars Holand had stated.[18] Furthermore if the State Park Board took Holand's charges as an expression of the sentiment of the people of northern Door County, "they will establish the park at Clark's Lake or Kangaroo Lake, where there will be no danger of bloodshed that Mr. Holand threatens. I will not ask space in your paper to reply to Mr. Holand's foolish arguments!"

Local support for the park continued to wane, in part due to Holand's influence. The Young Men's Progressive Club of Ephraim, meeting at the village school, debated a resolution on the park and voted unanimously that it would not benefit the community. They also agreed to send a resolution to the governor, the state senator, and Reynolds, asking them to oppose the portions of the pending park bills that related to Door County.[19]

Holand's charges drew criticism from Alfred M. Weborg, the Gibraltar town clerk and a resident in the proposed park site. Writing to the *Advocate,* Weborg stated that Holand had grossly overestimated the amount of taxes the township would lose.[20] He noted that 1908 tax records indicated that with the exception of school and road district taxes, the actual amount levied for the year amounted to only "a few cents over $385." He also said that residents were "not shedding any tears" about moving since "with a few exceptions the people are well satisfied with their bargains." Regarding future hotel sites, he pointed out that the rooms presently available for one hundred persons in Gibraltar could easily be enlarged to accommodate five hundred or more visitors. Tourism expansion would not be a problem since "Egg Harbor, Sister Bay and Ellison Bay" had lodging for many more visitors.

Attempting to clear the air, Pinney published "Facts about State Park" on the front page, a lengthy article based on a meticulous examination of land values and assessment records.[21] "So many misstatements have been written by one H. R. Holand, and gladly published by *The Advocate,*" he began, "that the *Democrat* feels it duty bound to come to the rescue and set things right." He noted that Holand "claimed that his property was worth 14½ times assessed value." Andrew Johnson, whose forty-four acres with its small log barn with a tiny frame addition and hen house was assessed for $305, was demanding eight thousand dollars—more than twenty-six times the assessment. Yet, said Pinney, Johnson could have optioned for more than three times its assessment. Pinney was also critical of the views expressed by both *Advocate* editor Frank Long and Holand, who "endeavors to misrepresent everything pertaining to the state park project."

Lashing out in still another letter to the *Advocate*, Holand complained bitterly that options on the land were secured "by intimidation and coercion."[22] During the preceding summer, he explained, Long and several others from the area, including Roy Thorp, "drove around and in a courteous way asked the local residents what they wanted for their land." According to Holand, the total exceeded one hundred thousand dollars; however, the owners would rather not sell. He then noted that Pinney had taken three weeks to help negotiate the options—an unusually long period of time, he believed—and used "unsavory means" and "deliberate falsehoods to persuade a non-resident to sell his property."

Several days later Dr. G. R. Egeland of Ephraim, who would later be appointed to the State Park Board, interviewed Governor Davidson in Madison about the park. He wrote in the *Democrat,* that Davidson stated, "There has been no end of misrepresentation on the proposed park site purchase."[23] He also indicated that Davidson said that the state will never "rob a man or family of a home" and "will pay every dollar a place is worth." Assuring readers that Reynolds was working faithfully for his constituents, he asked why their legislator "should be so misrepresented . . . and attacked?" Holand responded in the *Advocate* with an article critical of Egeland, calling him "the medicine man of Ephraim," and charged that Egeland "can diagnose the ailments that beset the human body with precision, but when it comes to his diagnosis of the faults with the matter at issue I think there is room for improvement."[24]

By now other state newspapers had joined the park controversy. An editorial against the park in the *Green Bay Gazette,* for example, said that the state should "drop the Door County site."[25] The *Milwaukee Free Press* staunchly supported the park. "It would be a thousand pities," it stated, "if the difficulty of acquiring land in Door county at a reasonable figure should cause the plan for locating a state park in that picturesque region to be abandoned."[26] Newspaper coverage for and against the park continued. In June the legislature finally passed Reynolds's bill.

Meeting with Governor Davidson on July 23, 1909, the State Park Board gave permission to complete the purchases and obtain deeds to the properties.

With the governor's approval, Attorney General J. A. Frear began arrangements to acquire the land on behalf of the State of Wisconsin.[27] Assistant Attorney General J. E. Messerschmidt went to Door County to close on options for 2,287 acres of the park and begin negotiations to purchase the remaining 1,413 unoptioned acres. The first action taken to secure property where the price could not be agreed upon was service of a notice on E. F. Folda to cease work on the summer cottage he was erecting on Eagle Island. Folda offered to donate the thirty-seven-acre island tract if he could retain life tenure on the "home and the enclosure, the remainder being used for park purposes."[28] Folda sold the island for a fair price—five thousand dollars—with the provision that he and his wife continue to use it as a life estate and be exempt from real estate taxes.[29]

Before the summer of 1909 ended, Davidson made an important change to the State Park Board by appointing Egeland to fill the vacancy created by the resignation of E. E. Brown of Waupaca. This was an astute political move because Egeland was respected throughout the peninsula and had followed the park project closely since its inception. In addition, he was personally acquainted with many of the landowners and could greatly assist with the remaining property acquisitions. Largely due to Egeland's efforts, the state was able to reach a satisfactory agreement with Folda for the Horseshoe Island purchase.

The board continued negotiations; most of the land was eventually purchased from the remaining occupants. Many relocated north of the park but sometimes only after condemnation proceedings were initiated and a deadline set for appealing the board's offering price. Some of the remaining owners, often assisted by Attorney John Reynolds of Green Bay, won their appeal. For example, Olaf Hanson contested the board's $6,700 offer, and the circuit court awarded him a settlement of $8,500. By the end of 1910, only seven families remained on the park tract.[30] Some owners who vacated their property arranged to move or salvage material from their buildings. Albert Hansen, for example, hauled his lumber to the beach early the following year to transport it over the ice to his new home at Ellison Bay. Hans B. Olson stayed by arranging to lease his house, barn, and outbuildings while receiving fifty dollars per month to work as the park warden.[31] With most residents of the park gone, the district school was closed and rural mail delivery service was discontinued.[32] One of the last holdouts was H. R. Holand, who even traveled to Madison to discuss the matter with Governor Francis McGovern. When state acquisition of his land appeared imminent, Holand cleverly proceeded to purchase several nearby parcels, accumulating a total of 169 acres. After the court dismissed condemnation proceedings for his land, he made two propositions to the board: to sell his land for $21,000 in cash, or to sell it for $14,600 with a tax-free twenty-five-year lease for the large orchard on his premises. In an amicable settlement, the board agreed to the latter proposition. However, Holand's resentment about the park lingered for several years. Later he even sued the state for trespassing at his leased orchard.[33]

A few private property "islands" remained in the park for several more decades. Vandalism prompted the conservation department to negotiate with the Folda family to obtain immediate possession of Eagle Island rather than wait until their life lease expired. In the early 1940s, subdivision of some of the mainland parcels caused growing concern. A tavern in the park on land formerly owned by Oscar Ohman caused the Conservation Department embarrassment because it was thought to attract "an unsuitable type of traffic."[34] In November of 1943 the tavern was purchased from its owner, August Lautenback of Egg Harbor. The following year Horseshoe Island and the 120-acre John Kodanko farm on Middle Road were acquired. By then the remaining inholders had sold thirteen mostly one-acre lots. Ohman sold seven on Highland Road the previous year. The remaining six, along the north side of Highway 42 near the golf course, were purchased from Oletta Gustafson. In subsequent years, the state bought additional parcels, but private land ownership in the park continued well into the 1950s, when the last parcel was acquired.

CHAPTER 8

❧

The Doolittle Years

W ith Peninsula State Park formally established, it was essential to select someone to oversee the many tasks required for its development. This individual had to be proficient in construction, forestry, conservation practices, public relations, and political acumen—somewhat of a "renaissance ranger." A. E. Doolittle proved to be just such an individual.

Doolittle first arrived on the scene in 1913, to supervise improvements at the park. That summer state forester E. F. Griffith had told the Ephraim Men's Club what needed to be done. The forestry department was in charge of all improvements for Wisconsin's fledgling state park system, and Griffith was familiar with the park site, having visited it with the board and other officials on their 1908 inspection trip. First, he told the group, underbrush and dead timber must be cleared away under the supervision of a state forest ranger. Next, temporary repairs would be made to the roughest areas of the roads, as would the surveying for road alignments and development of camping areas. Also being considered for the park was a horticultural experiment station.[1] Several weeks later three state employees, plus several student workers, were stationed in the park to begin the work. Al Doolittle, a state ranger at that time, would supervise them.[2]

A native of Elroy, Wisconsin, Doolittle married Lettie Hastings of Cadott in 1893. Two years later, the young couple moved to Vilas County, where Doolittle worked in lumber camps and established the Rocky Reef Resort on Trout Lake, a modest combination hotel in their home that later had several rustic cabins. Doolittle then became a state forest ranger and managed the state fish hatchery at Trout Lake.[3] After taking the exam to become a park superintendent, he was appointed Peninsula's first superintendent, a position he held for three decades.[4]

Doolittle selected one of the houses on land the state had purchased for the family's residence, but after his wife and seven children joined him the house proved to be too small. In 1914 they moved into a larger house, which was moved one-quarter of a mile over the ice from another location in the park and then remodeled to make it a "modern" residence.[5] It still serves as the park superintendent's house.

As superintendent, Doolittle proved to be a man of remarkable vision and dedication throughout his thirty-year career at Peninsula. Strong willed and feisty, he worked tirelessly to promote the park and secure funds for its maintenance and development. He also had a keen sensitivity for its natural features and breathtaking beauty. Doolittle planned many of the early features of the park. Under his direction, miles of its roads, scenic lookouts, early campgrounds, the towers, and initial portions of the golf course were constructed.

An enterprising individual, Doolittle also established a small motel complex near the Fish Creek entrance. Nearby he built a service station where gasoline, auto accessories, refreshments, and camping equipment were sold. It also provided restrooms for travelers and park visitors.

In anticipation of a tourism boom, an unusual but visionary proposal was made for northern Door County in the fall of 1913. The E. E. Galle Company

A. E. Doolittle (center) with his wife, several children, and relatives. (Courtesy Peninsula State Park office)

of Minneapolis, working with the Sturgeon Bay Commercial Club, undertook a feasibility study for an interurban railroad through the northern peninsula.[6]

What probably helped generate this idea were the hazards and unpredictability of travel by boat at that time. In fact, one of the Great Lakes' worst storms occurred early in November of that very year. It resulted in the disappearance of twelve ships, serious damage to twenty-five more vessels, and the loss of an estimated 250 to 300 people. Decrying the area's remoteness, H. R. Holand began promoting the railroad from Sturgeon Bay to "the farthest limits of the peninsula." If "two sturdy arms of steel" were built, he maintained, considerable business would come to the city's merchants from towns in "the large stretch of fertile country" to the north. The proposal had been met with "a most liberal and ready welcome," he maintained, since it would "bring prosperity to the struggling thousands there."[7]

To capitalize the planned "Sturgeon Bay and Northern Railroad," a stock subscription was proposed. "Where cash was lacking, there was considerable good will" about the venture, he added. Citizens could raise the money, if "a promising heifer, perhaps, was disposed of; the seed for next spring was skimped a little; or the tattered garments were patched up and made to do for another year—and thus, by saving and pinching and begging and borrowing, the ten dollars" could be found for their first payment on a share.[8]

Meanwhile, a survey was completed for the main line of the proposed railroad that would run from Sturgeon Bay through most of the townships en route to Newport.[9] Later, branch routes running from the main line into most of the northern communities were to be surveyed. A vote backing the project was taken at a spirited meeting of the Ephraim Men's Club.

Much to the chagrin of many present-day visitors to the peninsula who dread long drives to get there, the visionary railroad concept never became a reality. With the demise of that endeavor, Holand turned his attention to another project: establishing a state horticultural experiment station in the park. This was important, he maintained, for the county's extensive fruit-growing industry. In fact, several orchards existed in the park, including Holand's and another owned by Dr. H. C. Welcker. Dean Harry L. Russell of the university's College of Agriculture favored the idea, and another unsuccessful attempt was made to obtain funds from the legislature.

Meanwhile, at its February 1914 meeting, the State Park Board took up several important matters regarding the new park. It approved granting leases for some of the remaining buildings and instructed Doolittle to sell the others to the highest bidder. It also authorized the erection of two lookout towers to help prevent fires.[10]

By now the new park's fame had spread throughout the region. The *Minneapolis Journal*, for example, proclaimed it "will become the rendezvous during the summer months of people from all over the northwest."[11] In the spring, with an eighteen-thousand-dollar appropriation from the legislature, work on park improvements began in earnest. Thirteen buildings were sold, including log and frame houses, barns, and a workshop that had been used by the park's resident farmers and fishermen. Bids were sought to lease six remaining residences in relatively good condition during the summer.[12]

That season, some forty-four thousand three- and four-year-old trees were shipped to the park from the state nursery at Trout Lake—white and Norway pine, Scotch pine, Western yellow pine, Colorado blue spruce, and Norway spruce. Fifteen thousand of the trees were to be planted on Eagle Island.

Campsites were also made ready, and by the end of July about two hundred people were visiting the park each day, while some ten to fifty automobiles passed through daily. Several campers had also pitched their tents at Shanty Bay, Weborg Point, and a third location called Cedar Glen. Campers paid five dollars per year to pitch their tents, while those who towed "portable cottages" behind their automobiles paid ten dollars. If they cleaned up their site before leaving, the money was refunded. Using the new trails and roads, sightseers enjoyed visiting such places as "Sween's [Sven's] Bluff, [the] Lighthouse, Eagle Bay, Welcker's Point, Norway Bluff, Herman's Spring, Cedar Glen and Devil's Pulpit."[13]

That summer stumps were removed and rough grading was done along the south boundary road of the park. Then, crushed rock was hauled in and rolled, and culverts and guardrails were installed before several miles of the road were macadamized. This roadwork used more than half of the park's eighteen-thousand-dollar budget. Meanwhile, brush and dead trees were removed from ten miles of the dirt interior roads of the park. To keep down grass and weeds, Doolittle sought to bring one thousand sheep to the park. Seven miles of trails were also cut through the park and several footbridges were erected across creeks. The two observation towers were also completed.[14] Eagle Tower, the taller of the two, was erected at the crest of Eagle Bluff. It was seventy-six-feet tall, and its top level reached 225 feet above the water. Sven's Tower, built at Sven's Bluff, was forty-five-feet tall and more than 200 feet above the water. This high, westerly facing vantage point provided breathtaking views of sunsets, plus the three Strawberry Islands and the village of Fish Creek. The towers were similar in appearance, with three viewing platforms supported by four long corner posts. Eagle Tower had intermediate stair landings between its three viewing platforms, and a long flagpole extended from its top level.[15]

Sven's Tower, built in 1914. The tower provided breathtaking views of sunsets, Fish Creek, and the adjoining islands in Green Bay. After three decades it deteriorated, became hazardous, and was dismantled in 1947. (Photo by Merl Deusing, courtesy Milwaukee Public Museum)

The towers were built without modern machinery. Logs and boards for their construction were cut from timber in the park. They were erected by first raising a long gin (center) pole. This was done by placing the bottom end in a deep hole and raising the top end several feet with jacks. A cable was then fastened to the top end, and a tractor pulled the gin pole into an upright position. It was secured and cables were attached to it to raise the four poles at the square tower's corners. These were stabilized with long diagonal cables running to the ground. Next the horizontal landing support beams were attached. Heavy planks were nailed to them to form the decking at each of the three levels, and railings were added. To prolong their durability the towers were given a coat of creosote preservative.[16] The cost to build the landmark Eagle Tower came to $1,061.92—an incredible value since many thousands of visitors would climb its steps to enjoy spectacular views from its exhilarating height.[17]

Both towers were valuable as lookouts for forest fires, since the park was full of dry, dead grass and brush. They were connected by telephone to the superintendent's residence and to the local exchange for a quick response if suspicious smoke was spotted.[18] However, it is not known if they were ever used for that purpose. Sven's Tower was taken down in 1947 after withstanding nearly two decades of wear and weathering. Eagle Tower gradually deteriorated and was dismantled in 1932 and completely rebuilt. Massive logs were transported from the State of Washington for the corner posts, and wider

View from Sven's Tower looking north to Tennison Bay. (Author's collection)

viewing platforms were constructed. With further restoration work over the years, it remains one of the park's most popular attractions.

Other summer projects included removing old foundations, taking down wire fences, and gathering driftwood and rubbish that had accumulated for years along the shore. With interest in the park growing rapidly, these improvements were an important start toward making it available to the large number of anticipated visitors.

Early in 1915, park supporters and county legislators battled again in Madison to obtain adequate funds for the park. Holand and the Ephraim Men's Club also continued their efforts to secure an appropriation for a horticultural experiment station. By now, both the university and the State Horticultural Society were backing the project. However, because of the newly elected legislature's frugal attitude and the many other budget requests before it, only four thousand dollars was appropriated for the park for the next fiscal year. From this, $1,250 was to be used to extend the Shore Road from Eagle Bluff Lighthouse to Shanty Bay. With his reputation for efficiency established, twelve hundred dollars was approved for Doolittle's salary for another year.[19]

By summer, electricity had been installed for lights at Fish Creek, and the park's macadamized south boundary road running from Fish Creek to Ephraim was completed. Timber was cut and stumps were blasted out for the route

View from Sven's Tower looking north. Initially resident fishermen probably occupied the buildings. (Courtesy Peninsula State Park office)

of the main road through the park. According to the *Door County News*, this road would "be a thing of beauty and a joy forever. It enters the park near the Ephraim end, skirts the golf links for a half-mile and then plunges into the grandest piece of natural timber in the county. It follows the cliffs that over-hang the water all the way with magnificent vistas across the water to wooded islands and dark headlands. When completed it will easily be the most charm-ing driveway in the state."[20] Since most of the road remained unpaved, frequent oiling was necessary to keep the down the dust. When gravel was needed, it was obtained from a gravel pit near Blossomburg Cemetery. Two stone pillars were also erected to mark the Ephraim entrance to the park.

Important changes that would affect the park were also underway in Madi-son. Legislation was passed combining the State Park Board, the Fisheries Commission, the State Game Warden Department, and the State Board of Forestry, to form the Conservation Commission. Meanwhile, park attendance grew steadily. An estimated nine thousand people visited the park that sum-mer. In fact in 1915, more people "from all parts of the United States" visited Peninsula than in any previous year.[21] The park also received its first official visit from the new Conservation Commission.

While funding remained severely curtailed for about a decade after the park was established, some limited improvements were made each year. The construction and maintenance of roads and trails became virtually an annual task. Work to remove stumps and grade the Eagle Bluff dirt road took several years. Because of the ever-present danger of forest fires, each spring roadsides and some four hundred acres of fields were burned for fire protection. This involved first plowing two furrows eight to ten feet apart and then burning the vegetation between them. Dead and downed timber was also removed, and some of it was sawed into boards. Eight to twelve hundred seedlings per acre were also planted. For several years, it was hoped that a concrete dock for yachts could be constructed at Eagle Bay, but this project was never realized.

By 1916, the park was being widely advertised and becoming better known as a premier natural and recreational attraction. In April, the *Door County Democrat* called it "one of the finest of all the natural state parks in the middle west and the pride of the Wisconsin State Conservation Commission."[22] Yet, considerable funding was needed for the park to realize its full potential. Standing at the top of Eagle Tower late in June, Conservation Commissioner F. B. Moody exclaimed, "Money! Money! That's all we want. If we can get the appropriation [twenty thousand dollars was being sought], we will make this the garden spot of the world."[23] However, 507 acres and seven platted lots within the boundary of the park still had to be acquired. By now, average land costs within the park had gone up to more than thirty dollars per acre. It was estimated that the cost of these acquisitions alone could exceed the twenty thousand dollars being sought from the legislature. The lack of funds frustrated many park devotees, including Moody, who stated that "the state should either sell Peninsula Park or develop it."[24]

The *Appleton Post Crescent,* another park supporter, commented on this dilemma in an editorial: "There is one thing . . . [for] which there ought to be strong public protest and that is the manifest niggardliness of the state's treatment of beautiful Peninsula Park. . . . It looks as though not a single penny had been spent on this park since a year ago at this time."[25] It criticized the "boundary road" along the Green Bay side which, it said, was full of chuckholes and several hills that were "absolutely dangerous" for motorists. Concerned about criticism regarding the lack of progress at the park, Doolittle wrote a detailed letter to the *Advocate* describing his approach to the situation.[26] He asked "auto tourists" to contact their senators and assemblymen for a suitable appropriation so that "a good road can be built right away around this park. This means eight miles." It should have good ditches and culverts, he wrote, so "it will stand up for just one good rain" before a few "heavy autos" turn it into "a mud hole proper." He went on to describe the work that needed to be done, far more than the two-thousand-dollar appropriation for the coming year would cover: "I have to keep the weeds cut down, fields all burned over, paths cleaned out and have had men continually on the golf links and others making tables, benches and stairways, and it keeps me guessing to keep from going broke against the amount of money that is available." At the top of his list of needs was "an appropriation for a good macadam road on the shore line of Peninsula State Park." Later that year, evidently in appreciation for the good work he had been doing, the board furnished Doolittle with a new truck bearing the name Wisconsin Conservation Commission.

By now, Wisconsin had six state parks: Peninsula, Devils Lake, Marquette, Interstate, Brule, and Cushing. The commissioners' growing responsibilities did not deter them from planning some unusual projects. For example, they wanted to erect a large sign on the bluff at Peninsula, to advertise the park to passing steamers. Assemblyman Frank Graass had several projects in mind, including the experiment station and a game reserve. The latter would consist of a fence around twenty acres in which there would be deer, plus "a few head of elk . . . from the Yellowstone National Park." Other animals would also be added.[27] The commission requested a budget of eighteen thousand dollars for the next biennium, a figure that was cut to eight thousand dollars, due to "the extra heavy financial burden that the state of Wisconsin will be placed under due to war conditions."[28] This amount was barely enough to cover expenses and maintenance for the next two years, and it eliminated any additional road construction.

The popularity of the park grew during the summer of 1917. To promote local interest, Doolittle proposed a Sturgeon Bay Days event for the first Sunday in July at Eagle Terrace. Hundreds of county citizens and others attended. Buses and more than thirty cars, each carrying a capacity load, motored north to the park. The Sturgeon Bay Band led the way in a huge convertible owned by Dr. A. J. Gordon, the city's highly regarded dentist. At the park, they were joined by scores of carloads of picnickers. The crowd ate lunch at the benches and tables near the terrace, and drank fresh water from Eagle springs and hot coffee furnished by Doolittle. The visitors were then escorted to interesting points in the park, before parading home out the Fish Creek entrance. The name of this event was later changed to Door County Day to give it a more countywide appeal.

That summer it was estimated that seventy-five automobiles motored through the park's shady roads daily. All of the "cottages" in the park were rented. Even yachting parties were popular there, since boat owners found it an ideal place to spend time while anchored offshore. Others enjoyed "splendid fishing" and picking the abundant wild berries. "With the very small amount that has been appropriated by the state for the upkeep of this beautiful spot, Mr. Doolittle and his assistants have done remarkably well," the *News* commented in an editorial.[29]

While World War I raged in Europe, 1918 proved to be an important year for the park and many new projects were undertaken. In an article entitled "Peninsular" published in the Conservation Commission's biennial report, Doolittle gave a glowing description of the "largest of state parks" and the improvements he and the other park workers had undertaken. "Each year sees a marked increase in the number of visitors," he reported. "Once here, there are attractions to meet the desires of all lovers of outdoor life." He then gave some interesting insights into the work he had supervised and the activities of park visitors. Note his sensitivity regarding roadside scenery:

War conditions have interfered somewhat with the road building program . . . Nevertheless some beautiful scenic driveways have been opened and still others are in contemplation. . . . Further [road] repair work consisted in the trimming of some of the main driveways. Some were not trimmed because to have done so would have destroyed the scenic effect. There are twelve miles of trails in this park. About four miles of these were old logging and "tote" roads of the lumbering days. . . . The fishermen's houses remaining near the beach after the purchase of the park lands have been repaired and made habitable. . . . Camping privileges have not been used to the extent that was expected though those who have camped here have spoken enthusiastically of the pleasures thus enjoyed. One reason that more people do not come with camping outfits may be attributed to the poor docking facilities. During the past two years much damage has been done to the docks by the ice of Green Bay. While pleasure boats were common visitors a few years ago, they very seldom stop now, because of the difficulty in docking.

Some improvements have been made on the grounds at Eagle Cliff, and other places to accommodate picnic parties have been put in shape.

The plans for . . . the planting of certain portions of the park with seedling pine and certain cutting of the mature timber are underway. . . . Ninety-five thousand trees have been planted on the Park during the past two years. . . . As to the cutting of mature timber, about twenty thousand log feet were taken last winter. . . . The Commission . . . believes that when the lumber needed for park improvements can be cut in the park without impairing its forest growth, or its beauty, it is wise to make use of it. An additional twenty thousand feet will be cut this year. Other improvements made in the last two years consist in the painting of all buildings used for the housing of tools . . . [and the] house used by the park superintendent. Several wells were drilled. Holland [*sic*] Orchard was pruned. Signs were also posted directing visitors to places of interest about the park. Stairways at Eagle Terrace and a number of benches and tables were constructed to add to the convenience of visitors. A telephone system covers the park for fire protection purposes. Two high towers have also been erected . . . [and] there is maintained a tank wagon and a truckload of cans which are always filled with water . . . in case of fire. Also in the early spring all fields that are not seeded with pine are burned to rid them of the dry grass.

With all of this work for fire prevention, fires sometimes occur. During the last two years there were several that came so near getting beyond control, that apparently the only condition which saved the park was a change in the direction of the wind.

At the extreme headland of Eagle Point stands Eagle Tower. This tower was built four years ago and the top story of it rises high above the towering trees. . . . Another point of interest is along Eagle Driveway . . . At one time last summer there were five thousand cars parked along this driveway.

It will be as pleasing to the people of the state generally as it is to the Commission to learn that the popularity of this great playground is increasing. Thousands of visitors are each year making use of it.[30]

After reading about timber cutting in Doolittle's report, the Ephraim Men's Club expressed strong opposition to the plan to manage a sustained yield of forest products. It charged that the endeavor looked "more like a forestry project than it does from the standpoint of a park."[31] One million feet of the park's big hardwood trees, "not to be below fourteen or fifteen inches in diameter," was to be harvested from the park's 2,770 wooded acres. The plan also called for reforesting the open fields of the park. After club members conferred with Doolittle, tree cutting was stopped, and the Conservation Commission was consulted about the matter.

An event that was significant for the entire county was the dedication, on September 22, 1918, of the new Gibraltar High School building. Classes had begun several days before, with thirty-five students enrolled. Designed by Sturgeon Bay architect F. D. Crandall, the two-story structure was built at the south edge of the park, just north of Fish Creek, at a cost of roughly fourteen thousand dollars. An overflow crowd attended the ceremony. The interior of the new building was handsomely decorated with flowers, ferns, and autumn leaves, under the skillful hand of Mrs. Crunden, one of the dedicated teachers. The impressive dedication opened with an invocation, brief addresses by several prominent county officials, and piano and violin solos. H. R. Holand, who had vigorously promoted the establishment of the much-needed high

George Larson and a work crew at the temporary sawmill set up at Shanty Bay to produce lumber from timber cut in the park. (Author's collection)

school, spoke about the history of the Gibraltar High School. Gifts were presented that included a one hundred dollar donation from Sturgeon Bay banks for purchasing a bell and a donation from the Ephraim Men's Club for purchase of a piano or other suitable gift. The event concluded with a tour of the new building.[32]

The year 1919 brought the end of World War I and several noteworthy events related to the park. The first, in January, was the death of Thomas Reynolds, considered the father of Peninsula State Park. In May, a delegation of county officials, representatives from the fruit growing industries, and Doolittle met with officials in Madison to discuss establishment of an experimental farm in the park. Door County was said to have "the largest cherry orchards in the United States,"[33] and the orchards in the park were thriving. Two months later the Conservation Commission visited the park to look over the proposed site. Commission members also planned to establish a zoo in the park.

Aerial view of Gibraltar High School, ca. 1947. Designed by F. D. Crandall, the original building (center) was dedicated on September 22, 1918. The school was built at a cost of fourteen thousand dollars on land deeded to the school district by the Wisconsin Conservation Department. (Photo from the 1948 Viking yearbook, courtesy Lee Tishler)

In August, a huge Peace Day Celebration commemorated Victory Day and the end of the war. Nearly four thousand people attended, "the largest crowd that has ever gathered in the northern part of the county," according to the *News*.[34] Doolittle estimated that about one thousand automobiles came to the park. The visitors picnicked at Eagle Terrace overlooking Eagle Bay, while bands from Sturgeon Bay and Forestville provided music. A "half-mile row of stands" served coffee and other nonalcoholic refreshments (Prohibition was in effect). After choral renditions of patriotic songs by campers at Camp Meenahga, Lieutenant James H. McGillian gave a rousing address. A prominent Green Bay attorney who had served in the navy during the war, McGillian emphasized the importance of the League of Nations, praised President Woodrow Wilson's support for the organization, and paid tribute to the men and women who fought in the war, to the delight of the many veterans present. After a flag drill by riders from Camp Meenahga carrying flags of the allied nations, the crowd watched two ball games on the spacious golf links near the Ephraim entrance to the park. Reflecting the sentiments of the crowd, local newspapers called the occasion a "stunning success."

Superintendent Doolittle estimated that fully twenty thousand people had visited the park during the 1919 season, which marked the end of the park's first decade. Peninsula was well on its way toward becoming one of the Midwest's premier outdoor playgrounds.

The year 1920 saw another attempt to establish an agricultural experiment station in the park. President Edward A. Birge, Dean Harry L. Russell of the College of Agriculture, and several university regents visited Door County that summer as guests of the Chamber of Commerce. After a luncheon with members of the county board and several town chairmen at the Hotel Swoboda in Sturgeon Bay, they inspected three potential sites in the park. The university was already undertaking extensive research with the peninsula's cherry and apple orchards, and several of its scientists were working on combating the troublesome pea moth that was reducing yields of an important local crop. The experiment station never became a reality at the park, but it was finally established on Highway 42 several miles north of Sturgeon Bay, where its first one hundred acres were purchased in 1922. It has been an active agricultural research center since that time.

The early 1920s proved to be eventful not only for Peninsula State Park but also for the nation's conservation movement. In 1921, Governor William L. Harding of Iowa invited a group of about two hundred conservation-minded people to a conference to address the growing interest in state parks. Stephen Mather, director of the National Park Service, was the instigator and guiding spirit for this gathering. Besieged with requests from many states that wanted a national park, he envisioned that state parks could help fulfill this need. They could, he believed, provide recreation areas that might not have the grandeur of a national park but could be patterned after the national park system. At the Iowa meeting, the National Conference on State Parks was organized. This group played an important role in developing state parks throughout the nation.

By now, Door County Days, first proposed by Doolittle in 1917, had become an annual tradition at the park. The fourth such gathering, in 1920, drew a crowd that the *News* estimated at more than seven thousand people from throughout the county and "all parts of the middle west."[35] The program, prepared by Doolittle, began with a picnic at Eagle Terrace. Throughout the day, bands from Sturgeon Bay and Forestville provided "peppy" music. The main feature was an address by junior U.S. Senator Irvine Lenroot, who praised Door County's beauty and then focused on reconstruction problems. He also warned against disloyalty, criticizing radical sources that, he maintained, were sowing seeds of discontent in the country. These individuals, he said, were working within labor and farm organizations in Wisconsin. They should "go to Russia which . . . is symbolic of the principles which they stand for." A baseball game followed, with county champions Baileys Harbor defeating Casco, said to be the best team in Kewaunee County. The day's events closed with singing by girls from Camp Meenahga.

By 1922, Door County Days had become the All Door County Picnic, and it was held on Memorial Day under the auspices of the Door County Farm Bureau. A picnic was followed by games and contests between the townships, such as a tug of war and horseshoe pitching, known locally as Barn Yard Golf.[36] A representative of the North American Fruit Exchange gave an address on marketing farm products, a topic of special interest to the local fruit-growing industry. The event concluded with the usual much-anticipated ball game.

That same year, U.S. Representative David Classon of Oconto introduced a bill to establish a Coast Guard station in the Strawberry Passage, a route running through the body of water between the mainland and the three Strawberry Islands. Extensive boat traffic in the vicinity included the large fishing fleet operating in Green Bay, plus the thousands of tourists who used motor boats and yachts in the area. There was strong local support for the facility, which was to be built in the park adjoining the Eagle Bluff Lighthouse. Its cost was estimated at thirty-five thousand dollars—far less than other Coast Guard stations being considered, including one at Grand Island, Michigan. The bill passed but no funding was provided. U.S. Representative George Schneider of Appleton continued to appeal for funds and eventually secured an appropriation, but the director of the budget denied the request.[37] Efforts to build the station continued for more than a decade but without funding it never came to fruition. Bitter over the project's failure, Holand later wrote: "The country is not ruled by Congress but by a stern gentleman known as director of the budget who possesses a vicious dexterity in the use of a blue pencil"[38]

The following summer, fires became a serious problem on the peninsula. Always dreaded in the park, one fire swept across thirty acres near Camp Meenahga. As it spread, there was concern that it would consume the buildings of the camp. The youthful campers and an army of volunteers that included tourists finally succeeded in quenching the roaring blaze.

During the early 1920s, the low water level in Lake Michigan became a growing concern. Many believed the Chicago drainage canal was causing the problem. With its roughly 250 miles of shoreline, shallow water in the peninsula's bays and harbors began to interfere with navigation. A major concern was water depth in the Strawberry Passage. Keeping this waterway open for large vessels such as those of the Goodrich Passenger Line was essential for Door County's economic welfare. Should the passage be abandoned for the deeper route around Chambers Island, the *Advocate* proclaimed, "thousands of people who take a lake trip on these boats will be deprived of the greatest scenic beauty . . . enjoyed on the trip from Chicago to Mackinac Island."[39] Many tourists, it pointed out, were attracted to Door County after viewing its scenery from the passing steamers. The line also played an important role in the northern peninsula's commerce, hauling hundreds of tons of freight to and from Washington Harbor, Sister Bay, Ephraim, and Egg Harbor. Yet, the Goodrich Company maintained that the fourteen-foot depth at that time was insufficient to operate its steamers safely. To remedy the problem, the ever-vigilant Ephraim Men's Club contacted Congressman Schneider to determine whether the government would dredge the channel deeper. Expense made such a project prohibitive.

In winter, with the bay frozen over and the steamers unable to operate, merchants had always crossed the ice to Marinette in horse-drawn sleighs and carriages to deliver eggs and produce and pick up merchandise from Marinette's wholesale houses. Cracks in the ice were sometimes eight to ten feet wide, so horses were trained to walk across a makeshift bridge of planks. The arduous forty-eight-mile journey from Detroit Harbor could take twelve to sixteen hours or longer. With time for resting the teams, it could take up to three days. In the winter of 1925, merchants began using new "motor trucks" for the journey.[40]

The year 1926 proved to be important for both the park and its adjoining communities. In the spring, Doolittle erected a filling station at the Fish Creek entrance. The Parkside Service Station was described as "the largest and most beautiful service station in the county."[41] It was managed by Doolittle's son Jay, who sold gasoline, car accessories, refreshments, and camping equipment, and it provided restrooms for travelers and park visitors. Doolittle later joined Lester Anderson in a partnership to develop adjoining land into the Anderson cottages.

That summer, twelve inmates from the Wisconsin State Reformatory began working in the park. Headquartered in several of the park's remaining farm buildings, the men cleaned up abandoned orchards. Supervised by only one officer, the prisoners were under an honor system—their good behavior could lead to an early parole. Needless to say, the effort aroused considerable controversy in nearby communities.

The previous summer, an infestation of worms began ravaging hemlocks in the park, destroying nearly sixty acres of trees. In June, an airplane arrived to dust some five hundred acres to destroy the deadly, hairlike insects. Seven and one-half tons of calcium arsenate were used. Flying just above the treetops, the plane spread a path of the deadly dust twenty-five feet wide and four miles long. Dead worm specimens were then sent to Washington where they were identified as the hemlock spanworm. Many insectivorous birds, especially warblers, were known to nest in the hemlock-wooded areas. The effect of the poison on birds was not known at that time, and probably not given much attention. More than three decades later, Rachel Carson's crusade against the wholesale use of pesticides finally brought public attention to the dangers of using such insecticides.

In October 1926, the Door County Historical Society was organized, largely due to the efforts of H. R. Holand, its first president. Later the group would play an important role in events at the park. In Ephraim, ground was broken for the new village hall, which was patterned after "Norse architecture."[42] The structure, with a footprint in the shape of a cross, would have an auditorium running east-west, and a post office and reading room running north-south.

By the end of the year, the county board also acted to change the name of Shanty Bay to Nicolet Bay.[43] The name had been used for decades and originated when early fishermen operated out of several shanties at the harbor, but now it was considered somewhat derogatory. Since it was believed that early explorers had stopped there, Nicolet Bay seemed to be a more appropriate and sophisticated name.

Because more people were using parks and more natural areas were needed for public use, several proposals for new parks were initiated late in the 1920s.

The most sweeping of these was an attempt to establish a lakefront park extending from Milwaukee to Sturgeon Bay. To implement this far-reaching endeavor, a bill was proposed in 1927 for purchasing a lengthy three-hundred-foot-wide swath of land along the lake. Meanwhile, legislation was proposed to establish a Northern Lakes Park and two additional state parks, Seven Pines Park in Polk County and Kettle Moraine Park in southeastern Wisconsin.

The flurry of park bills generated a far-reaching state "conservation bill" to establish a nonpolitical, nonsalaried board to oversee Wisconsin's various conservation programs. It would have wide powers, including supervising management of the state parks. Promoted by the Isaac Walton League, whose secretary-treasurer was former Assemblyman Frank N. Graass of Sturgeon Bay, the legislation received broad support. According to the *Door County News,* those opposing the bill used "every scheme and parliamentary tactic to defeat the measure." Enactment came after a five-month battle, "one of the most spirited fights that has taken place in the Wisconsin Legislature for many years," the newspaper stated.[44]

Late in 1929, the nation slid into a devastating depression. The sharp economic downturn affected the entire population and ultimately had a important impact on Wisconsin's parks. The Depression grew steadily worse until the early months of 1933 when the New Deal was inaugurated. This program attempted to boost the economy and provide employment. It established numerous federal agencies, one of the most significant being the Works Progress Administration (WPA). Some programs were involved with significant conservation work and park development. Chief among these were the Emergency Conservation Work Agency and its successor, the Civilian Conservation Corps (CCC). The CCC undertook significant work on an array of projects at Peninsula State Park.

During the early years of the Depression, concern was growing over the fate of the park's wildlife, particularly its deer. At that time, deer were not plentiful in Door County but a small number of them existed in the park. For many families in dire economic straits, a regular diet of meat became a luxury and some resorted to poaching deer in the park. Eventually their numbers were depleted to the point that news of a sighting made the front page of the *News.* One article referred to a group of deer as "one of the most unusual sights ever seen on the Door County peninsula."[45] The deer population on Rock Island, however, was exploding. The owner of the island, Chester Thordarson, had complained that deer were eating his shrubs and flowers and had vaulted fences in search of food. A park employee trapped and moved several deer from Rock Island to Peninsula in hopes of increasing their numbers there.

To propagate more wild animals and birds, the Conservation Commission established a game farm in the park. Wallace Grange of Ladysmith (a cousin of Red Grange of football fame) became its manager. The farm was stocked with wild birds that were kept in large pens. Eggs from pheasants, quail, and wild turkeys were to be hatched at the farm. Eventually, the commission hoped to release upward of eight thousand birds each year. To protect the pheasants, Harry Johnson, the farm's gamekeeper, began trapping predators at the Hotz Game Refuge near Ellison Bay. Johnson was told to capture as many foxes and wolves as possible, plus "mink, weasels, housecats, skunks and raccoon and, if possible, to kill great horned and barred owls and any hawks."[46]

The game farm quickly became a popular attraction for park visitors. Eventually the Conservation Commission's game committee, which included Aldo Leopold, the "father of game management," recommended that the state's two game farms (the other was at Kewaskum) be gradually consolidated at one central location. After spending nearly a year examining potential sites, they recommended locating it on a 110-acre tract just east of Poynette in Columbia County. Peninsula State Park's game farm then became just an empty field and pleasant memories for its many visitors.

Pens for raising pheasants and quail at the game farm in the park. (Photo by Merl Deusing, courtesy Milwaukee Public Museum)

In 1929, a new project threatened to encroach on the park. Led by Holand, chair of the county's park commission, a group that included Doolittle and representatives from the Ephraim and Fish Creek men's clubs met with C. L. Harrington of the Conservation Commission to discuss developing an airport. They maintained that the facility was necessary for northern Door County and suggested that it be located in the park. Harrington indicated that the project could be undertaken on a fifteen-year lease basis. Before proceeding, however, he wanted aviation experts to review the proposal. After examining the park, they recommended that a landing strip be built on a 150-acre tract known as Poplar Flats near the Fish Creek entrance to the park.[47] The Ephraim Men's Club voted to donate twenty-five dollars to help fund the project. Although the Conservation Commission turned down the proposal, eventually an airport was built, in 1945, on a 128-acre parcel of land just southeast of the park.

Some buildings remained in the park for several decades. Select individuals leased them, mostly on a seasonal basis. By 1930, nearly a dozen families, many from Illinois, had taken advantage of this arrangement. Initially, they paid from sixty to seventy-five dollars for the season, but rates gradually increased over the years. In 1930, the commission approved an unusual request from a Green Bay family to erect a small cottage for a disabled World War I veteran. When the veteran died two years later, his family was allowed to continue using the cottage for the nominal rental fee of twenty dollars. Over the years these cottages were repaired and improved at their occupants' expense.

Some of the leaseholders were colorful personalities with close ties to the park. As mentioned earlier, Vida Weborg was an accomplished artist and held a life tenancy with her sisters. Charles Lesaar, the artist who helped design the memorial pole in the park, leased a cabin near Weborg Marsh until 1941. By then, he was in poor health, and late that summer the *Advocate* reported that he had taken his life by drowning: "The body was found on the beach near Weborg Point . . . a rope around the neck and a loop in the other end as though it had been tied to a stone."[48] Others in the "art colony" of the park included Marie Gatter, a weaver from Evanston, Illinois, with a fondness for owls, who named her Shore Road cabin the Owl's Nest. Gatter moved the former Nelson barn and rebuilt it into a cottage, garage, and "out cabin."[49] Agnes Kuechler, a professional musician, had lived in the park since 1927 and occupied what was known as the old Amundson house cabin atop Sven's Bluff. A rugged individual, she eventually became a yearlong resident in the park and taught piano lessons to area children.

Leasing buildings to private parties proved to be a vexing issue for Doolittle and the Conservation Commission. Their policy was both controversial and difficult to implement. Questions arose over the ownership of improvements paid for by the leaseholders. Insurance and subleasing to friends and relatives were also thorny issues. Some people had unusual requests, such as Ted Cornils's attempt to stable some of his riding horses near Camp Meenahga. Another individual, who made the request through his assemblyman, wanted to build a cottage near Weborg Point with a twenty- to twenty-five-year lease arrangement. Harrington responded that he did "not feel it advisable," noting that "there is a definite conflict of interest between the transient user of an area . . . and those who put up a building that has more or less of a rather permanent character."[50] It is interesting to note that in the same letter Harrington stated, "We have thought somewhat of laying out a regular area back from the water . . . for just such a purpose . . . but as yet this has not taken on any tangible form." A few years earlier, Harrington had expressed concern about leasing problems in a letter to a member of the assembly. "As a general rule," he said, "as the years go by, this department is attempting to close out these leases as in a great many respects they have not proved satisfactory."[51] He noted that certain Conservation Commission employees had taken over several buildings for their work, such as that of the custodian at the Nicolet Bay campground. Conservation Commission employees who came to the park on official business used another cabin, affectionately known as the Little-To-Do-Inn. "This department is not in the business or renting cottages," Harrington concluded, "particularly in the park in Door County." Thus, the number of leases gradually diminished.

The perplexing lease situation at state parks led to establishing a special subcommittee of the commission to investigate private leases. Its report, issued in 1954, recommended that all recreational land leases in the Peninsula State Park end by December 31, 1964. The last lease arrangement in the park, made with Alice Kuechler, was officially terminated that year.

During the 1930s, greater demands were placed on the park and more events were held, resulting in proposals for an array of new facilities. The scenic lakeshore drive along Lake Michigan, which evolved from the lakeshore park proposed in the legislature in 1927, continued to get support. This road would be a boon for Chicagoans, said the *Chicago Tribune,* which wanted the project completed in time to accommodate traffic for the 1933 World's Fair.[52] Since Chicago's North Shore Drive already carried heavy traffic, a link with the new lakefront highway would enable motorists to drive directly into the heart of the city. Despite objections from the State Highway Commission, support for the lakeshore drive idea continued, backed by a citizen group called the Lake Michigan Shore Drive Association. Eventually governors of four states met to consider developing a scenic drive around the shore of Lake Michigan.[53] Such a project, they believed, could generate much-needed employment while providing motorists with an important recreation amenity.

The possibility of a wildlife museum at Peninsula Park was explored, at the suggestion of the Milwaukee Public Museum. Display cases would exhibit animals and birds native to the park, along with indigenous geological and botanical specimens. The Door County Historical Society agreed to add an exhibit of historical relics. The Conservation Commission supported the idea at first, for it seemed in keeping with its policy to stress educational aspects of the state parks. Instead of a museum, a zoo grew out of these interests and game farm superintendent Grange began stocking it with native birds and animals. The public was encouraged to donate birds or animals, and if Peninsula Park did not need them, the Vilas Park Zoo in Madison did, for it was finding it "difficult to obtain native Wisconsin specimens."[54] Topping the list of creatures sought was a wildcat. For some time, hunters had seen one in the Sawyer canal swamp. Once established, the zoo began drawing "thousands of visitors," who drove to the park just to see its display of wildlife. According to the *Advocate,* by the summer of 1930 the zoo had "twenty-one different birds and animals in it. These included several white tailed deer, a great horned and barred owl, red tailed hawks, ruffed grouse, one golden and one bald eagle, black bear, wild cats, muskrats, mink, skunk, woodchucks, porcupine, snow shoe and cottontail rabbits, gray squirrels, raccoon, coyotes and red foxes."[55]

In the summer of 1930 Harry Johnson, who had worked at the game farm for nearly two years, succeeded manager Wallace Grange, who resigned to take a position with the Federal Bureau of Biological Research. About this time, eleven hundred ringneck pheasants were obtained for breeding stock. During the 1930 season, the farm produced nearly forty thousand pheasant eggs, many of which were shipped to sportsmen's groups throughout the state. Late in the fall, the escape of the zoo's two bear cubs caused a lot of excitement. Acquired when they were only six months old, they could not survive in the woods on their own. To capture the hungry cubs, Johnson set out baited box traps near the pens so they could be returned to their farm dens before they might "sneak up and give someone a bear hug," as the *Advocate* jokingly put it.[56]

It was not long before the zoo drew the wrath of Jens Jensen. For years, Jensen had praised the beauty of Wisconsin's landscape, continuously warning of the need to protect its scenic quality and special natural areas. As early as 1921, he gave an illustrated lecture about the beauty of Door County to a capacity audience at the Art Institute of Chicago. The Door County Club of Chicago—Chicagoans with ties to the peninsula—organized his presentation.[57]

Soon, his views on conservation became feature articles in state newspapers. For example, the *Milwaukee Journal* interviewed Jensen and reported his concerns regarding Wisconsin's "selling her soul by permitting the commercialization of her natural beauty spots." At the same time, he castigated the state's conservation program for permitting the degradation "of those beauty spots which the state makes a gesture at preserving for the people."[58] Continuing his tirade regarding developments in Peninsula Park, he wrote to the *Milwaukee Journal*, "A zoo in the wilderness! Caged animals where animals should be free! And we call this civilization!" He went on to state bitterly, "And there are more surprises. Raising foreign birds to take the place of our own beautiful native game birds. Can you beat that? No you cannot." He equated seeing native wildlife in the park's natural surroundings with viewing "a masterpiece in the art institute." In his final paragraph Jensen noted: "Are we hastening the day when the only place we can see the wild life of our country is in cages or, still worse, stuffed and in our museums?"[59] Jensen's criticism of the management of Peninsula State Park, and state conservation policies in general, continued into the 1940s. It consisted of periodic columns in the *Capital Times* and sharply worded letters to various newspapers, the governor, plus commission members and staff of the Conservation Department. He was particularly concerned about unlawful deer hunting, the introduction of nonnative species, the influence of the Wisconsin Conservation League (then an organization of mostly hunters), and campgrounds that he called "slums."

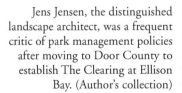

Jens Jensen, the distinguished landscape architect, was a frequent critic of park management policies after moving to Door County to establish The Clearing at Ellison Bay. (Author's collection)

Ignoring Jensen's criticism, the Conservation Commission decided to en-large the zoo. Its plan was to improve the game bird displays but discontinue displaying many animal species. The lack of refrigeration made it difficult to keep horsemeat to feed the carnivorous animals and, without concrete floors, unsanitary and smelly conditions prevailed. However, the main attractions of the zoo, the bear cubs and deer, would remain. By now, three bear cubs from Wisconsin were on display. They drew large crowds that watched them cuff playfully at each other, wrestle, and glide on their rustic swing.

About this time, a public arboretum was also envisioned for the park.[60] Sev-eral groups, including the Wisconsin Nurseryman's Association, garden clubs, and horticulturists at Madison, backed this venture. Like many other early proposals for new attractions in the park, it never became a reality.

Because camping enabled people to enjoy a relatively inexpensive vacation, it rapidly became popular at the park. Each summer hundreds of campers pitched their tents in its cool, green setting to escape the heat in their homes, offices, and factories that rarely were air-conditioned. The *Green Bay Press Gazette* noted that "happily there are cars from the scorching prairies of Kansas and Nebraska and others from the stifling streets of Ohio and Missouri" in the park.[61] According to Doolittle, tourist business at Fish Creek was greater dur-ing the summer of 1933 than it had been for several seasons. Campsites were often completely filled. Many campers spent several weeks or even the entire summer in the park. Initially there was no charge and practically no restric-tions; they could pitch their tents where they pleased within the camping areas. Starting in 1936, however, those staying longer than two weeks were charged eighteen dollars per season. They would also have to pitch their tents or park their trailers in designated areas, and certain places were roped off for the more permanent campers. Several years later, camping fees were raised to twenty-five cents per day, or one dollar per week.

For many, camping at the park became the highlight of their summer. Most of them cherished the many opportunities for socializing as well as the park's delightful setting. Lasting friendships were made and, for children, the expe-rience was an exciting outdoor adventure. When they were not swimming, hik-ing, or boating they could enjoy card parties, wiener roasts, Chinese checkers contests, and social gatherings. The *Advocate* said that camping in the park was like "one large family reunion."[62] A much-anticipated event each evening was gathering around a huge bonfire for various forms of entertainment and group singing. A Chicago friend of the author's, whose family had camped at Nicolet Bay for many years, was kind enough to share one of their favorite tunes, the "Nicolet Bay Song." Sung to the tune of "Shanty Town," the words were:

Just an old canvas shanty, at old Nicolet Bay
   Some rounded, some slanted, some every which way.
And when spring rolls around, you can always be found.
   Planning a trip to that old camping ground.
You'll pack up your troubles and worries behind,
   And hide us away to the moon and the pine.
We're all friends when we meet at that perfect retreat—
   'Round the campfire at the old Nicolet Bay.

One creative camper, who spent several weeks in the park each summer, was S. J. Huber of Portage. In 1930, Huber began organizing the evening performances on a stage that he improvised at Weborg Point. Later the park erected an artistically detailed, rustic structure, built of cedar posts with a slab roof. With gas lantern footlights and an improvised curtain, it was a perfect stage for outdoor productions. The decorative structure soon became a popular landmark in the park. In 1934, county newspapers described one of the theater's biggest productions. Huber had arranged an impressive show with a cast of forty, including several professional singers from the Chicago Lyric Opera and

Campers in the park could attend evening performances at the Huber Theater at Weborg Point. In 1930 S. J. Huber, a regular camper at the point, began organizing impressive productions featuring talented campers and occasionally professional performers. (Author's collection)

Metropolitan Opera companies. Other campers with stage experience and musical talent completed the cast. The production was similar to a big-city minstrel show, complete with music, jokes, and dancing. The public was welcomed to the event and there was no charge for admission, but a free will offering was taken to help defray costs. Some fifteen hundred persons attended the show. Huber was pleasantly surprised when a four-by-eight-foot sign of white birchbark appeared on the roof with the words Huber Theatre. During the performance, Doolittle called him up before the audience, and the structure was respectfully dedicated to him in appreciation of his many efforts to entertain campers, tourists, and local residents.

Several years later, the camping area at Nicolet Bay was enlarged. Doing so involved moving the main road from the lake edge to circle around the campground and return to the shore beyond the dock on the west side of the harbor. Camping was prohibited on the ridge along the swimming area. The new campsites were laid out according to National Park Service guidelines, and several council fire areas were proposed.

To provide additional entertainment for park visitors and tourists, a huge "outdoor stage shell" was proposed for the park. Its supporters proclaimed that it would rival "that of the famous shell at Hollywood, California." The project was endorsed by a number of prominent individuals, including Frederick Stock, music director of the Chicago Symphony Orchestra. Ephraim architect William Bernhard drew a sketch of the facility to be on "the natural slope just west of Eagle bluff."[63] This area could accommodate several thousand persons, and the shell would be built at the bottom of the slope on the edge of the bluff. This proposal was never realized.

By now the park was a popular tourist destination and the number of visitors increased steadily each year. Eventually records were kept of their numbers, and in 1934 they reached more than sixty-seven thousand. Attendance declined a bit during World War II, when gasoline and tire rationing limited vehicular travel and many young men had gone off to war.

Landscape architect Kenneth Greaves and architect William Bernhard were hired to oversee many park improvements during the 1930s. In 1935, the Conservation Commission received a large federal grant for park improvements that provided funds for a new repair shop and garage for park vehicles. Designed to harmonize with its natural surroundings, Bernhard proposed a large, handsome, "English cottage" type of structure.[64] The long stone building had a cross-shaped footprint and a steeply pitched roof. The steep roof of the short arm of the cross, comprising the main entry area, rose above the rest of the building. A tall cupola capped with an ornate weather vane and massive stone chimney highlighted the peak of its roofline. A smaller and less elaborate version of the design was eventually built.

By 1935 it was time to expand Gibraltar High School. Since the school was close to the park boundary, the school board requested two acres of parkland for the expansion. C. L. Harrington approved the request, and a fifteen-year lease was granted for the nominal fee of one dollar per year. The law did not permit a longer lease, and the school would have first renewal rights after fifteen years. The new addition housed a gymnasium and classroom.

Under the Roosevelt administration, the federal government, through the Department of the Interior, initiated several planning efforts involving the states and their parks. One such program was the Wisconsin Park, Parkway, and Recreation Area Study, carried out by the National Park Service in cooperation with Wisconsin's State Planning Board. It involved "making comprehensive studies as a basis for state and local planning for park, parkway, and recreational-area facilities and in aiding in the planning of such areas."[65] A major thrust of this effort was to secure basic data to help meet the recreational needs of the people. Consequently, several useful attendance and park user studies were carried out. One survey, for example, pointed out that in 1938 most people visited Wisconsin's state parks for "scenic appreciation."[66] The next most popular activities, in order, were picnicking, swimming, hiking, and camping. It also found that 1,295,562 individuals visited the parks that year, with attendance peaking during the last days of July. Of the eleven state parks existing at the time, Devils Lake had the largest number of visitors, followed by Interstate and then Peninsula, which had 148,042 visitors. Peninsula also had the highest percentage (52.4) of out-of-state visitors. Other useful information from these studies indicated that Wisconsin ranked low in expenditures for its state parks. For example, of the eleven states surveyed, Wisconsin ranked tenth in expenditures for maintenance costs per park patron. The state was near the bottom in virtually every type of park expenditure, including total spending for maintenance and operation, and for maintenance and operating costs per capita. As of 1937, Wisconsin also ranked low in actual state park acreage. On the other hand, another analysis pointed out that out of fourteen states, Wisconsin had the fifth highest traveler expenditures per capita for 1938.

A ferocious storm swept through the Upper Midwest on November 11, 1940. One of the worst storms in the recorded history of Lake Michigan, it claimed five vessels and sixty-six lives. The mighty gale ripped an unsightly swath through the park and downed some five hundred acres of timber. Because the fallen trees represented a dangerous fire hazard, Doolittle requested WPA funds, mostly for labor to help clear the timber. Salvageable wood was made into lumber on the park's portable sawmill. The rest was used for firewood to be distributed to needy families by the Door County Relief Department, or made available to campers.

By 1942, the Conservation Department had established detailed policies for the state park system. It determined that the dominant values of the parks could be inspirational, recreational, educational, or scientific. As John Nolen said earlier, state parks also should be large—not less than one thousand acres. Other components of the system would include recreation areas, monuments, historic sites, roadside parks, waysides, and parkways. The policies also established guidelines for park planning and development, tree cutting, concessions, wildlife management, and the elimination of inholdings. These guidelines undoubtedly were influenced by the many years of experience gained at Peninsula State Park.

The following year, A. E. Doolittle retired after working thirty years as Peninsula's first superintendent. It marked the end of an important era in the history of the park. Under Doolittle's dedicated supervision, the park was transformed from a series of farms and forests into what for many years was Wisconsin's largest state park.

Doolittle had directed the development of miles of roads, the golf course, observation towers, campgrounds, and many other improvements. He was also

Parkside cabins and cottages originally built by A. E. Doolittle and managed by his son Jay. (Author's collection)

responsible for many of the improvements at Potawatomi State Park, which came under his supervision shortly after his coming to Door County.

Doolittle was confronted with the overwhelming challenge of opening the wild parks to the public. While he was not formally schooled in park planning, his good judgment and keen sensitivity of their beauty and natural features resulted in improvements that, for the most part, did not detract from the many qualities nature had bestowed on them.

After retiring, Doolittle continued his involvement with Peninsula State Park, but on an informal basis. He also gave more attention to managing the family's cottage resort in Fish Creek, but his heart remained with his beloved park. Unfortunately, he would enjoy his retirement only briefly. He died in March 1944 at the age of seventy-four—less than a year after he and his wife celebrated their golden wedding anniversary.

An artist's rendition of Camp Meenahga. (Courtesy Peninsula State Park office)

CHAPTER 9

❧

Camp Meenahga

Few people today remember the bustling summer camp for girls that operated in the park from 1916 through 1948. Known as Camp Meenahga, it was organized by two gracious and resourceful women from St. Louis: Mrs. Warren L. (Alice) Clark and Mrs. H. C. (Fanny) Mabley. Both were widows with young children.[1]

With two children and no source of income, Alice Clark conceived of "starting a girls' camp" in 1915.[2] Inexperienced in such an endeavor, especially preparing food for large groups of hungry girls, she discussed the idea with her friend Fanny "Kidy" Mabley, who managed the cafeteria at McKinley High School in St. Louis. Mabley was seeking summer work at a camp, and the two decided to join forces for the new enterprise. After corresponding to find potential locations, they initially chose a site on the Door County peninsula at Sawyer, a community that was annexed many years earlier by the city of Sturgeon Bay. Clark's daughter spoke of the camp's beginnings at its twenty-fifth anniversary banquet in 1940. "Camps for girls were practically unheard of, especially in the Middle West," she stated. Therefore, the founders of the camp had to "educate both girls and parents to the aims and benefits of summer camps. . . . The fathers especially had to be won over, for it was unheard of to think of their daughters sleeping in the open."[3]

The Clark family had early ties to the Fish Creek area. Among their friends were Mr. and Mrs. Frank Crunden from St. Louis, who had summered at Fish Creek since the late 1890s. Crunden was president of the Crunden-Martin Company, a woodenware manufacturer. Upon hearing of the Sawyer location, which Mrs. Crunden considered an undesirable "mosquito hole," she suggested establishing the camp in Peninsula State Park and urged the women to discuss the matter with A. E. Doolittle. Mrs. Crunden also gave Clark money for a train ticket to Sturgeon Bay and wrote to a Mr. Vorous of Fish Creek to pick Alice up at the railroad station and drive her to the Thorp Hotel to meet Doolittle. In April, Clark spent two days driving through the park with Mrs. Thorp and Doolittle. Enthused about the proposed camp, he believed it would benefit both the park and nearby communities.

Alice Clark found the Evenson farm just off Shore Road to be the ideal place for her camp. Originally an eighty-acre parcel of land, it was settled by Simon Evenson and his wife, Emily, in the early 1870s. Alice later wrote her impressions of this idyllic place: "That old farm seemed to have everything I could imagine a camp would need. A huge threshing barn for the dining room and recreation hall, with cowsheds, stable and woodshed all connected to the barn. Across the lawn was the (circa 1837) farm cottage, which seemed adequate for the living quarters of the two [Clark and Mabley] families, except for the camp girls who would live in tents. Also there was room for an office, a nice sitting room and small bedrooms upstairs."[4]

After further discussions, Doolittle, with support from the Crundens, Mrs. Thorp, and others, negotiated approval for the camp from the State Park Commission. Anxious to see the camp become a success, the Crundens loaned Clark one thousand dollars to finance the venture. The two women then began ordering equipment, ranging from "kerosene stoves to small granite potties," from Sears-Roebuck. "When we unpacked at Camp," she later recalled, "we found the potties were baby size—we never stopped laughing."[5]

The name *Meenahga* was from an Ojibwa word meaning "the blueberry." (The term appears in the "Vocabulary and Notes" section at the end of Longfellow's epic poem *The Song of Hiawatha*.) The two women had chosen the name when considering the Sawyer site, where blueberries grew in abundance. In addition, they had already purchased an assortment of dishes decorated with the letter *M*, possibly from a defunct Lake Michigan shipping line.

The camp opened for the summer of 1916 with the arrival of fifteen girls accompanied by eight adults. Early in July, twenty-two more young women joined the group. They came from St. Louis, Dallas, San Antonio, Chicago, Buffalo, and other cities. Professor Carl Stephenson of Washington University in St. Louis was the camp's head counselor, and his wife supervised boating, fishing, and hiking activities. Other counselors were in charge of swimming, artistic dancing, physical training, tennis, and music. In its first year, the women spent fifteen hundred dollars renovating the buildings and planned to spend more on improvements in subsequent years. According to the *Door County Democrat*, the camp, in its delightful setting, became "probably the merriest place on the whole Door county peninsula."[6] At the beginning of

September, Mabley returned to St. Louis with thirty-five of the young ladies. All "were jubilant over their stay in this county," the *News* reported, and they "regretted that the coming school term necessitated their leaving." Mrs. Clark supervised the remaining girls, who stayed several more weeks at the camp.[7]

The next year, on the morning of July 4, Chicago and Alton Company sleeping cars filled with girls left Union Station in St. Louis for Sturgeon Bay. In the North Western station in Chicago, they had breakfast before proceeding to the train to Sturgeon Bay. Young women from locations other than St. Louis gathered in Chicago, where they took a Goodrich Line boat to Sturgeon Bay. From there the group was driven north to the park. Alice Clark Peddle later recalled arriving at the camp: "On the way to Camp Meenahga we passed the Doolittle house, then the swamp, and finally Mengelberg Lane, leading to Blossomburg Cemetery. Then, passing the limekiln on the Green Bay side, we made an abrupt right turn up a little hill and we were there. Tired and hungry, we bounded out of the autos and rang and rang the old ship's bell that Mr. Doolittle had found for us from a sunken boat."[8]

The eight-week camp season in 1917 ended in August. For those wishing to stay longer, a two-week postseason camp was scheduled. A booklet about

Alice Clark, cofounder of Camp Meenahga. (Courtesy Laurence C. Day)

the camp issued that year stated that the "aim at Camp Meenahga is to give a limited number of girls from the ages of twelve to twenty, a wholesome, happy vacation under the guidance of councilors of culture, refinement and winsome leadership. It gives our girls a vacation from fashions and boys. It creates a love of nature and the out-of-doors." It also contained the rules of the camp, including the stipulation that "no girl may leave our grounds without special permission and accompanied by a councilor." Three references were required for admission. Charges for the eight weeks were two hundred dollars, or twenty-five dollars per week, with no refunds for late arrivals or dismissals. The brochure was illustrated with photographs of camp scenes, including a view of the long, renovated Evenson barn, referred to as the One-Hundred Foot Lodge.[9]

In 1920, camp enrollment peaked with some 118 young women and more than twenty counselors. Upon arriving at the Sturgeon Bay railway station, the girls were met by Yellow Cab Company vehicles. All of the company's cars and trucks were needed to transport the merry girls. The *Door County News* reported that the procession hauled 111 trunks of clothing and personal items to the northern part of the county that day, most going to the camp.[10] The girls, screaming with excitement, hopped out of the vehicles hugging and kissing. Then they swarmed into the lodge for a hearty dinner where they jabbered and raved about the camp and the exciting times they anticipated. Exhausted but happy, they retired to their tents. The same newspaper reported that at least 150 girls were expected at the camp the following year.

To provide instruction and assist with camp programs, nearly twenty counselors adept at sports activities were hired, mostly college-age women and a few young men. Many were students at the University of Wisconsin. One counselor, Clark Clifford of St. Louis, who was camp master in 1927, later achieved prominence as an attorney, political advisor to several presidents beginning with Harry Truman, and secretary of defense under President Lyndon Johnson. His sister Alice was also a counselor at the camp.

The stay at Meenahga, "in the great north woods," was a delightful experience for the young women, most of whom came from cities.[11] Its location was a refreshing reprieve from the hot, muggy cities to the south before the days of air-conditioning. Some of the campers returned for several summers. By the 1940s, early campers were enrolling their daughters at Meenahga, making it a family tradition.

So successful and inviting was the summer camp experience that other youth camps soon were established in northern Door County. These included Camp Wildwood for boys near Juddville; Camp Hellenic at Jackson Harbor on Washington Island; the Adventure Island Camp for boys, established in 1925; Camp Greenwood at Ellison Bay, started in 1921; Camp Shoreland Acres at Jacksonport; the Mabel Katherine Pearse camp for girls on Washington Island, established in 1924; and Camp Kewahdin for girls on Chambers Island.

In 1922, two boatloads of girls from the Chambers Island camp visited Camp Meenahga for a tennis match on clay courts. Later tournaments were held for basketball, baseball, and swimming. In 1927, the Wildwood boys visited Meenahga and were regaled with cheering, singing, and a basketball game. Four days later, the girls visited Wildwood. After inspecting the camp one girl wrote that the neatness of their tents "was such as we had never dreamed existed." Then they were entertained with a rowing and diving meet, and Wildwood's tennis finals. "Meenahga and Wildwood agreed that inter-camp affairs were great fun and should be continued," she concluded.[12]

Many insights into camp life were recorded in *Pack and Paddle,* the camp's newsy pamphlet published each year from 1917 to 1945. Written and edited by the campers, it was illustrated with photographs and sketches as a "remembrance of delightful days and happy friendships." At the back of each issue were advertisements from various camp boosters and Door County merchants. These frequently included the Hotel Thorp and Cottages, Door County State Bank, Mrs. C. A. Lundberg's General Merchandise, L. E. Schreiber Dry Goods, the Happy Hour Tea Shop, L. M. Washburn's Shopping Center, the Eagle Inn, and Pleck Ice Cream and Dairy.

A typical day at camp began when the girls were roused from their warm cots by the old ship's bell mounted on a tall pole near the lodge. The sleepy campers then donned bathing suits and caps and dashed down to the pier for a cool, eye-opening dip in the bay. Returning to their tents, they kicked off their wet swimming gear and jumped into their uniforms: a white middy blouse with a long narrow scarf tied near its ends, green bloomers fastened below the knee (later, shorter white bloomers were worn), and long socks. Then they rushed to make the 7:10 morning drill. By the time they had saluted the flag and done in-unison exercises, they had worked up huge appetites for breakfast.[13] Tent inspections followed, and then it was time for swimming, diving, canoeing, or playing tennis, basketball, softball, or volleyball. Watchful camp counselors provided instruction for these activities, especially the water sports.

To promote competition and sportsmanship, the girls were divided into two teams, the Purples and the Yellows, and wore identifying purple or yellow scarves. They elected cheerleaders and captains for basketball, baseball and swimming.[14] Sometimes competitions were held between the girls and their counselors. Each side cheered on their teammates, who worked hard to win "star awards" for their team.

The noon bell summoned the campers to dinner, and the three o'clock bell sounded the end of the afternoon rest period. Swimming and mail filled the time until supper at six. After eating, the girls could relax and write letters home, or just loaf until the call to bed. In the darkness, they made their way to their tents down trails lit by kerosene lanterns. The lights-out bell rang at ten o'clock. A golden silence crept over the camp, pierced with occasional giggles and, if the tent flaps were open, glimpses of the dazzling northern lights. Later, a bugle sounded both reveille and taps.[15]

Everyday life at camp provided a good introduction to the wonders of nature. The trees, flowers, abundant wildlife, clean water, and invigorating air offered a delightful environment for the young women, many of whom came from urban areas. Yet, the camp was not without its nuisance creatures. The girls swatted mosquitoes (sometimes referred to as "camp livestock") and chased spiders from their beds. There was time to watch squirrels, chipmunks, bats, snakes, and toads. Campers could also romp with the dogs. As many as five were kept in kennels, including Fette, Alice Clark's beloved Highland terrier.[16] Mischievous capers were common, such as sneaking into the lodge at midnight for fudge and lemonade, making ghostlike noises at other camper's tents, pillow fights, painting a sleeping camper's nose with iodine, or night swims minus bathing suits.

Campers at Camp Meenahga started the day with in-unison exercises after a refreshing dip in Green Bay. (Courtesy Laurence C. Day)

One of the great adventures at camp was the canoe trip north along the shore of the peninsula. Only expert canoeists were allowed to make these arduous treks. One such outing was described in the 1917 issue of *Pack and Paddle*. On a July morning nine young women set out in the green canoes with "light hearts and full stomachs" for the long paddle. Since the day was hot, several of them decided to shed their shirts until an occasional boat came by which sometimes "seemed to be full of staring eyes and interested smiles." Their first stop was to stretch their legs and climb up to Eagle Cave. By noon, they had worked up huge appetites and the group halted at Cedar Springs, opposite Ephraim, for lunch prepared over a small fire. From there they crossed to Ephraim and splurged on ice cream. After more hours of furious paddling, they stopped at a pebble beach for a swim. Those who had forgotten their bathing suits went into the water "a la Venus." At half past seven, a suitable place to sleep was found. The girls awoke the next morning covered with dew and started back to camp. Just before they reached Shanty Bay, a storm came up, but with skillful paddling, they overcame the waves. When they came within shouting distance of camp, they gave the camp yell, bringing everyone down to the pier. "The canoes were welcomed hilariously and enthusiastically."

Canoe trips to Gills Rock could last as long as three days. The first stop was usually Ephraim, for refreshments at Wilson's, then on to camp on a beach suitable for swimming. After supper they told "hair-raising ghost stories around the camp fire, before crawling between their blankets." The return trip included dinner at Pebbly Beach in Little Sister Bay, and later the traditional stop at Wilson's for more sundaes and banana splits.[17]

On one occasion in 1923, the girls boarded a "lumber boat" for a late-afternoon ride to Ellison Bay. Watching the sunset on the way, they piled out for dinner at their destination on the beach. With their ravenous appetites satisfied, they gathered around a huge campfire and, according to one girl's account, "sang till way after 'lights out' time, until the whistle from the boat called us aboard. The ride home by moonlight," she wrote, "was extremely romantic and wonderful."[18]

Hikes in the park—a veritable wilderness to the young city dwellers—became another adventure that campers relished. One young woman described the experience in glowing terms: "The winding trails, where the leaves brush my face, and my feet sink down into the cool, damp earth; the alternate light and shade, silvery birches with the sunlight filtering through, and the dusky pines, the deep silence, oh, the joy of it all!"[19] Day hikes included climbing up Sven's Tower just before sunset to look from the dizzying height at the winding shoreline stretching into the distant haze. Treks were sometimes made to the Fish Creek bluff, or for a tasty lunch at Cedar Springs or for ice cream in the evening. Other destinations included the seven-mile jaunt to Ephraim or to their favorite raspberry patch for fresh fruit for sundaes at dinner. Sometimes they walked to the lighthouse or along Sunset Trail or to Shanty Bay in the late afternoon to swim or to play tag on the sandy beach. Occasionally, they even marched off to the orchards to pick and eat Door County's famous cherries. They paid regular visits to such favorite wooded haunts as Thistle-Cave-In, the Brig, and the Owl's Nest cottage, or rested on the Balsam Bench on Hemlock Trail to enjoy a treetop view of the bay and Fish Creek, then stopped at the Devil's Pulpit.[20]

Some of the hikes were "all nighters" to Sven's Tower, a favorite destination that included passing a "haunted" house on the way. There they could spend the night sleeping on the tower's first level while a counselor slept at the top. To initiate novice campers, nighttime "snipe hunts" were held, whereby the girls tripped over trails and through the woods with laundry bags and flashlights to catch the "small birds." The 1930 *Pack and Paddle* recounted one such hunt:

> These fowl were described to the uninitiated . . . as being rather like sandpipers and we were told that they were delicious to eat . . . Most of the new campers fully expected to eat fried snipe for breakfast the next morning.
>
> As we went from the riding field to the graveyard, we were cautioned to silence. Finally, the fun began. We threw ourselves into blackberry bushes, trees, poison ivy, *everything,* laundry bags and flashlights in readiness.
>
> By this time, nearly everyone was beginning to feel rather dubious, and so at last we started home. Ghostly howls came from the hill as we passed through the graveyard, but we had expected them. We had a delightful, if slightly exhausting, evening.[21]

During 1918, with World War I raging in Europe, campers were sometimes occupied with war relief projects. A special Red Cross room was set up where they sewed and knit muslin slings, dresses for French orphans, undergarments, and a quilt. Seventy dollars from the Patriotic Pageant was donated to the war relief fund. Money was also raised from vaudeville acts, a gypsy party where one girl acted as a fortune-teller, and auctions of ice cream and pies at dinner. That year, a *Pack and Paddle* writer noted: "Although camp is too far away to be constantly in the atmosphere of the war, there were many inspiring ways in which our feelings were aroused; beginning . . . with the raising and saluting of the flag and closing at night with accounts [read] of the daily war activities."[22] On Sunday nights the campers gathered in the lodge and sang "The Star Spangled Banner" and "God Save Our Noble Men." While the war seemed remote from the campers' carefree world they still, as one girl wrote, "had that overwhelming feeling which is a mixture of love and devotion and grief and pride and, above all, an unconquerable desire to do our part in winning a glorious, honorable victory." Expressions of patriotism became an important part of the camp experience. In later years, there were sometimes fireworks on the beach on the Fourth of July. On one July evening in 1925, the excited girls deserted the camp to greet a fleet of Navy submarine chasers docked at Fish Creek. During World War II, the girls helped the war effort by purchasing savings stamps each week.

The camp hosted an array of social programs. Often Alice Clark and Fanny Mabley invited groups to their cottage for afternoon tea and entertained them with funny stories about early camping days and tales about their children and themselves. Local residents, parents, and other visitors frequently attended elaborate events. A huge countywide celebration to commemorate Victory Day in August of 1919 featured patriotic singing, a special tableau presented by the young ladies of the camp, and a flag parade on horseback under the direction of the camp's riding master, Hans Berg, who had brought horses from the Berg Riding School on Warren Avenue in Milwaukee. In this impressive mounted flag drill, the young horsewomen carried flags of the Allies. They rode down a path in the woods into a field and, with flags fluttering, faced the large audience. It was an impressive sight.[23]

Equestrian activities were always popular at the camp. Sometimes the girls took daylong rides through the woods and fields to Baileys Harbor or Egg Harbor. By 1924, the camp was holding an annual Derby Day near the end of the season. This display of riding skills drew large crowds of parents, lovers of fine horses, Fish Creek and Ephraim residents, and tourists from nearby resorts. The visitors parked their cars in a circle around the riding ring. The girls watched the impressive event unfold from the hill above the ring. Initially, Berg served as master of ceremonies for this event. Later Chris Christiansen, from the Lakeshore Riding Academy in Chicago, became the riding master. Ted Cornils succeeded him.

The derby started with a bagpiper leading a parade around the ring and playing his Scotch Highland bagpipe. Then, at the sound of a bugle, which added pomp to the affair, riders dressed in riding pants, blouses, and tall boots trotted out in single file. After forming in rows, they competed in riding contests. The competitions included "the Drill, the Apple Chase, the Ribbon Chase, and the Ball Game [which resembled polo]."[24] The spectacular Ribbon

Chase, held at the end of the derby, was a rigorous event for some of the best horsewomen of the camp. The leader dashed off with a ribbon tied to her arm, with the other riders in hot pursuit attempting to snatch it. The event required sudden bursts of speed and quick turns.

In the 1920s, jumping events were added. By the 1940s, the girls were using horses from Cornils Riding Academy on Highway 42. Cornils sometimes gave special riding demonstrations on his show horse Countess. The event concluded with the presentation of prizes, pins, and trophies for the junior, intermediate, and senior riding championships. The Camp Meenahga Silver Cup was awarded for best senior blue ribbon winner.

The campers also took part in the annual Ephraim Regatta, an annual summer tradition in August, in which they challenged boys and girls from Ephraim and neighboring towns. Pennants were awarded to the young women who won the swimming, diving, and canoeing events and the "watermelon race."[25]

Beginning in 1934, sailing on the waters of Green Bay became a popular camp pastime. In 1938, the camp acquired a Sea-Gull class sloop christened the *Loch Maid.* Campers enjoyed all-day sails to Chambers or Horseshoe islands for picnic lunches cooked on shore or, weather permitting, delightful moonlight sails. The girls also sailed in the biweekly Seagull races at Fish Creek, later competing with a second camp boat, the *Kelpie.*[26] In 1941, the *Windward,* identical in design to the *Kelpie,* was added to the fleet. Using these two boats, the Yellows could race the Purples on a course to a gas buoy in the Strawberry Channel and back.

Theatrical events were an important part of camp life, and many were open to the public. Dance pageants—plays using artistic stage scenery and an array of other dramatic presentations (with the girls sometimes dressed as clowns and nymphs)—took place at the outdoor theater, with its improvised stage, in front of a thick row of balsam trees.[27] These innovative and colorful performances, directed by the music and drama teachers of the camp, gave the campers an opportunity to display their dramatic ability. In addition to performing, the girls helped with costuming, settings, and makeup. Other events included musical farces, pantomimes, vaudeville acts, patriotic pageants, and fashion shows with the campers acting as models complete with makeup. Minstrel shows featured sunburned young maidens with faces blackened with burned cork from the kitchen vinegar jug. Swimmers who took morning dips the next day sometimes chided that the bay tasted slightly of burnt cork.

Other group events on the camp's busy social calendar included pajama parties, the counselors' party in the lodge, auctions, beach suppers, and midnight beach parties around "a dying campfire [with] tired, happy faces lit up by the last rays, and the dense black around and above," where they would "sit cross-legged and gaze into the embers, wrapped in thought."[28]

The girls were often invited to visit the Foldas, a prominent Omaha, Nebraska, family who owned Folda's Island (Horseshoe Island). Their yacht *Brigydon* ferried the campers from Ephraim or Shanty Bay. Writing in the 1922 *Pack and Paddle,* a camper described one such visit:

> Soon we arrived at the island—too soon almost—for the yacht was a pleasure to ride in. Those of us who had visited Mr. Folda before began to recall delightful memories of other years.
>
> We walked up a little wooded path to the house, which seemed to blend in with the pine and hemlock trees surrounding it. Mrs. Folda, Mrs. Sherman and Marcelle Folda received us. The house was delightful, especially the large living room, which has an immense fireplace at one end and is filled with all kinds of curios. There were rows and rows of interesting books lining the walls and as many cushions as one could desire. It is certainly an ideal room.
>
> Mr. Folda entertained us with interesting stories of the times when Indians inhabited this region. He also showed us some interesting objects, such as prehistoric pottery and petrified wood.
>
> We returned to the house and received delicious refreshments, after which we decided to walk around the island. The wild beauty of it sends out a natural appeal to every one.

Pageants put on by students from the drama program were an important part of Camp Meenahga's social life. (Courtesy Laurence C. Day)

We had a glorious time and are all indebted to Mr. Folda for his cordiality and kind hospitality.

Many clever camp songs reflected camp life or local geographic features. One popular early number was sung to the tune of "Moonlight Bay":

> We were drifting along on Ephraim Bay,
> We could hear our comrades calling,
> They seemed to say,
> We have paddled enough
> So let us stay,
> And at Cedar Springs, we'll camp,
> On Ephraim Bay.[29]

Some songs became traditional Meenahga favorites. At the camp's twenty-fifth anniversary banquet, it was noted that "the first Camp song was composed on the road to Fish Creek. Its tune was a current favorite, 'In the Blue Ridge Mountains of Virginia,' and the words we put to it began, 'In the Sweet Grass Meadows of Wisconsin.'"[30]

By 1921, a junior camp had been established for younger girls, who were referred to as the juniors. Initially, it was located near Nicolet Bay, and the young campers were housed in an older park building that had been moved to a location near the shore.[31] Another building served as their dining room. Later, the juniors were moved to Tin Can Alley at the main camp, and the junior camp buildings were then used for the state game farm. At their new location, the group stayed in a cluster of ten tents, and they published their own yearbook, *Junior Pack and Paddle,* as a section of *Pack and Paddle.*[32]

Those campers who were fortunate enough to afford the time stayed on for the two-week postcamp session. After the majority of girls had departed, the posters, as they called themselves, gathered their cots into two tents separated by a third, which was used as a dressing room. For competition, the two teams used the names Wampuses and Gaboons, instead of Purples and Yellows. Their days were filled with games of tennis, baseball, swimming, hikes, and evening songfests around a roaring fire followed by an occasional snipe hunt.

Initially, Camp Meenahga operated under a five-year lease from the Wisconsin Conservation Commission. Under its terms, Alice Clark paid a deposit of six hundred dollars each year for the "Camp Meenahga Lease Improvement Fund." The State of Wisconsin used the money for building materials and labor costs. The camp continued under a series of five-year leases. When each

lease ended, Alice Day and Fanny Mabley had to plead with the Conservation Commission for its renewal. This was always tenuous, since leasing state
park land for a privately operated enterprise could be controversial and was not
typical of state park policy. However, the camp had made many friends in the
area and its business was important for local merchants.

In the fall of 1931, a crisis occurred when the Door County State Bank, where
Meenahga's funds were deposited, closed. The closing froze the deposits of the
camp and complicated its financial situation, for the bank was unable to pay
on checks written to merchants for camp supplies. Thanks to the resourceful-
ness of Clark and Mabley, Camp Meenahga barely survived this financial crisis.

When a new five-year lease was negotiated the next year, the annual payment of the camp was lowered to five hundred dollars. Yet, the Great Depression made operating Camp Meenahga in the black a challenge for some time.

Over the years, changes and improvements were made to the camp. What
had been fields and pastures became ball diamonds, clay tennis courts, basketball courts, and a riding ring enclosed by a white wood fence. New roofing
was added to many of the old Evenson buildings.

After a few years, the tents were set up on slightly elevated wood platforms
with a step in front that served as a convenient bench. Inside were two rows
of sleeping cots and trunks for the campers' personal possessions. Eventually
a more secure tarpaulin covered the tents for added protection. Later, the tent

A group of Meenahga campers posing before their tents. Their uniforms consisted
of a white middy blouse with a long scarf, green bloomers fastened below the knee,
and long socks. (Courtesy Laurence C. Day)

shelters consisted of canvas stretched tightly over a wood frame. The numbered white tents were placed in several locations, with the main group lining Fifth Avenue, behind the lodge.

The log end of the barn was converted into the camp kitchen and the rest of the long structure became the dining room. A massive fireplace was erected at its north end. A huge, old ship's propeller—donated by Doolittle, who painted it green to resemble a shamrock—sat on the fireplace mantle between two tall iron candleholders. The walls of the rustic building were decorated with colorful posters, many made by campers in their art classes. In 1919, a screen porch was added along its east side. Three years later, a large frame wing was built on the north end for a reading room. It was furnished with wicker chairs and wood tables supported by log legs with decorative details made from branches.

A rustic shelter with open sides was constructed around the windmill of the farm. Nearby, a deep depression in the hillside served as a natural amphitheater. Other camp structures included an icehouse, a shed with wood stacked at its side, and a small garage. Some of these buildings had been part of the farm. Others were built for the camp, including the clubhouse set back in the woods and a small hospital.[33] The Evensons' original home was remodeled

The one-hundred-foot lodge. Originally a threshing barn on the Evenson farm, the building was expanded with a long porch and several other additions. (Courtesy Laurence C. Day)

and enlarged to become the two-story director's cottage with a wing on the back for the camp office.

Rustic benches and flowerbeds edged with rocks were situated about the camp. Tall, handsome hollyhocks grew by the main lodge. The floral displays added a colorful touch to the sea of green vegetation surrounding the camp. Birdhouses, the camp bell, and the flag topped long wood poles near the lodge.

Near the lakeshore was a handsome gazebo. Its base was a seat-height stone wall, and cedar posts held its five-sided peaked roof. Several benches near the gazebo served as seating for watching water activities and sunsets. Attractive stone steps led down to the pier, which extended well out from shore. At its end were two wide ladders for slipping gradually into the water. Anchored in deeper water was the raft with its diving board and metal water slide.

At various times, a number of local residents worked on camp improvements. Some were seasonal park employees. They included such familiar Fish Creek area stalwarts as Hubert Woerfel (who sometimes was a project foreman), Elmer and Leslie Anderson, Clarence Beyer, William Carlson, Merritt Churches, Harry Doolittle, Ronald Doolittle, Sheldon Doughty, Sam Erickson, George Froemming, Thorvald Hanson, Clarence Hedeen, Sylvester Judd, Alson Kinsey, Emil Krause, Herman Krause, Louis Larson, Robert Newberry,

Campers relaxing before the huge fireplace in the reading room—a frame addition to the north end of the log barn. (Courtesy Laurence C. Day)

Albert Ohnesorge, Carl Olson, James Polster, Al Smith, Thomas Wesa, and Stuart Woerfel. A great deal of construction and remodeling occurred in 1927–28 and in later years, particularly 1931.

In time, more counselors were added and changes were made in the kitchen staff that cooked and did other housekeeping chores. Capable young women from the area were hired for these tasks. They included, among others, Evelyn and Elizabeth Bhirdo, Gertrude Franke, Emma Hanson, Kathleen Hanson Kodanko, Olive Bhirdo Koessel, Julia Williams Peil, Alice Reinhard, Hilda Reinhard, Elsie Krause Tishler, and Sylvia Williams. Alice Clark's good friend Adeline Edmunds of Baileys Harbor supervised the kitchen workers.

Edmunds described some of her experiences as head cook in *The Loving Spice of Life,* the book she wrote about her kindly mother, the legendary "Grandma Peil." "The old woodshed attached to the kitchen," she noted, "held a cord or more of wood to fire the double-oven kitchen range; and despite the lack of convenience, it [the kitchen] held a charm all it's own." The "magic cooks" prepared sumptuous meals for the girl's ravenous appetites. The menu often included "freshly baked cherry pies and sour cream doughnuts served with applesauce every Sunday morning."[34] Blueberry muffins, Parker House rolls, and roast beef with gravy were also popular. The girls pitched in to help wash the dishes, and the kitchen staff scrubbed the pots and pans.

MOONLIGHT ON THE BAY · PENINSULA STATE PARK · WIS.   3491

This handsome gazebo was a favorite place for Meenahga campers to meet and to watch the spectacular sky as the sun set into the watery horizon. (Author's collection)

While most of the camp traditions remained unchanged over the years, some new features were added. One enduring camp fixture was the old, black, wood-paneled Ford Model T station wagon. Sometimes this "metal Elizabeth" had to be cranked or pushed down the entry drive to start. It was used for fun rides, hauling campers to various destinations, and the morning "milk run" for fresh milk or groceries at Schreiber's. By 1923, art classes were being taught in the art tent by Helen Stern, who had studied under Charles M. Lesaar of Fish Creek. By 1925, archery and sewing were added. Carpentry was taught as a craft in the Woodpecker Tent. The girls made birdhouses, towel racks, trellises, toothbrush holders, and benches.[35]

As the end of the camp season neared, the campers looked forward to their traditional closing banquet. Everyone donned their best Sunday dresses and assembled on the front porch of the lodge. Forming two rows, they allowed the guests to enter first and then, with great anticipation, walked by twos into the dining room.

The kitchen workers. Fish Creek area young women were hired to manage cooking and dining room chores at Camp Meenahga. During World War II, however, many Door County women went to work in the shipyards at Sturgeon Bay and help had to be imported from cities farther south. Front row left to right: Julia Peil, Hilda Reinhard. Back row: Alice Reinhard Frea, Katherine Hanson Kodanko, unidentified, unidentified, Evelyn Bhirdo, and another Bhirdo woman. (Courtesy of Dianne Peil)

For this special night—their last at Meenahga—the counselors and kitchen staff transformed the plain dining room, with its exposed rafters, into an enchanting fairy bower. Counselors and camp masters were seated at a table before the fireplace. At the opposite end of the hall were the directors and their guests, who looked down on the long tables of campers. The walls and ceiling were covered with pine boughs and the fireplace was banked with goldenrod. The dining tables, once the scene of "pancake rolls" and water fights, were decorated with purple and yellow flowers. Rows of candles on the tables threw a soft light over the campers' sunburned faces. As place cards, little birchbark canoes bore a name and a yellow or purple ribbon. Great merriment prevailed throughout the evening.[36]

After dinner, the girls and counselors sang camp songs. Mabley and Clark served as the witty toastmistresses and introduced two of the camp's staunch friends, Doolittle (the "angel" of the camp) and Crunden. Both men would make a few heartfelt remarks, which were followed by toasts. Beginning in the 1930s, Clark often read congratulatory telegrams from former campers. Sometimes camp alumnae attended the banquet.

Finally, Clark and Mabley arose with their usual dignity and, to the hushed room, presented the M Awards—always an eagerly awaited event. These were given for such activities as dancing, dramatics, diving, swimming, canoeing, basketball, hiking, music, tennis, and literary contributions. An award was also given to the yellow or purple team that had won the most stars. The most cherished award, however, was the Camp Spirit M Award to the girl who best exemplified the camp's lofty goals of integrity and good sportsmanship. It reflected one of the fundamental lessons the camp emphasized: always doing one's best in all aspects of life. Marian Wickham, editor of the 1921 *Pack and Paddle*, stated this goal succinctly when she wrote, "It is only after doing one's best in one's own sphere, be it home, school or camp, that one is fitted for playing a greater part in service to the world."[37] Girls who won the large *M* letters pinned them to their uniforms, to be displayed proudly. The lodge rang with cheers for each camper as she was honored. With the event over the girls left, some in tears since this was their last evening at camp, "every one of them, knowing inwardly that they would surely return the next year."[38]

The author received several letters from women who had been campers at Camp Meenahga. Writing from New York, one recalled, "When V-J Day came people gathered on a large field. Many, who were close to some one in the war, cried."[39] She wrote of other lingering memories, including "skinny dipping." Another sent a page from the *Chicago Tribune* of August 31, 1947. It featured

photographs of the happy campers, many of them on the pier in their bathing
suits. She had worked as a counselor that summer and was "paid a total of
$60," plus lodging. She also remembered that "the best solution to the little
'no-see-ums' (tiny black creatures with a devastating bite) was 612 Lotion
smeared all over the bed sheets."[40]

Visiting the site of Camp Meenahga today, it is difficult to visualize it as
the setting where thousands of young women spent many joyful summers—
a place of laughter, delightful outdoor adventures, close friendships, and lessons about how to live a better life. Now, instead of laughter, singing, girlish
pranks, and the sound of excited young women at play, there is silence. Some
evidence of the camp can still be found in a few remnants scattered about the
site. These include broken steps by the lakeshore, foundation rubble, depres-
sions where buildings once stood, overgrown rows of cedars, tattered beds of
plants, pieces of rusted metal, broken glass, the remains of an early stone fence,
and the large hillside depression that was once the amphitheater. The buildings are all gone, and trees and shrubbery have reclaimed the lawns and fields.
Only the breathtaking sunsets, starry night sky, large trees, lapping of crystal-
line waters on the pebbly beach, and plaintive call of gulls bear witness to the
glorious past of Camp Meenahga.

Betty Fairfield, the camp's business manager, aptly summed up the Camp
Meenahga experience in a whimsical but thoughtful essay in the 1919 edition
of *Pack and Paddle:*

> Once there was a very beautiful place in a very beautiful country. There were
> great trees, a lake, a fine climate, and peace and beauty everywhere. Now, some
> very discerning people, having seen this place—not casually, but with real
> understanding—decided that it was the best place in the world (and so it was)
> for a girls' camp. Many girls came; some, because their parents, being older and
> wiser, knew it would be good for them; and others, who knew already the cus-
> toms and joys of out of door life, thought they might teach and help others
> to love it with them. More and more came from year to year, leaving behind
> their books and lessons, their city clothes, and their worries and responsibilities.
> As they became stronger in body and more unselfish in spirit, their every-day
> pettiness and selfishness was dropped as if by magic. Through their sports and
> games, their gaiety and happy idleness, and wise and loving leadership came a
> love of the life and of the country and knowledge of the close and friendly inti-
> macy with nature. They learned to love good sportsmanship and to give of
> themselves more than ever before. They learned a truer and deeper friendship
> based on play and work together and mutual aspirations. And last and greatest

of all, they learned not only to love, but also to know their fellowmen. Surely, a greater thing cannot be accomplished in the world.

Fanny Mabley retired from her association with the camp during the Depression, and moved to Iowa. She returned periodically for visits, however, especially to attend the closing banquets. To assist Alice Clark, Ruth Warren Becker of St. Louis became a camp codirector in 1941. Clark's daughter succeeded her.

Alice Orr Clark remained in charge of the camp for thirty-three years. Upon her retirement in 1948—the last year the camp was operated—she sent out the following announcement:

DEAR CAMP MEENAHGA GIRLS ALL, from 1916 through 1948: There is always a beginning and by that same token, there must be an ending. So after thirty-three years of running Meenahga, many of them with my dear friend Mrs. F. W. Mabley as my partner, I feel that it is time to close and have our camp a very happy memory.

I hope all the girls and counselors who have passed through its paths and forests will look back and feel, as do I, that Camp Meenahga has given them a wealth of joy, growth and progress. I am sure that no one woman has gleaned as much solid satisfaction and happiness as I have. Each girl in the many years has given me more than she knows.

Thanks to you all from the very first Meenahga-ite in 1916 to the very last one in 1948. My love and undying interest follow each one. My daughter, Alice Day, joins me in all that I say, and adds that she too will miss you and camp.

Yours in happy days, ALICE ORR CLARK

❧

CHAPTER 10

The Golf Course

ONE OF WISCONSIN'S FINEST

Versions of the game of golf are centuries old and golfing as we know it today has its origins in England and Scotland. The sport was introduced to Wisconsin in the late nineteenth century and today the state has nearly five hundred courses. As its popularity grew, a surge in golf course building began in the early decades of the twentieth century. During that time it was introduced to Door County, and Ephraim summer vacationers and businessmen sought to establish a local golf course.

The park was considered to be an ideal location, and work on a golf course began as early as 1914. That year, at its February meeting, the Conservation Commission authorized superintendent Doolittle to "lay out two golf links of sixty acres each, one near Fish Creek, and the other near Ephraim and to select buildings which would be suitable for club houses and locker rooms."[1]

Doolittle's notebook containing various records and payments indicates that work was undertaken that year on both the Fish Creek links, located east of what became the site of Camp Meenahga, and the Ephraim links.[2] Work that summer included clearing fields of stone and excessive vegetation and "erecting two small houses" at each course.[3] Arrangements were also made with hotel owners in the two communities to take charge of both of the proposed golf links.[4] Eager to assist the project, the Ephraim Men's Club appointed a committee consisting of Adolph Anderson, Ole Olson, and Elias Helgeson to oversee the links and find someone to "keep them in proper shape." E. F. Folda agreed to furnish the club with $150 to pay a groundskeeper for a three-month period for three successive years.[5] While still in a rough state, the first crude holes were "made good use of by the tourists and visitors" who practiced whacking their golf balls around the area.[6]

After visiting the park on an inspection trip the following year, Conservation

Commissioner Frank B. Moody recommended "that both Ephraim and Fish Creek golf links be put in shape for next summer's use."[7] Doolittle then requested five hundred dollars from the commission for grubbing out stumps, clearing brush, and grading the first part of the Ephraim course. This area extended from an existing building used for the clubhouse into Holand's farm and orchard.[8] The crude greens and tees were located and shaped with a ten-ton road roller.

In the spring of 1916, the two new golf courses were anticipated as a boon to tourism in the area. The front page of the *Door County News* proclaimed that the golf links "will be in great demand by the many visitors and tourists. A great deal of work has to be done before the grounds are in good condition, but when they are turned over for play they ought to be in fit condition for any professional player." Because of the "peculiar condition of the [previous] winter and the ice sheet that covered the course," however, the grass seed that was sown in the fall had rotted and 140 pounds of new seed was ordered to establish an adequate cover of turf.[9] Because of budget cutbacks, Fish Creek and Ephraim businessmen and summer visitors had offered "several hundred to be used in fitting up the links.[10] After more site work, both golf courses were opened that summer.[11] Early the following year the *Democrat* noted that "the golf links, on either side of the park are now being used by the followers of the game."[12]

Golfers and their caddies at the park golf course with Ephraim in the background beyond Eagle Harbor, ca. 1946. (Author's collection)

Expanding and improving the two golf courses proved to be a tremendous undertaking, and Doolittle asked for four hundred dollars more to continue the work.[13] This amount was to be part of the annual seventeen-thousand-dollar park work appropriation requested for the following year. The Conservation Commission supported this request and Assemblyman Frank Graass brought it before the legislature. With the outbreak of World War I, money was tight and only eight thousand dollars was allotted after road improvement funds were eliminated. This lack of funds, and difficulty in obtaining water for the greens, led to the abandonment of the Fish Creek course.

By the summer of 1917, the Ephraim links were in better condition and were being "used almost constantly."[14] Work on the course continued with a few holes added each year. It soon became evident, however, that an overall plan for its layout and development was needed. In 1921, W. R. Lovekin of Green Bay was hired for this task. Impressed with the work Doolittle and the park staff had already done, Lovekin stated that "residents of the North would have every reason to feel proud of their links."[15] The new plan estimated that the course would have a total distance of thirty-five hundred yards, making it one of the longest nine-hole courses in the state. In June implementation of the plan began. That same year Alex Cunningham was hired as the course's first pro. He would serve in that capacity until 1929.

By this time, the fields that were converted into the nine-hole course were in good shape for use as fairways, but new greens and tees had to be built. A big drawback was the lack of water for keeping the greens in shape. In 1923 this was remedied by substituting sand and oil for the grass. This type of "green" had been used successfully elsewhere and it provided smooth areas for putting. Thus, the park's golf course—at least the first nine holes—can be dated to 1923. It remains the oldest links on the peninsula, predating the Alpine course, which opened in 1926, and Maxwelton Braes, which opened in June of 1929.[16]

Under the efficient management of E. F. Folda, the course became almost self-supporting. Since considerable new construction was still required, Conservation Commissioner Elmer S. Hall promised one thousand dollars in aid. But, with no money available, the assistance had to be given in labor by men on the park's payroll rather than in cash. Hall was so pleased with the success of the park's new golf course that he championed bringing before the legislature "the matter of creating and maintaining golf links at all of the state parks."[17]

Course maintenance and adequate financial support remained a difficult problem during the early 1920s. Commenting on this situation in 1925, the *Advocate* reported, "Up to last summer, these links for various reasons have been an eyesore and source of grumbling instead of a pleasant playground."[18] Seeing it as a boon to local tourism, the Ephraim Men's Club continued managing the links and took action to make improvements. A committee solicited subscriptions from northern Door County hotel owners and raised nineteen hundred dollars for a watering system for all the greens. The system involved building a pump house on the beach that pushed lake water into a tank on a large steel tower on the bluff above the links. To further assist course maintenance, a nonresident club member donated a twelve-hundred-dollar Worthington tractor and mowing machine. At the club's urging, the Conservation Commission also provided one thousand dollars in labor for course improvements. Work that year included constructing a new main road along the upper edge of the links to replace the many twisting roads which cut up the course, exasperating golfers and creating a hazard for passing traffic. An old granary, which had been converted into a clubhouse, was also moved from the center of the course to a location above the new road. With its large screened-in porch, the white building was an attractive and homey feature. Because it had no electricity, kerosene lamps were used and it was necessary to cool refreshments with ice purchased from a local grocery store. Water came from a nearby pump close to the first tee. Later, a rustic shelter with seats was built around the pump. This became a popular place to sit and watch golfers tee off on the first

Rustic cedar log shelter where spectators could watch golfers tee off. (Author's collection)

and tenth tees. A seventy-car parking space adjacent to the clubhouse was also completed. Toilet facilities consisted of two outhouses located up the wooded hill beyond the parking lot. Because of the improvements, 1924 was a very successful season, with "thousands of tourists" using the links. The income derived from the golf course was even adequate to cover its considerable expenses.

The first annual golf tournament for the championship of Door County was held at the course late in August of 1925. It was open to the general public and offered four prizes for the winners, with the Ephraim Men's Club awarding the grand prize: an attractive loving cup. To keep the cup permanently, one had to win three times. Under the watchful management of Harold C. Wilson, and with the Ephraim Men's Club's continuing support, the course flourished that season. The income from approximately twenty-four hundred day tickets, ninety-five week privileges, and twenty-five season tickets was thirty-five hundred dollars.[19]

By the end of the 1926 season, it had become evident that the popular nine-hole course was too small to accommodate the large number of golfers. Its beauty and spectacular setting had become widely known and on some days, reported the *Door County News*, "as high as 130 people were using the golf links at one time." The golf course "is the pride of Mr. Doolittle and the wonder of visiting tourists from all over the United States," said the front page story, adding that it promised to be "one of the best and most unique golf courses to be found in the United States."[20]

Enthusiastic park supporters began lobbying the legislature to return to the park all income from course memberships and fees. This, it was hoped, would help defray the costs of enlarging and improving the course. Senator John Cashman of Denmark introduced such a bill, but the measure was defeated. Doolittle then called a meeting of county representatives to establish an organization that would lease the golf links from the Conservation Commission. Doing so, he maintained, would help secure income for improving the links. Incorporation papers were filed with the register of deeds, and the nonprofit organization elected officers: Frank C. Blakefield of Baileys Harbor, president; Doolittle, vice president; Sam Hogenson and Everett Valentine of Ephraim, secretary and treasurer, respectively.

Meanwhile, plans for the additional nine holes were being carried out. Fairways were cut through the woods above the existing course and the stumps were blasted out. Several new holes were added each year. The park's annual golf tournament continued, and in 1929 Olaf Christianson became pro for that season. He also supervised construction of some of the holes designed by Cunningham.

The second nine holes were opened in 1930, and separate tournaments were established for men and women.[21] Ed West, a student at Lawrence College, became the new pro. West continued as the park's pro until the end of the 1935 season, when he passed the state bar examination after completing his law degree at the University of Michigan. West went on to a successful career in the corporate world, but he remained a lifelong booster of the course. By the time he left, young men from the area were serving as caddies. Eager to have this source of income, they earned seventy-five cents for carrying a player's clubs for eighteen holes. However, they felt this task was worth one dollar, and when West refused to approve this increase, the caddies went on strike. It lasted for only one day![22]

Don Nelson of Sturgeon Bay succeeded West as pro in 1936. That was also the year that a sixteen-year-old caddie from Maxwelton Braes, Johnny Brann, created a sensation by reaching the finals of the twelfth annual tournament. The young golfer continued playing championship golf at the course for more than a decade. By the mid-1930s, the park was also hosting exhibition matches that included golf pros from courses in northeastern Wisconsin, such as Art Saunders from Maxwelton Braes, the Alpine's Art Schlueter, and George Leonard from Sturgeon Bay's Lucerne course.

The turnover of new pros continued at the park, with some working there for only one season. Gilbert Baltzer served for the summer of 1937, before

Ephraim entrance to the park off Highway 42, at the edge of the golf course. Note the stone entrance markers. (Author's collection)

departing for a similar position at Three Lakes, Wisconsin. Godwin "Buck" Nilsson from Superior took on the pro's responsibilities for another year, and was succeeded by Charles Clemenson of Ephraim.

Finally, in 1941, Doolittle hired a golf pro who stayed for many seasons. Jack Notabaart, an outstanding athlete and instructor at the Appleton Vocational and Adult School, was recommended for the job by Ed West, who occasionally played golf with Notabaart at Appleton's Riverview Country Club.[23] After meeting Doolittle at the park office Notabaart was offered the job. His income would be derived entirely from concessions, golf supplies, and lessons. All golf tickets, which then cost one dollar for eighteen holes, were to be handled by Ralph Halvorsen, a state employee who later become superintendent at Peninsula. For several years, Notabaart and his wife lived in cramped quarters above the clubhouse. Later they rented a cottage from H. R. Holand.

The year Notabaart arrived, there was considerable speculation about a new and much larger clubhouse.[24] The preparation of plans for this long-sought facility was approved by the Conservation Commission. A state architect visited the course and picked a location for the structure—a short distance north of the existing clubhouse. According to preliminary plans, the "rustic" building would have a canopy covering the roadway, enabling golfers to drive directly to the entrance. At the time, sentiment favored using stone for the lower part of the structure and "rustic logs" above. These materials could be obtained at the park, thus cutting construction costs. Unfortunately funding was never obtained to build the clubhouse, and it was not until 1955 that a new one was constructed.

The course opened each day at about seven thirty and play was generally over by five o'clock. For several years a group of players had a "twilight league," playing when it was less crowded while enjoying the dramatic sunsets. Notabaart continued to provide caddies, and in 1948 he purchased twenty-five pull carts for rental. He sold pop, candy bars, cigars, and cigarettes. He also sold beer, until local authorities complained that the village of Ephraim, which included the golf course, prohibited the sale of alcoholic beverages—much to the chagrin of many thirsty golfers.

Notabaart started a series of immensely popular weekly tourneys at the park. Special ladies' day tournaments attracted some of the area's best women golfers. The highlight of every summer, however, was the Resorters Golf Tournament, which took place during the second full week of August. Northern Door County hotel operators and merchants donated prizes for the winners. Spencer Gould and his wife, who were championship golfers from Ephraim and St. Louis, were great boosters of the course, and for many years Gould served as master of ceremonies when prizes were awarded. Notabaart worked at the park for fourteen years, until 1954, the same year the present clubhouse opened for use.

After Notabaart left, Jane Bielefeld began her nine-year tenure as resident pro. By this time Lowell Hansen had become the park's superintendent. An avid golfer and a trained landscape architect, Hansen continued improving the course and emphasized retaining a qualified golf course architect for assistance. Edward L. Packard, of Packard and Wadsworth, a Chicago firm that had worked on over fifty courses throughout the country, was hired for consultation. With Packard's recommendations, Hansen finalized a new long-range master plan that provided for eliminating three holes, constructing three new ones, building new tees and greens, and constructing other improvements to make the course longer. Implementation of the plan proceeded slowly, because it remained "a low priority project." Unforeseen complications sometimes arose as the changes were carried out. For example, Hansen said "deer seem to take a fancy" to "stomping in the soft topsoil used in building the greens and they almost ruined the green." With his background in landscape architecture, Hansen remained sensitive to the integrity of the course's special scenic features. He summed up his work stating, "The changes in the course carefully maintain the flavor of Door County and conform to the bluff and woods character that has made the course so well known. The rolling fairways thru the hardwoods and pines, the limestone bluffs and the magnificent views over Green Bay and Ephraim have all been retained."[25]

In the early 1980s, Wisconsin's Department of Natural Resources turned over course operations to a nonprofit corporation, the Peninsula Golf Association (PGA). The PGA hired the course's first professional greenskeeper and continued the long tradition of annual improvements. Thanks to their dedicated involvement and skillful financial management, Peninsula State Park remains one of Wisconsin's most scenic and popular golf courses. Its spectacular setting incorporates wooded areas, hilly terrain, and stunning views of Eagle Harbor and the picturesque village of Ephraim. One journalist, in his regular column in the *Milwaukee Journal,* aptly summed up the beauty and excellent layout of the course when he referred to it as "designed by Mother Nature."[26]

◠

CHAPTER II

Potawatomi

PENINSULA'S SISTER PARK

A decade after Peninsula was established, a second state park—Potawatomi—was designated in Door County. This 1,046-acre tract consists of two and three-quarter miles of shoreline and a majestic bluff rising some 150 feet above the waters of Sturgeon Bay. The high-forested plateau at its top is broken by open stretches of meadow resplendent with masses of trillium and daisies in season. Quarrying—Door County's first industry and its first export—began here in 1834.[1] Over the years it furnished quality limestone for river and harbor construction, including the breakwaters of Michigan City. Once known as Government Bluff, the land had been owned by the United States since 1837.[2] At that time it was considered a prime location for a fort in case of war with Canada, and it remained under the control of the War Department for nearly a century.[3]

In fact, an early Army Corps of Engineers map refers to the bluff as Quarry Point.[4] When quarry operations ceased, the site remained under the administration of the War Department, which classified it as an abandoned military reservation. In the early 1880s, Frank Hogan opened a stone quarry at Government Bluff. Being only a squatter, he was driven off and started the Green Stone Company quarry at Sawyer.[5]

The area once was the site of extensive Native American activity. Onanguisse, principal chief of the Potawatomi, had his winter camp in the Idlewild area just north of the park. Henry Tonty and two priests, Bibourde and Membre, with three other starving Frenchmen, were brought to the camp in November 1680. They remained there for the winter as guests of Onanguisse. Father Membre then left for De Pere, where he founded a Jesuit Mission, while the others left for Mackinac late the following spring.

Many artifacts have been found in the Sand Bay area west of the park.

There, during the late winter spawning season, Native American families came to catch northern pike and other large fish. According to local residents, sturgeon were piled up on the shore like cordwood. Natives placed fish, meat, and other food in deep holes that they dug in the sand, filled with moist sand, and marked for location. This primitive refrigeration method provided a source of food for later consumption.

Early industrial activity began in 1836, when Peter Sherwood settled on the point just north of the park and worked as a cooper. The point was named after him. Around 1849–50, Frank Sawyer settled near the shore west of Government Bluff, where he farmed and carried on a vigorous trade with Native Americans. Sawyer Harbor, the cove between Potawatomi Park and the Idlewild Peninsula, was named for him. One mile west of the park, Hainesville became a thriving Norwegian settlement. It was founded by Tallak Haines, who came from Bamle Parish in southern Norway and settled at Sawyer Harbor in the early 1860s. Haines made several trips back to Norway, returning to Door County with many of his old neighbors.[6]

By the turn of the century, individuals who were living on the tract as squatters were harvesting its remaining timber. Noting this unsavory activity in 1904, the *Advocate* wrote: "It is reported that the government reservation is being depleted of the timber that still remains, the parties engaged in the nefarious work being people who are utterly irresponsible and who have been squatting on the lands for some time past. If the timber is to be taken off it should be by everybody and not a few never-to-do wells, as has been the case for the past several years, and who apparently have no fear of the law, everything being grist that comes to their mill."[7]

Because the federal property was being neglected, some considered it a "wasteland." In an editorial early in 1909, the *Advocate* echoed local concern about the tract when it wrote:

It is a question whether it is at all beneficial to a town or county to have a considerable area of waste lands lying within its borders remain in the keeping of the state or nation. A fair illustration of this is . . . the government reservation. Here is a tract of more than two full sections which is not being utilized for any purpose whatsoever, although there is a great and growing demand that it be put on the market and utilized for agricultural purpose; but to all these appeals the officials turn a deaf ear. Were the property looked after and kept up there would be some sense in the government continuing to own it; but nothing of the kind has ever been done from the time it obtained possession of the lands, many years ago, until the present moment. Having no one to look after it this reservation has become a menace to the neighboring farmers by reason of the forest fires, which occur regularly every summer whenever a prolonged drought prevails, and the people have to fight for their property with no help from the owner of this large area of desolate and neglected territory. The reservation is also a habitation for wolves and other noxious animals that continually prey on the farmsteads of that entire region under certain conditions, and whenever there is a severe and stringent winter with deep snows covering the ground. There are several other reasons why such reserves as the one in question are not a good thing for the townships within which they are situated, but it is not necessary to refer to these at this time.[8]

A plan to locate the Great Lakes Naval Station near the bluff was proposed, but instead its present location at Glencoe, Illinois, was chosen.[9]

Being federally owned, Government Bluff was considered a prime candidate for a national rather than a state park. Sturgeon Bay attorney Thomas A. Sanderson spearheaded the move to establish a national park on the tract. Early in the summer of 1923, Sanderson outlined the concept of a national park for the site before the Door County Chamber of Commerce, which eagerly backed the idea. He then wrote to U.S. Senator Irvine Lenroot, asking him to consider the proposal and inviting him to vacation in Door County where the matter could be discussed further. To garner broader support for the proposal, the Chamber of Commerce invited the Wisconsin Press Association to convene in the county. The newspaper editors and their families arrived in Sturgeon Bay on a Sunday evening in mid-July for a three-day tour of the county. The following morning their thirty-five-car caravan lined up on Cedar Street, where a band played as a sendoff for the sightseeing trip to the northern part of the county. After visiting Martin Orchards, the Leathem Smith Stone Company, and Murphy Farms at Horseshoe Bay, the group stopped for dinner at the Alpine Resort in Egg Harbor. Sanderson gave an eloquent speech about Government Bluff's potential as a national park and urged the group to support efforts to establish it.

The *Green Bay Press Gazette* reported on the trip and included excerpts of Sanderson's talk. He began, they noted, by praising the county, calling it "Wisconsin's wonderland." Regarding the park proposal, he noted that:

> All the beauty, the glory of this region, is not available to the public [to] use. To you, the Press of Wisconsin, we submit for your consideration an additional beauty spot, that the people of this great state—the people of the middle west, of the nation, may find the joy, the invigorating spirit, that comes with the enjoyment of the great out doors.

He went on to describe the Government Bluff area:

> Upon Green bay, at the entrance of Sturgeon Bay lies a vast tract of some
> thirteen hundred acres of land now owned by the United States government,
> that possesses all that the nature lover might ask. Here lies a mighty bluff; at its
> feet the placid waters of Sturgeon bay and Sawyer's Harbor; just beyond the
> restless waters of Green bay, far in the rear, visible, the rolling waters of Lake
> Michigan. . . . In the distance: the islands of Sawyer's Harbor are at our feet, for-
> est, hill, valley, dingle and dale add to the charm. Here are miles of shore line;
> deep water; good fishing abounds.

Then, he pleaded, "our appeal to you, the press of the state, is to assist in making this tract of land available as a national park." He added, "The purchase
would cost nothing, as the government already owns the land. Legislation by
congress is needed to make it available as a national park." Sanderson pointed
out that there was no national park east of the Dakotas or north of Arkansas,
except for one in the state of Maine. He also emphasized that there was no
national park in the Great Lakes region. "Give to the people . . . a place upon
these Great Lakes where they may come to enjoy the invigorating, exhilarating atmosphere, the magnificent scenery, [and] participate in the pleasures

View from the water of the towering bluffs in what would become Potawatomi
Park, referred to initially as Nicolet Park. (Author's collection)

held in store by nature." We need to "give it to the people," he argued, and he concluded by stating, "This then is our project. We know your vision; we know your love of your state; we feel your desire to foster projects of merit. We seek your co-operation; we solicit your enthusiasm; we hope for your support." He suggested the name Nicolet National Park, since it was believed that Jean Nicolet had stopped at or near this location in 1634 before his historic arrival at the Winnebago village at Red Banks. As the editors and their families left for home, four boxes of cherries were placed in each auto.[10]

Sanderson's appeal brought results. Several newspapers, including the *De Pere Journal-Democrat,* the *Green Bay Press Gazette,* and the *Manitowoc Herald News,* brought statewide attention to the park proposal.[11] In September, Senator Lenroot visited the site accompanied by a committee of twelve from the Chamber of Commerce. Lenroot was impressed with the location and influenced by the extensive information and convincing case for making it a park that Sanderson had prepared. That evening, before a large audience at the Door Theater, Lenroot announced that he would introduce a bill to establish the park when Congress convened in December. "I will use my best efforts to have the bill favorably reported," he stated.[12]

Growing speculation about the park gave it prominence as a valuable piece of property. Sturgeon Bay resident David Cody, who was part Menomonee Indian, claimed a legal right to the title of a portion of it. In a letter to the *Door County Advocate,* he pointed out, "In 1842, or while the state of Wisconsin was yet a territory, they [his Menomonee ancestors] were promised protection and their land reserved for them by the War Department. . . . This land never was paid for by the Government. Therefore, I claim the title rights of a portion of this land as a United States citizen."[13] Cody's family had located at Government Bluff in 1910 and, he pointed out, his Indian ancestors had lived there until they were drafted into the Civil War. He also noted that his family had applied for timber money from the government in 1910, which was being paid to other Menomonee Reservation Indians, but had never been paid to the Cody family. "If we are not successful," Cody stated, "we shall all settle on the vacant land known as Government Bluff and file our claim in Congress, since . . . our ancestors who settled there . . . never sold a bit of it [and] the inheritance laws should give us title." The Cody family stuck to their claim for several years, but never received the allotments they requested.

By the end of 1923, Senator Lenroot had introduced the Nicolet National Park bill. In doing so, he eloquently described its features, explaining that "the scenic sweep of water, unusual shore line, headlands, coves, bays, islands, varieties of hill and country and forests are unexcelled anywhere in the United

States."[14] In April the following year Congressman George J. Schneider introduced a companion bill to establish the park. Assemblyman Frank N. Graass strongly endorsed the measure, which provided that the land be placed under control of the secretary of the interior with an annual appropriation, not to exceed ten thousand dollars per year, for its maintenance and supervision. The bill also authorized the interior secretary to use this money, if necessary, for allotments to the Wisconsin band of Potawatomi Indians.

During that legislative session, Congress took little action on the bill since both the War Department and the Interior had to report on it. However, Interior officials objected to the bill because they considered the site too small for a national park. To continue local support for the bill, businessman Leathem D. Smith went to Washington on a business trip, where he met in Lenroot's office with Stephen T. Mather, director of the National Park Service. Mather reiterated that the reservation was too small for a national park and suggested that the bluff be turned over to the state. The idea did not appeal to Smith because it had already been difficult to get adequate state funding for nearby Peninsula State Park.

A short time later, Congressman Schneider met with the Chamber of Commerce to discuss the park situation, which at this point looked doubtful. He proposed an alternative plan to open the bluff land to the public as a forestry preserve. This, he maintained, would require building roads for fire protection, making it accessible to the public. The group objected to this plan.[15]

Schneider doggedly continued to support the park proposal. In 1928, he introduced another bill to enable the government to turn over title to the bluff to the State of Wisconsin for $1.25 per acre. As the *Door County News* noted, "Some difficulty may be experienced . . . in getting the bill passed due to the fact that it is so near to the Peninsula State Park."[16] At the same time, the conservation commission appointed Graass and Albert Kalmback, both park supporters, to a newly established advisory commission made up of a number of prominent Wisconsinites including noted conservationist Aldo Leopold.

Finally, after a favorable recommendation by the Committee on Military Affairs, Schneider's park bill was passed by the House of Representatives and, on April 4, 1928, by the senate, with "the hearty support of Senators Blaine and La Follette."[17] In an interview about his long career in public service, Graass later recalled that President Coolidge wired the Wisconsin Conservation Commission to inform them that if they would purchase the land he would sign the bill. Commission chairman L. B. Nagler then telephoned Graass regarding the advisability of the purchase. Upon Graass's advice, Nagler wired the president, stating the park would be acquired. In a letter to the *Door County Advocate,*

Nagler wrote that the purchase "will be completed almost immediately," and the deed of Government Bluff, now referred to as Nicolet Park, was finally turned over to the State of Wisconsin to be managed in conjunction with Peninsula State Park.[18] The War Department, however, reserved the right to use the quarry at a future date if necessary. There was also a provision that if the State of Wisconsin failed "to keep and hold the said land for park purposes or devote it to any use inconsistent with said purpose, then title to said land shall revert to" the War Department. It cost a mere fifteen hundred dollars.

Later that summer the Wisconsin Conservation Commission visited Door County and toured the future park. It recommended a road leading along the shore through the "Daisy field," up the bluff, and around to the Sawyer Harbor side, where it would connect with the town road. They also proposed developing a campsite, as money became available. The group then boarded a ninety-foot yacht owned by Robert and Edward Uihlein of Milwaukee for a three-hour trip along the shore to Ephraim. There they were met by A. E. Doolittle and taken to Peninsula State Park, where they spent the rest of the day before returning to Green Bay. In support of the proposed road, the *Door County News* said that because "it is impossible to reach the bluff without walking a considerable distance, few have ever witnessed the beautiful scenery in this vicinity." It also suggested erecting "a look-out tower similar to the one at the Peninsula State Park."[19] Later, in a front-page editorial, the *Milwaukee Journal* decried these developments proclaiming, "Those who really care deeply about forests and scenery do not need roads. . . . In fact, many a fine wilderness tract [has been] spoiled by roads with tourists pitching camps, tossing tin cans about, setting fire to the woodlands, [and] leaving desolation in their wake."[20] In a lengthy editorial, the *Door County Advocate* vehemently disagreed with the *Journal*'s position, while vigorously supporting the proposed developments.[21]

The name for the new park became the topic of considerable debate. Some felt that Nicolet, which Schneider had suggested, might create confusion for tourists since there already was a Nicolet Bay at Peninsula Park. The Conservation Commission sought suggestions. The name Potawatomi State Park was proposed by Sanderson, endorsed by the Chamber of Commerce, and suggested to the commission. Other suggestions were La Salle, Allouez, Marquette, Andre, Townty, and Onanguisse. Several of these were proposed by H. R. Holand, who pointed out that La Salle was the name of a park in Clay Banks. Townty, he explained, was a former lieutenant in the Robert La Salle expedition, while Onanguisse was a great Potawatomi Indian chief. In accordance with the resolution passed by the Chamber of Commerce, Assemblyman M. B. Goff introduced a bill to use the name Potawatomi State Park. The Door

County Historical Society preferred Nicolet, but by the end of April, the conservation commission had made its decision. Potawatomi it would be.

A two-thousand-dollar appropriation for the road would build only one and a half miles of road—to what was known as Daisy Field. It would be brushed out to a width of twenty feet and, where necessary, would gradually be surfaced with crushed stone. As more funds became available, the road would be extended. At the same time, a trail would be cut for the half mile leading to the top of the bluff. If possible, a well would be drilled at Daisy Field. Meanwhile, the Sawyer Commercial Club was considering erecting an observation tower. These accomplishments generated considerable local enthusiasm, which was reflected in a *Door County News* editorial: "The park opens a wealth of additional natural treasures in this county that has been witnessed by few people. It is needless to say that it will become a haven for hundreds of tourists and local people each year."[22]

Official dedication of the new park involved an unusual ceremony late in May 1929, during the county's annual Cherry Blossom Festival. The arrival of Governor Walter J. Kohler at Sturgeon Bay's Cherryland Airport in his own Ryan monoplane highlighted the event. A large crowd and the Nicolet High School band from West De Pere greeted him. The governor immediately consented to dedicate the new park by dropping a wreath on the site from the air. Followed by an entourage of six other planes, the governor dropped the wreath, appropriately made of pinecones, from a height of twelve hundred feet. Due to strong winds, it almost missed its mark, landing close to the water.

When the planes returned, Kenneth Greaves, on behalf of the Door County Chamber of Commerce, dropped a floral wreath to dedicate Cherryland Airport. The visitors then traveled by auto to Ephraim, where lunch was served to a delegation of two hundred citizens at the Eagle Inn. The governor and his party visited Peninsula State Park and returned to Sturgeon Bay to join the celebration.

Continuing his dedicated service to the new park, Schneider sought to capitalize on its scenic potential. On one visit, he wisely suggested that "a landscape artist be engaged to lay out roads and trails through the property that would give it an outstanding scenic attraction different than that in other parks. Most roads laid out through a wooded district, or along water frontage," he maintained, "have a great similarity about them, when the work is done by road builders in place of landscape artists."[23]

Later in 1929, the Conservation Commission appropriated twenty thousand dollars to continue road construction. Doolittle began the work immediately with seventeen men working on the six-mile project under foreman Ralph

Haskell. Their effort involved blazing six miles of road through the timber and then pulling out stumps before the grading could begin. It was hoped that the grading and surfacing could be completed by August of the next year. The *Advocate* described the road:

> Starting at the south border of the park the road is constructed along a natural ridge that runs from 100 to 200 feet back from the shore. It winds up the side of the top of the 200-foot bluff, with a stonewall constructed on the outer edge. Continuing along the edge of the bluff for half a mile, it turns into a beautiful stand of timber leaving about five acres between the road and the edges of the bluff for parking purposes and picnic grounds. The road comes out to the edge of the bluff again at the extreme west end overlooking the low land and farmlands out toward Little Sturgeon Bay. From here the road continues along the bluff . . . connecting with a town line road by means of a short spur. The main highway will continue through the park, winding through heavy timber until it again comes out at the south entrance.[24]

In the summer of 1930, Potawatomi Park was finally available for use by the public. The next year the seventy-foot observation tower was built on the peak of the bluff. It was designed to be the same height as the tower at Peninsula State Park. Financed by the Sawyer Commercial Club, its erection was

Campers at the Daisy Field campsite, ca. 1950. (Author's collection)

Potawatomi Tower. Built in 1931, it is seventy-five feet high—just one foot shorter than its twin at Peninsula State Park. (Author's collection)

supervised by Louis Hanson of Racine, assisted by Ralph Haskell and volunteers from Sawyer. Holes were blasted for the concrete foundation, a gin-pole was erected, and the four seventy-five-foot support poles were then raised. With its three main landings, the tower rose well above the treetops. Between each landing were separate flights of stairs of eight to ten steps. Six steel tie-rods were installed to counteract swaying and wind strain, and the entire structure was given a coat of creosote to prevent rotting.[25]

After seven weeks of work, the tower was opened to the public. Visitors who climbed it on the first Sunday after it opened were treated to a spectacular sunset. As reported by the *Door County Advocate,* the sun went "down in the waters of Green Bay like a huge ball of fire, so the few still on the tower at that time had a scenic treat that will long be remembered."[26] At the end of the 1936 season—six years after the park opened—attendance had shot up to 41,679 visitors—more than half of the number of visitors at Peninsula, its sister park. The following year WPA workers helped build a bathing beach in the little bay at the campsite. Eventually winter sports became popular at Potawatomi and its ski hill and exhilarating toboggan slide became area attractions.

Boy Scout jamboree at Daisy Field, ca. 1950. Troop 29 of Baileys Harbor camped in the pup tents on the left, while scout troops from other Door County towns camped beyond and across from them. (Author's collection)

Road building continued around the bottom of the bluff, extending to the park's west boundary, and other improvements were gradually made.

The dramatic landscape of Potawatomi State Park continues to be a haven for family gatherings, campers, picnickers, hikers, boaters, skiers, and a variety of other outdoor enthusiasts. It remains one of the jewels in Wisconsin's renowned state park system.

◆

CHAPTER 12

Camp Peninsular and the CCC

The Civilian Conservation Corps was one of the many New Deal programs created by President Franklin Delano Roosevelt in response to the
Great Depression. Signed into law early in 1933, it became one of Roosevelt's
first New Deal initiatives, and it operated until 1942. This peacetime "tree
army" was one of the new president's most popular programs because it was
developed to enhance both natural and human resources. Certainly, it was
one of the most idealistic. In proposing this agency, Roosevelt noted the vital
natural resources efforts to be undertaken, but also emphasized the more important moral and spiritual value of such work to the multitude of jobless
young men—really boys, as they were called then—who would enroll. The
program proved to be a boon for Peninsula State Park and all of Door County.
Noting the serious local and national economic situation and the dire unemployment situation, the *News* commented, "Unless something is done . . .
the winter of 1933–34 will be the worst in the history of the country." It added,
"The state of Wisconsin faces an especially trying situation. Practically every
taxing unit in the state is without funds with which to carry on its normal
governmental activity, because of the enormous amount of tax delinquencies,
to say nothing about providing relief for unemployed."[1]

Once established, the CCC program provided employment and training
for over three million young men.[2] In its early years, enrollment was limited
to those selected from local relief rolls who were between seventeen and twenty-
three years of age. Their involvement was also a great help to their families
since most of their monthly pay was sent directly home.[3]

CCC camps were placed in the heart of wilderness areas, parks, and at the
edge of small towns. There, groups of about two hundred young men lived
in neat rows of military barracks-like dwellings. Each camp was, essentially, a

municipality in itself and was self-supporting in subsistence and administration. In April 1933, during the height of the Great Depression, enrollment started for thousands of unemployed young men from families on relief. By July, the full quota of three hundred thousand men had been selected and the initial enrollment task was completed. They were distributed among fifteen hundred camps.[4] Before the year ended, forty U.S. Forest Service CCC camps had been established in Wisconsin.[5]

By the end of the summer of 1934, there were CCC camps in 102 national parks and 268 state parks in forty states.[6] Eventually, thousands of these installations were located in every state and territorial possession. While every state had at least one project undertaken by the CCC, Wisconsin had many. Ninety-one CCC camps operated in Wisconsin, employing about fourteen thousand enrollees per year.[7] Most of the camps were established in Wisconsin's state forests, but a few of them were in state parks. In addition to the one at Peninsula State Park—Camp Peninsular—there were camps at Devils Lake, Copper Falls, Interstate, Perrot, Rib Mountain, and Wyalusing, as well as the University of Wisconsin–Madison's Arboretum. In all, about 75,242 Wisconsin young men took part in this noble environmental and social effort.[8]

To administer the program and, where essential, cooperate with the many state and local governments, four "districts" were created that divided the country geographically. At first Wisconsin's district headquarters was in Indianapolis, but beginning in April 1, 1935, after CCC administration was decentralized, all of Wisconsin north of a line running east and west through Baraboo, which included Door County, was organized into the Sparta CCC District. That fall the district's headquarters, originally at Camp McCoy, was moved to American Suppliers Incorporated, in Sparta.[9]

At the parks, the CCC boys cut trails and roads, hauled massive stones for paths and staircases, cleared brush and stumps, and built bridges and shelters still in use today. Erosion controls were put in place and bluffs were stabilized, usually without the help of mechanical equipment. An inspector compared the building of steep trails at Perrot State Park to the "labors of the ancient Egyptians in the building of the pyramids."[10] Other crews worked on city parks such as Whitnall, Sheridan, Estabrook, and Klezsch in Milwaukee.

It has been said that the Civilian Conservation Corps advanced the nation's state park movement by a half-century.[11] Their work was a classic example of how buildings and landscapes designed with a "sense of place" can reflect the indigenous qualities of a given location. In fact, visitors to our parks today might see and enjoy examples of CCC work without ever realizing that it was not provided by nature but built with human hands. While little evidence of the CCC camps survives, what does remain is an incredible legacy etched with great sensitivity on the American landscape. Miles of shelterbelts, dams, fire roads, billions of planted trees, and hundreds of park shelters, walls, bridges, trails, and other features remain throughout the United States.

Administration of CCC camp logistics and work was a dual responsibility of the U.S. Army and a civilian project superintendent.[12] The army company consisted of a commander (either a regular army or reserve officer), junior officer, camp doctor, and educational adviser. The company operated the camp, in military fashion, essentially controlling everything having to do with the enrollees when they weren't working. The project superintendent was in charge of all the actual work projects. He was a trained specialist who supervised a small group of foremen, usually experienced local men. The foremen were in charge of the work crews. In addition to the camp's majority of basic laborers, there were special classifications for the storekeeper, steward, assistant cook, leader, and assistant leader. Sometimes this management system resulted in conflicts between the army and technical service personnel. There was also the problem of coordinating with local officials. Certainly, these conflicts arose at Camp Peninsular, much to the chagrin of superintendent Doolittle, and sometimes to C. L. Harrington, superintendent of forests and parks for the Wisconsin Conservation Department.

Young men seeking enrollment in the CCC program first applied to their local selection agency. The enlistment period was six months, with the option of reenlisting for another six months up to a maximum of two years. If accepted, they were sent to conditioning camps at army bases. Many of Camp Peninsular's enrollees started at Fort Sheridan, Illinois. Later, the enrollment often took place at the actual camp.

After arriving at the base, a new enrollee was given a hot meal, a medical exam with vaccinations, a bunk assignment, a CCC serial number, basic equipment, and clothing. The latter usually consisted of blue denim pants, jacket, hat, and a renovated surplus army olive drab dress uniform. The winter outfit included heavy wool long johns and undershirt, a thick wool sweater, an army overcoat, lined mittens or gloves, heavy wool socks, and shoepacs. Winter headgear consisted of an army cap with earflaps and a visor.[13]

Assembling in a military formation, the CCC boys then raised their right hand and took the oath of enrollment. Later, they signed a written oath (those who were illiterate made an X).[14] They then started raking, sweeping, mopping, and undertaking other chores. The objective was to keep the enrollees so busy that they would have little time to ponder problems and aches, or get homesick. After this initial indoctrination period, the young men were sent to one of the many work camps.

Early in the CCC program, or where new camps were being established, the enrollees lived in neat rows of tents. This was the case during the initial months at Camp Peninsular. More typically, however, the young men lived in four or five wooden barracks. Accessory buildings usually included a mess hall, administration buildings, officers' quarters, a hospital, a garage, and sometimes a schoolhouse. These structures were typically arranged in a rough U shape around an open space. Sometimes the buildings were painted brown or green, but more often they simply were given a coat of creosote, or covered with tar paper. They were usually electrified, as at Camp Peninsular, with current from gasoline-powered generators.

Each day started with reveille at 6 A.M. The boys had thirty minutes to wash, shave, and dress in their work clothes before physical training at 6:30. Then they trooped off to a hearty breakfast. They ate at tables for six to twelve enrollees. CCC food was plain but wholesome and served in large quantities. After breakfast the young men policed the grounds, tidied up their barracks, and then formed in platoons for roll call and inspection. At about 7:45 they walked or left in trucks to work on various projects in the park. At noon, work stopped for lunch, which was often trucked out to the work site. After the one-hour lunch break the men worked until 4 P.M, when they returned to camp.[15]

The rigid, geometric layout of Camp Peninsular, CCC camp SP-10, 1935. Enrollees lived in the four long tarpaper-covered buildings centered on an axis leading to the kitchen in the background. In the foreground is the exercise yard and flagpole with a small entry building. (Courtesy National Archives)

Before dinner there might be free time for sports or other leisure activities. At dinner, which was usually served after 5:30 P.M., the enrollees had to wear their dress uniforms. Afterward many attended classes, but recreation, such as table tennis and pool, was also popular. The camp lights were flashed off and on at 9:45 P.M., and turned off at 10. Taps was sounded fifteen minutes later.[16] Youths who did not return to camp by lights out could lose certain privileges. CCC camps had no facilities for physical restraint, guardhouses, or jails, or even a CCC equivalent of military police. Punishment could consist of fines (the maximum was three dollars for any given month), restriction to camp, or extra duty. The worst possible penalty was a dishonorable discharge.[17]

Early in 1935, the *Door County Advocate* speculated that a CCC camp might be established at Peninsula State Park. "Superintendent Doolittle," it noted, "could be depended upon to lay out a program, the work of which would greatly improve the attractiveness of both [Peninsula and Potawatomi] parks."[18] A *News* editorial, however, remarked, "Candidly we believe there is just about as much show of getting one of those camps in this community as there is of getting any federal project that will employ some of the men in the community. The New Deal, as far as Door County is concerned, thus far this year is a 'Raw' Deal. Other counties get projects and we sit twiddling our thumbs waiting for some fairy to come along and drop money in our lap."[19] But before long, quoting from a letter from Harrington, the *Advocate* said Peninsula Park was "high on the priority list" for a camp. It also noted that camp workers would not "be entirely restricted to park work," but could also help assist with other "conservation improvements everywhere in the county," including county parks.[20]

A short time later three federal officials visited the park and conferred with Doolittle about the camp's location, construction, and operation. They envisioned cleaning up underbrush in certain areas, cutting trails, constructing docks, and working at "most everything with the exception of building roads."[21] They also supported a plan to build a large stone machine shop and garage for park equipment. Possibly crews could be involved in other projects, such as the ski and toboggan slides being considered for Peninsula and Potawatomi parks.

The location chosen for the camp was just north and west of Gibraltar High School. A road near the school led to the site, which was on top of a ridge and would be screened from the highway by a large planting of trees. It would be called Camp Peninsular and numbered SP-10, in accordance with standard CCC camp nomenclature. CCC camps in the state parks were designated with the letters *SP;* camps in national forests were designated with an *F,* and those in state forests with an *S.*

On August 10, 1935, the first detail of nineteen young men in Peninsula State Park's new CCC Company 3648 arrived from Camp Finley (Camp 2614, the parent company) in Juneau County. A second detail arrived in a convoy of trucks two days later. The trucks were piled high with cots, mattresses, stoves, buckets, tents, and CCC youths who let out an occasional "Fish Creek here we come" yell![22] Enrollees at Camp Peninsular now totaled ninety. In command was Captain A. J. Rasmussen, with Second Lieutenant R. W. Stebbings serving as junior officer and Dr. Warren Baker, a civilian physician, taking charge of the medical department. A virtual tent city of army pyramid or bell tents sprang up overnight. By the end of the month, some hundred new "rookies" arrived from Herrin, Kewanee, Peoria, and Springfield in Illinois. Army personnel who were later transferred to the camp included Captain E. C. Grafton, commander; Lieutenant Miles J. Krug, adjutant; and Lieutenant R. E. Martin, camp surgeon. D. S. Burnett, an engineer from Wausau, was the acting camp superintendent. Later, Lieutenant Maurice Stone became camp commander, and after he was transferred to Camp Pattison early in 1937 Lieutenant William Kelly took charge. The civilian camp staff included

Camp supervisory personnel, 1935. Front row, left to right: David Urban, junior foreman; Arnold Ackley, subforeman. Back row: Elmer Anderson, mechanic; Gilbert Larson, junior foreman; George H. Nickell of the National Park Service; D. S. Burnett, camp superintendent; and Kenneth Greaves, landscape architect. (Courtesy National Archives)

Kenneth W. Greaves, a landscape architect from Sturgeon Bay, and architect William Bernhard of Ephraim as senior foreman. Other supervisory personnel included: Howard E. Reed, foreman; Gilbert Larson and David Urban, junior foremen; Arnold Ackley, subforeman; Elmer Anderson, mechanic; and E. J. Schuster, educational advisor. The CCC boys were immediately formed into crews to work on roadside clearance, foot trails, and building stone steps at Eagle Terrace.

Construction also started on the permanent camp buildings. Bids went out for building materials, including lumber and millwork, hardware, screening, roofing, sheet metal, hearths and chimneys, electric supplies, and plumbing. According to Captain Rasmussen, the sixteen-building camp was "expected to be one of the finest in the state." The compound would consist of four barracks, each 20 by 30 feet; a 22-by-40-foot garage; two latrines, each 20 by 36 feet; a 16-by-16-foot pumping and light plant; a 20-by-100-foot recreation building; a mess hall and kitchen, 20 by 120 feet with a 20-by-40-foot wing; officers' quarters, 20 by 50 feet; foresters' quarters, 20 by 90 feet; a 20-by-30-foot army office and orderly building; a 20-by-30-foot first aid and medical building; a 20-by-36-foot bathhouse; and a 20-by-40-foot warehouse.[23] The Barker Lumber and Fuel Company was awarded the contract for furnishing the lumber and millwork, and the Fuller-Goodman Company won the contract for part of the building materials and all of the roofing. "Carpenters and contractors of Door county," were "engaged to carry out the construction program," noted the News.[24] The author's father, William John Tishler, was one of the carpenters employed on the project.

The workers built the long, one-story structures and covered them with tar paper. Two parallel barracks buildings were placed on each side of a central grassy area that fronted on what was probably the kitchen/mess hall. At the other end of the space, a central gravel walk crossed the road running parallel to the first set of barracks to a large open space with a tall flagpole in the middle. Other smaller accessory buildings were placed at the entrance to the camp and at other locations adjoining the main buildings. The entire complex soon took on the appearance of a small, campuslike encampment.

In just a few months, the work was nearly completed and the CCC boys moved into their new quarters in October before the first snow of that year. The buildings had not yet been insulated, and with the temperature dropping rapidly, it became difficult for the young men to sleep and eat in cold tents and the chilly outdoors. To make matters worse, six of the canvas shelters, including the kitchen tent, were blown down during a severe electrical storm with heavy winds.

Camp Peninsular's recreation hall was equipped with a salvaged pool table and makeshift tables for table tennis. An appeal went out for donations of used books, including reference books and magazines, to be dropped off at the county Chamber of Commerce office. Superintendent of schools J. A. VanNatta gave the camp some 150 textbooks, and the Sturgeon Bay library arranged to lend twenty-five books of fiction at a time. "A piano or organ, victrolas and odd pieces of furniture" were also sought.[25] Later, the reading room had a fireplace and a radio.

B. L. Bion of Chicago, the educational director, organized classes for subjects the enrollees wanted to study. These included typing and shorthand, taught by John Pivonka, and agriculture, trigonometry, physics, and chemistry, taught by Michael T. Madden (who also helped coach basketball). Both of these teachers were from Sturgeon Bay. Mildred Carlson of Fish Creek taught elementary subjects, and Olga Wickman of Ellison Bay taught music, mathematics, and high school English. Additional subjects included algebra, geometry, spelling, elementary and advanced psychology, penmanship, forestry (taught by foreman Reed), dramatics (Ackley and Reed), first aid (Dr. Baker), mechanical drawing, radio, leathercraft, wood carving and archery, landscaping (Greaves), and surveying (Burnett). Thus, the roster of instructors included WPA teachers, National Park Service staff, military and naval personnel, and even some of the camp's enrollees. Classes took place late in the afternoon and evening.

Early in 1936, the education program of the camp was reorganized with new courses in hygiene, public speaking, and mechanical drawing. In the ensuing months, improvements were gradually made to the camp. The recreation hall, with its reading room, was made more accommodating. The canteen was completely remodeled. Interiors of the headquarters, kitchen, bathhouse, and recreation hall were painted "robin's egg" blue.[26]

In May of 1937, one of Sparta District's four twenty-eight-watt radio transmitters was moved from the camp at Crivitz to Camp Peninsular, where it operated for a short time. It became part of a radio network used for official messages, but it also provided educational and vocational training for the CCC workers.[27]

Each enrollee was required to work forty-four hours per week. The program budgeted forty-six cents per day for his living expenses and approximately seventy-five dollars for clothing. From his monthly pay of thirty dollars, or one dollar per day, each man was required to send twenty-five dollars home, leaving five dollars for personal expenses such as candy, cigarettes, and other "luxuries."[28] For the fiscal year ending July 1, 1936, $19,575.80 was encumbered to operate the camp. This amount included the costs of supervision, tools and light equipment, gas and oil, maintenance and major repairs, supplies, and all project expenses—including skilled labor, equipment, and materials. Work at the park for the period totaled 24,978 man-days, and man-day costs were figured at $2.50 per day. Thus, the total cost to the federal government was $82,020.80, a tremendous bargain considering the social, economic, and environmental value of all this activity.

In October of 1936, a new quota of some hundred enrollees arrived at Camp Peninsular to replace part of the 125 who had completed their six-month enlistment period. At that time, many of the young men at the camp were from Illinois. Those in the new group came from several areas, including Portage, Baraboo, and Friendship in Wisconsin and Clinton, Illinois. Following established procedures, they were given a physical examination, sworn in, and outfitted with cots, blankets, and other items. As the *Camp Peninsular Breeze* noted, "It will only take them a month or two before a rookie will be indistinguishable from the 'oldest' of enrollees in appearance."[29]

Six months later, in April, the company lost nearly half its strength, as many of the enrollees left to seek positions in civilian life. The final day at camp was always memorable for the young men, since it started with "pay call" at 5 A.M. Then they received their discharge certificates, turned in their property, and, after an early dinner, were trucked to Sturgeon Bay where they caught the train for different parts of Wisconsin and Illinois. A few days later new rookies from Illinois and Wisconsin took their places. The majority of the new members were from Stevens Point (and referred to as the Polish Boys), with others from Madison, Milwaukee, Richland Center, and Sun Prairie.[30]

At the national level, the CCC was assigned to the National Park Service for guidance and supervision. Master planning became the responsibility of collaborative efforts of landscape architects, architects, engineers, foresters, wildlife technicians, geologists, and an occasional historian. Landscape architects and architects worked out detailed design considerations.

One of the many significant outgrowths of these efforts was the publication of an important government book, *Park Structures and Facilities,* in 1935. Intended as a guide for park construction, it was so well received that three years later it was expanded into three volumes entitled *Park and Recreation Structures.* Filled with plans and photographs of park features from throughout the country, it portrayed entranceways, signs, fences, fireplaces, drinking fountains, picnic tables, bridges, shelters, cabins, comfort stations, bathhouses, and other buildings.

The introduction to *Park and Recreation Structures* noted that the examples made "adequate provision for man's needs with a minimum sacrifice of the natural values present." While recognizing the importance of using materials in a "rustic" or "pioneer" fashion, the book warned against slavishly replicating these examples where function and materials dictated sensitive change. It made a strong argument for recognizing regional characteristics and designing and constructing facilities that are sympathetic with an area's "genus loci," or sense of place. For example, "In high, mountainous and forested regions the various structural elements of rustic construction—logs, timbers, rocks—must be reasonably overscaled to the structure itself to avoid being unreasonably underscaled to surrounding large trees and rough terrain." In addition, "The scale of the structural elements must be reduced proportionately as the ruggedness and scale of the surroundings diminish." It also noted the significance of an overall park plan: "The individual building or facility must bow deferentially before the broad park plan, which is the major objective, never to be lost sight of. The park plan determines the size, character, location, and use of each and every structure."[31] Written by Albert H. Good, the book had a significant influence on park design throughout the nation.

The landscape and architectural work at the park was planned by Greaves and Bernhard and carried out under the direction of George H. Nickell of the National Park Service.[32] Greaves planned for the improvement of trails, and he designed a new native stone stairway at Eagle Terrace, steps along the Eagle Bluff Trail, and a new "panoramic platform west of Eagle Tower to replace the old wooden one." Bernhard prepared preliminary sketches for the park's large garage and machine shed. He was also contemplating plans for rustic, stone trailside shelters and a large shelter house of stone and logs at the Nicolet Bay campsite.[33]

Late in 1935, Nickell reported that some of the CCC's first projects included "trail and fire hazard reduction work" and installation of more than a mile of telephone line.[34] Greaves's plan for enlarging and improving the recreational area near Nicolet Bay—then a rough irregular field filled with quack grass and poison ivy[35]—involved building a quarter-mile road into the area, where topsoil was dumped and graded over some five acres. According to the *Door County Advocate,* the main road was moved "back from the shoreline into the woods, circling the outer rim of the new camping area and returning to the shore beyond the old dock." The newspaper also noted, "Two latrines will be erected and an open council ring will be reserved for each group of camp sites. No camping will be allowed on the ridge along the beach as formerly. The camp will accommodate over 250 tents . . . and will cover an area of fifty acres."[36] Replacing Sven's Tower was also considered, but the National Park Service concluded that because of the natural height of the bluff and the good view already afforded from that point, only a stone lookout shelter should be located there.[37] It was never built.

That year, winter struck with a fury. The exceptionally low temperatures of January 1936, combined with winds at the exposed places where much of the work occurred, made the chill factor dangerous. Many of the men from southerly locations with less severe winters had to be taught how to dress to keep warm in the regulation clothing. Heavy snows made park roads impassable at times, and some weeks the men could work for only two days. Despite these conditions, by the end of that month a temporary frame garage and tool house was completed for storing heavy equipment and hand tools. Early in 1936, Greaves also drew up plans for proposed ski slides up to 130 feet in length, plus 1,200-foot toboggan and bobsled runs, and sent them to Madison for approval. They were to be "between Sky Line Trail and Hidden Bluff Road near Sven's Tower, sloping down to the Nicolet Bay campsite."[38] These facilities were endorsed enthusiastically by thirteen organizations headed by John Bertschinger of Egg Harbor, president of the Door County Winter Sports Club. They were also discussed at a Lions Club dinner at the camp in February of that year. Having completed plans for work during the coming six months, Greaves was transferred to Devils Lake State Park to do similar planning there.

During February and March, workers cleared and grubbed 1.3 miles of new park roads and nearly an acre of land for the ski jump run. Project completion reports for March indicated that the workforce, which consisted of sixty-six workers, finished twenty-two projects. The men also worked on "a large stone observation platform" at the Eagle Bluff panorama. There, as it was described in the *Peninsular Breeze*, a crew of men toiled "like ants at what seemed a hopeless job. Back breaking work to make a huge abutment on the side of a cliff where formerly stood an old rotting wooden structure. . . . The weather cold, good building stones hard to get . . . but they still worked on . . . There stands now a new Panorama, monolithic, beautiful. A colossal structure built to defy the fury of the elements, and the years."[39]

Other tasks completed by enrollees that winter included constructing two hundred tables for the picnic grounds at Nicolet Bay and Eagle Bluff, four toilet buildings, and the ski jump. They also continued the rerouting of roads around congested places. Later that year, under Commander Stone, workers enlarged the Nicolet Bay parking lot and edged it with boulders "from an old stone fence in the vicinity of Jacksonport."[40]

At the same time, Burnett announced two major projects for the next six months: a 22-by-48-foot bathhouse at Nicolet Bay and an eight-car garage and machine storage structure to replace the old buildings near Doolittle's residence near the Fish Creek entrance. Work continued into the fall on sanitation facilities at the Nicolet Bay campsite, stone steps at Eagle Bluff Terrace, and road improvements.[41] That winter a crew working under Larson completed a stone wall at the base of Eagle Tower, varying from two to four feet in height, with a flagstone walk along it.[42]

After Bernhard's plan for the garage and machine shed was approved, he began designing rustic stone trailside shelters and a large shelter house of stone and logs for the Nicolet Bay campsite. He also designed signs, specifying "all logs to be of cedar or Norway pine and to be heavily creosoted before setting up letters. Letters to be hand cut to a depth of 3/16 inch . . . and Block Type painted orange. Strap iron to be given two coats of Graphite Black Paint, etc."[43]

In January 1937, some of the men left for flood relief duty in the South. Others worked on the road between the panorama and the intersection of Skyline and Hidden Bluff roads. This section was straightened, a long curve was taken out, and the hill was cut down to establish a gradual incline to the panorama.

Early in the summer, twenty CCC members were called to Sturgeon Bay to search the woods in the western part of Sevastopol for a sixteen-year-old

CCC enrollees spreading dirt from dump trucks into low spots to level the recreation and parking area at Nicolet Bay, 1936. It was then edged with boulders from an old stone fence near Jacksonport. The site was once a rough field infested with poison ivy. (Courtesy National Archives)

boy. The youth was never found and was believed to have left the county. A week later, a fire destroyed barns and sheds on the E. C. Thorp farm and threatened the village of Fish Creek. Assisting the Fish Creek fire department, CCC enrollees helped prevent the spread of sparks and flames to the house occupied by Harold Thorp and to numerous nearby hotels, cottages, and business places. Again, the CCC young men proved to be a valuable asset to the community and the county.[44]

Various social programs helped to relieve the daily routine of work. The camp had a canteen, or exchange, where the men could spend tokens that had been issued to them in booklets. The facility occasionally offered free entertainment and "smokers." One winter evening, for example, a Chicago magician, C. W. Magrum, performed. Magrum had visited some two thousand of the nation's CCC camps. A smoker followed the program and each man was entitled to one pack of cigarettes. On Sunday nights, movies were shown in the mess hall. Enrollees often walked to Fish Creek or Ephraim for entertainment, but had to return by lights out. They were free on weekends, and some would travel to Sturgeon Bay. Many dated young women from the area and a few marriages even resulted.

The first issue of the camp newspaper appeared late in March of 1936. It contained a feature article about Burnett, the camp's acting superintendent, and announced a contest to name the paper, which would be published several times each month. The *Camp Peninsular Breeze* was chosen from the list of nominations. Many of the later issues were illustrated with a clever full-page sketch of some aspect of camp life. Originally mimeographed, the paper switched to a typeset format, plus sketches and photographs, with the November 1936 issue.

Special events in November of 1936 included an Armistice Day observance and a dance at the Congress ballroom in Sturgeon Bay. Aileen Malloy and Her Melody Maids (billed as America's finest girl band) provided music. The group also had two dazzling floor shows that included tap dancing, comedy, a gypsy acrobatic dance, a "cowboy line" number, and spectacular "Russian acts."[45] Many young women attended, as did other Door County residents. The event was a great success and another dance at the Congress was held the following spring, with Charles Van Caster and his eleven-piece orchestra from Green Bay providing the music. Profits from the event amounted to $12.20, and were used to purchase baseball equipment.

Sports activities were also an important part of camp life. These included football (although adequate equipment was lacking) played on the Gibraltar High School gridiron, basketball, baseball, and, to a lesser extent, tennis and golf. Some of the young men also participated in track meets, wrestling, and boxing events. Swimming, pool, table tennis, checkers, chess, and card playing were also popular. Occasional card parties were held on winter Sunday afternoons. Basketball practice took place in the Gibraltar gym. Each of the four barracks had a team and the squads practiced with each other. The camp team, however, played Door County community teams at Sturgeon Bay, Sevastapol, Sawyer, and Carlsville. Early in 1936, Camp Peninsular sent its basketball squad to a tournament at Rhinelander, and it won the CCC's first subdistrict championship.

Team members were on their way to capturing the district's championship when they were called to another urgent activity. On August 10, 1936, ninety enrollees, with Lieutenant Krug and several National Park Service foremen, left Camp Peninsular for Isle Royale to fight raging forest fires that threatened the island's majestic stand of virgin timber. Forty enrollees were transferred from Camp Madison to Camp Peninsular to replace the firefighters until their return, in September, when they resumed their regular duties. During this exceptionally dry year, the camp was also called to fight another fire near Sturgeon Bay late in August.

At Christmas, half of the company was issued a two-week leave; the other half had two weeks off over New Year's. A tragic event occurred when, en route to a New Year's Eve party in De Pere, Lieutenant Krug and a companion were killed in an auto accident. Krug was well liked and respected by the men, and the front page of the January 1937 *Camp Peninsular Breeze* carried a long article about the Green Bay native.

In April 1937, more than eight hundred people from throughout the county attended a celebration of the CCC's fourth anniversary. Held in the camp's mess hall, it consisted of an introduction by Lieutenant Kelly, guitar music and songs, and addresses by Burnett and James C. Langemak, principal of Gibraltar High School. After the program, many boarded army trucks for a ten-mile tour of the park to see what the CCC crews had accomplished. The program resulted in many accolades for the camp and its enrollees and praise for the entire CCC movement. Sturgeon Bay postmaster Harry Jones commended the enrollees on their "manly appearance and gentlemanly conduct" when they visited Sturgeon Bay. They "had won the respect of all with whom they had come in contact," he said.[46]

Baseball practice began in May. Camp Peninsular's team wore green trousers with blue stripes and orange basketball sweatshirts. That summer the team played against Egg Harbor, Sister Bay, Carlsville, and other county teams. Returning from a game at Sawyer, one of the big CCC trucks full of the players overturned at the corner of the Thorp Hotel in Fish Creek. Several young men received bruises and broken bones and spent the night at the Egeland Hospital. That year the team came home with the Sparta District's baseball championship.

On June 16, 1937, the commandant at Camp Peninsular received orders from the War Department in Washington to disband the camp and close quarters by Wednesday, June 30. Bold headlines in the *Door County Advocate* read: "C.C.C. Camp to be Abandoned June 30; Order Last Week a Surprise; Two Projects Are Unfinished."[47] Typical of such army directives, no reason was given for the shutdown. The men worked to finish the foundation for the garage and machine shop, leaving the rest of the building for the state to complete when funds became available. Then they were given their final paychecks. The only other unfinished project was the stone footbridge leading from the lower level of Eagle Terrace to the top. Commenting on disbanding the camp, the *Advocate* said it "means a loss to all of Door county. In dollars and cents it means the same as though a large industry closed down."[48] It also noted the end of the thousands of dollars in purchases the camp had made from Door county businesses.

Among the huge assortment of materials left behind were a huge stock of lumber, assorted hardware, paint, roofing paper, and 180 tons of soft coal. In July, camp inspector Noble Hollister directed that the responsibility for all camp buildings and federal property be turned over to the Wisconsin Conservation Commission. This, however, proved to be a long, bureaucratic process.

The fate of the abandoned camp raised considerable speculation in Door County. The newly organized Peninsula Arts Association wanted to transform it into a summer arts colony for aspiring artists, authors, and musicians.[49] The organization was supported by a group of distinguished officers and board directors: John Matter, president; William Bernhard, first vice president; Mrs. Arthur Byfield (a voice teacher from Chicago and honorary president of the Chicago Women's Symphony), second vice president; Mrs. Harold Wilson, recording secretary; and Herman Hochmeister, treasurer. The directors consisted of an august group of mostly summer residents, including Mrs. Donald Boynton, recognized both for her interest in music and her ability to paint; Leo Podolsky and Edward Collins, both well-known Chicago pianists; Colonel W. W. Yaschenko; and T. A. Sanderson, Sturgeon Bay attorney.

Concerned over the many delays and extensive red tape, Sanderson exclaimed in a letter to Harrington that the delays "illustrate why some citizens get disgusted with the administration of governmental affairs."[50] By March, equipment was being stripped from the vacant buildings. "Only 'shells' of buildings left," the *Door County Advocate* proclaimed on its front page.[51] To complicate the camp's future use, all the plumbing fixtures—sinks and lavatories, along with pipes and connections above ground—were trucked away, as were the electrical fixtures, exposed wiring, and stoves. Much to the frustration of the Peninsula Arts Association, even the pump was taken, the pipes pulled out, and the well hole plugged. Eventually, most of the buildings were dismantled. A few were adapted to other uses, such as one that served as the band room at Gibraltar High School for many years. Today, nature has reclaimed the site of this once-thriving encampment, and virtually no evidence remains to remind us of its controversial past.

The Civilian Conservation Corps left an enduring record on the landscape of Peninsula State Park. It enhanced the lives of hundreds of young men, some of whom were Door County residents. In a letter to National Park Service Superintendent Burnett, Henry Tiedke of Jacksonport commented on the many benefits derived from his CCC experience: "Ever since I completed my enlistment, I wanted to write informing you of how I appreciated the splendid co-operation I received while there. And [I] also want to comment on the benefit derived as far as having learned how to do many jobs such as mason work, tree planting, and landscaping and many other things too numerous to mention. I feel as tho it's a great school for young men, also for those that are able to qualify as local experienced men."[52]

The CCC camp was responsible for many important improvements at Peninsula State Park. The men completed two and three-quarters miles of park roads and thirteen and a half miles of foot and pony trails; a large (22½ by 86 feet) stone and frame bath house at Nicolet Bay and four comfort stations. They created three parking areas of about one and a half acres each; erected new speed limit and directional signs; established eight acres of picnic grounds; modernized forty campsites for tents and trailers, many with individual fireplaces; improved fifteen hundred feet of beach at Nicolet Bay; constructed forty combination tables and benches for picnic areas; and erected a championship ski slide. The men also spent one thousand man-days clearing poisonous plants and weeds, including two hundred acres of poison ivy, and twelve hundred man-days combing the park to eliminate twelve million gooseberry and black currant shrubs that harbored the deadly white pine blister rust. Many days were also spent eliminating forest fire hazards and fighting dangerous fires.[53]

One of their most attractive accomplishments was the panoramic viewing ledge west of Eagle Tower, with its spectacular view of Chambers Island, the

Strawberry Islands, Eagle Island, and Horseshoe Bay, of ships going and coming, and, in the far distance, the shores of the state of Michigan. The *Breeze*
called it "their final ideal," noting that "there stands now a new Panorama,
monolithic, beautiful. A colossal structure built to defy the fury of the elements, and the years."[54] Another is the five-hundred-foot stone retaining wall
along Shore Road, standing fourteen feet high in some places. Quite an engineering accomplishment, it has gutters along the sides connected to drains
underneath the wall. In 1937, Burnett estimated that if private builders had
built the wall, the cost would have been five thousand dollars.

The Civilian Conservation Corps program inevitably became a casualty of
World War II. In July of 1942, Congress ordered liquidation of the corps, and
by June of 1943, all the camps were closed.

The CCC left an indelible mark on Wisconsin's and the nation's landscape.
Perhaps even more important was the hope it brought to hundreds of thousands of enrollees and their families as they struggled through the financial
ruin and emotional heartbreaks of the Great Depression. Young men whose
families were not able to give them educational advantages benefited greatly
from the opportunities that enrollment in the camps fostered. Thanks in part
to the work of the CCC, state parks in several states are now listed as historic
districts. The legacy of Wisconsin's CCC men deserves similar recognition.

CCC workers built this sturdy Eagle Bluff panoramic viewing area in 1936. It
replaced a viewing platform of wood that was rotting from age. (Author's collection)

CCC workers built this attractive native limestone wall along Hidden Bluff Road.
(Author's collection)

CHAPTER 13

∾

The CCC Controversy

Virtually from its onset, the CCC program was subjected to criticism. Late in 1934, a *Saturday Evening Post* editorial accused the program, and its approximately 850,000 young men, of "Manicuring the Wilderness." While admitting the program "has accomplished much in the way of fire prevention, erosion control, road building and similar forest and park improvements," it cautioned that "there are almost certain to be unnecessary projects . . . and there is a tendency at times to overmanicure the wilderness."[1]

The CCC camp at Peninsula State Park was controversial from its very beginning. Upon hearing of the project, concerned residents of Ephraim and Fish Creek "entered a protest against a camp being located" at the park.[2] Even Jens Jensen entered the controversy. By now he had broken ground to start his "School of the Soil," The Clearing, where he would became a frequent critic of the park's policies. Regarding the CCC camp, he wrote a stinging letter to Governor Philip La Follette stating, "I have searched my mind as to why it is to be there." He was concerned that their "cleaning up" work would "destroy the last wilderness left," in the park, and he urged that instead they "reforest the poor lands of Door County."[3]

The *Advocate* expressed the opposite view. A week after the first CCC crew arrived, it declared that "Door County is fortunate in having this camp established within its borders, as it means many improvements in both Peninsula and Potawatomi parks that would not otherwise have been possible."[4] Two weeks later, referring to Jensen as "a Chicagoan, who spends his summers in Door County," the newspaper emphasized that the park had areas of thick underbrush, and clearing it away would remove fire hazards.

Striking back in two separate letters to the editor, the distinguished park designer questioned the purpose and management of the park. It should be, he stated in his usual poetic manner, "first of all, a place different from the man-made world where man may find and enjoy and study the work of the Great Master. It is also, or should be, a natural monument of outstanding character. . . . The thought that man can improve on the Master's Work, and thereby make it more fitting to himself, is only possible for those who lack an understanding of its true and profound value." Concerned by past "abuses" he had observed in park management, he went on to add that he had seen "camping grounds that are nothing less than slums, . . . a cleaning up . . . which destroys the very sustenance of the trees, . . . foreign trees unfitted to this environment, planted in [Peninsula] State Park, . . . [and] roads built for the sightseeing crowd, barring wild life from reaching the water and penetrating their secret haunts."[5] Other noted conservationists were also expressing concerns. Aldo Leopold, for example, was warning against excessive brush cutting and development of fire lanes in wild areas.

Early the following year, the *Door County News,* the *Advocate's* rival newspaper, praised the work of the camp in a lengthy front-page article entitled "Fine Service Rendered County by CCC Camp." The dispatch began: "Stability—permanency—usefulness! Such is the impression gained by a casual visitor to Peninsula camp of the Civilian Conservation Corps in Peninsula State Park." It went on to describe life at Camp Peninsula and the projects the young men there were completing. "Peninsula camp has brought about a great improvement in tourist conditions in Peninsula State Park," it concluded, "and local people feel that every encouragement should be given to make it permanent."[6]

On the eve of the newspaper's account, the Gibraltar Men's Club, an organization of Fish Creek residents, adopted a scathing anticamp resolution. The *News* published it one week later, as follows:

> No one can point to any benefit to anyone locally, and practically everyone is agreed that the establishment of the camp in this community has worked out to be a detriment to the State Park, the villages of Ephraim and Fish Creek, and the tourist business in the county and state. The beautiful new shop and garage . . . consists now of a pile of stone, which will probably have to be moved away at state expense. Trails are half finished. Camping grounds a mile long are half finished and no water or toilet facilities have been provided. . . . A natural scenic rock garden was destroyed to provide boulders for the construction of a panoramic view.

Fearing that the CCC contemplated radical changes, the resolution went on:

One of the projects . . . is the closing of the present main entrance of the park and building a single entrance between the villages of Fish Creek and Ephraim with . . . a sentry to collect admission fees from those entering the park, [plus] the abandonment of some of our most beautiful roads . . . [and] the patrol of public camping grounds with collectors for camping privileges. In short, they are going to take full charge of the supervision of this park.

Furthermore, it said, the camp was putting men formerly employed at the park out of work, was purchasing park supplies elsewhere, and was improperly disposing of sewage. It also stated that "there was no such thing as . . . discipline of any kind" at the camp, and there were "numerous cases of their [CCC enrollees] having broken into vacant summer cottages." The young men were walking on the "highways in all parts of the county at all hours of the night," and it likened their character to "inmates from a reformatory" and "convicts." Finally, "There is no redeeming feature in the present location of the CCC camp and if they are permitted to stay here much longer, local influence will have to be started for its permanent removal."

The resolution was distributed widely. Copies went to the *Door County Advocate,* the *Green Bay Press Gazette,* the Conservation Commission, CCC district headquarters at Sparta, men's clubs of various communities in Door County, Governor La Follette, and selected civic organizations. Inflaming the situation further, the Ephraim Association of Commerce passed a resolution the following week recommending "removal of the camp at the earliest opportunity."[7]

Joining in the fray, the *Door County Advocate* questioned the value of the camp: "When summer comes and thousands of tourists come to enjoy themselves in the park, the question is being asked 'Will it be advisable to have the two hundred CCC boys working in the park?'" It also expressed concern about future control of the park. "If the CCC camp becomes a permanent fixture in Peninsula State Park" it asked, "is the State of Wisconsin eventually going to surrender its jurisdiction over this park, and development and regulation pass into the hands of the National Park Service at Washington, D.C.?"[8] This issue was really at the heart of the controversy.

In response to the bad newspaper publicity, Captain Eldon Grafton, the camp commander, explained the situation in a confidential memo to the Sparta district commander. Doolittle had instigated the criticism, he said, and a member of the Gibraltar Men's Club was "a state employee of the park who it is believed has been engaged in an undercover campaign of malignment against . . . this camp." The memo refuted, in detail, most of the charges made in the men's club's resolution, noting that "several members of the Gibraltar

Men's Club have publicly disclaimed that such a resolution was ever officially passed or adopted by that organization."[9]

Two days after the resolution was drawn up, state and regional officials made a routine visit to the camp. In the group were L. I. Johnstone, regional inspector for the National Park Service; Noble P. Hollister, regional inspector for the CCC's fifth district headquarters; and state parks chief C. L. Harrington. They first visited with Harry Schuyler, president of the Gibraltar Men's Club, who also served as township councilman. Later, at an informal meeting of the club's directors, secretary E. D. Fuhr criticized the camp and stated that he "represented the feelings of Fish Creek, Sturgeon Bay and Door County."[10] Fuhr gave many reasons why the community was concerned about the presence of the camp. Hollister urged the group not to "meet exaggerations with further exaggerations, but to argue with cold facts which they could substantiate." Acting camp superintendent D. S. Burnett gave a forceful address on behalf of the camp and invited members of the club to visit the park and "see for themselves what was going on." But fears were expressed that the camp would be detrimental to the summer tourist business, a major source of income to the community. Finally, feelings calmed a bit and everyone shook hands at the close of the meeting, even though Fuhr complained that another villager had punched him in the nose for his opposition to the camp.

The following day, the inspectors toured the park and were "agreeably surprised at the quality and amount of work done."[11] Later, in Sturgeon Bay, they reassured Mr. Hansen, president of the Door County Chamber of Commerce, and editor Sanderson of the *Door County Advocate,* and they called on Assemblyman Frank Graass.

Back in Madison, Harrington declared that the camp would continue because county consensus favored it. He also noted that work scheduled for the camp could not be completed for another twelve to eighteen months.

In his report of the visit, Hollister said that "the resolution of the Gibraltar Men's Club was considered wild and as a misstatement of fact." One exception, he admitted, was an event that occurred "on Halloween evening of October 1935, [when] some of the enrollees had been guilty of disorderly conduct in the village of Fish Creek, and were reputed to have been intoxicated." He also stated that sometimes enrollees were seen walking down the highway at night, when some villagers saw them "as potential prowlers who might be guilty of several varieties of misdemeanors." However, no such misconduct had actually occurred. He also noted that "certain guarded statements and hints were dropped . . . to the effect that Supt. Doolittle had very likely aroused the sentiment expressed by the Gibraltar Men's Club in their resolution, because

Mr. Doolittle's ire had been aroused by the treatment accorded to him since the camp opened."[12]

Doolittle's anger was understandable. Apparently the camp's previous superintendent, G. H. Nickell, and the CCC's landscape architect had "shown deplorable lack of diplomacy in their attitude taken toward Mr. Doolittle."[13] After many years of exemplary, dedicated service, Doolittle had expected to be consulted about proposed projects for the park. Furthermore, the lines of authority for planning, coordinating, and supervising work in the park had not been established.

At its next weekly meeting, the Gibraltar Men's Club discussed a more cautious resolution to reserve judgment about the camp, but it was rejected by a vote of seventeen to twelve. This action, Burnett said, was "to act as the basis for instructions to Congressman George J. Schneider for the removal of the Camp."[14] Meanwhile several prominent individuals wrote to H. W. MacKenzie, head of the Wisconsin Conservation Department, and Governor La Follette to recommend that the State of Wisconsin and not the federal government operate the camp.

Again, Jens Jensen joined the debate, in a letter to Malcolm Dill, of the TVA's Division of Land Planning and Housing: "In most instances, [the CCC camps are] doing tremendous injury, and so is the Forest Service, in introducing recreation areas in the woods where . . . the growth of things, the mystery and beauty of it all, must be the only source for educational and spiritual purposes." He was especially critical of "including golf in our State Parks," which he called "sheer folly."[15]

Responding to fears of federal control of the park, Harrington assured Doolittle that "at no time was the national park service or the federal government to take administrative jurisdiction of the Peninsula State Park." He also told Walter Abramson that "closing down of this camp immediately would be a detrimental thing." Recognizing the opposition, however, "We now take the position that with any reduction in the CCC camp program, which we anticipate may occur during the next several months, our recommendation would be that this camp be the first one to be closed."[16]

In a letter to Harrington, H. R. Holand, Door County historian and chair of the Door County Park Commission, countered in detail charges made by the Ephraim Men's Club. Noting that he had voted against the resolution, Holand said Harrington had overestimated the opposition, which, Holand concluded, "mostly comes from one individual."[17] The *Milwaukee Journal* soon shed light on the actions of that individual, Doolittle, noting that he had "been a constant objector to the camp because of differences with the National Park Service on what work should be done to improve the area."[18] And the *Door County News,* in describing the meeting where the resolution originated, noted the superintendent's disgust with the CCC program: "Doolittle told of the destruction and mutilation of natural beauty spots as a result of the activities of the camp."[19]

Summer visitors expressed their fears in anticamp letters to WCD officials. The superintendent of schools at Two Rivers, who was a regular camper in the park, stated that "many of the campers make a practice of bringing their families, including many young girls, and because the CCC boys have a tendency to roam about the park very much at will, it seems to me very inadvisable" to have the camp located there. A similar concern was expressed in a letter from a Milwaukee insurance company executive whose daughter had attended Camp Meenahga: "I would dislike very much to send her up there . . . into a place where she might run into some unpleasantness or even worse due to the laxity of discipline in the CCC camp or through any lack of good manners towards girls or women in general on the part of the boys or men there."[20]

In the spring of 1936, local residents began taking a more positive view of the camp. In a conversation with Harrington, editor Sanderson intimated that many in Sturgeon Bay and Door County would regret the loss of Camp Peninsular. Clarence Mann, newly elected chairman of the Town of Baileys Harbor, indicated that the people there had not been concerned with the criticisms. However, in May of 1936 a group of northern Door County resort owners and other businessmen demanded that the camp be removed "not later than July 1, 1936."[21] They believed the camp to be "definitely injurious to the tourist patronage."[22] In response, the county board of supervisors passed a resolution condemning the camp and requesting its removal.

In late May, National Park Service inspector Johnstone provided the CCC's fifth regional office in Indianapolis with details about the controversy. "We have known all along that Doolittle is the prime mover" behind the petition, he noted, and because of Doolittle's "attitude and influence the work done by us in the park is practically valueless and in some cases actually harmful." He cited disagreements about the construction of roads, because Doolittle was concerned that there were "too many." The ski jump was another aggravation. After the project was approved and the site cleared and graded, Doolittle indicated that he "won't have it," deeming it unsafe and "demanding that it be built of masonry." Johnstone concluded, "Due to all this unwarranted interference it has been and still is impossible for the camp to function efficiently or usefully in Peninsula State Park." Thus, he recommended "that it be

withdrawn at once . . . and that the camp buildings be immediately dismantled and completely removed from the site."[23]

Controversy about the camp, both pro and con, continued into the summer. The indefatigable Earl M. LaPlant, president of the *Door County News,*
continued to express his strong support, declaring it "a crime the way they are
trying to ride the CCC camp in the Peninsula State Park."[24] The continuing
protests and the resolution passed by the county board brought action from
Washington. Robert Fechner, director of CCC Camps, sent a special investi-
gator, William P. Hannon, to Peninsula Park to look into the situation. Of all
the camps Hannon had visited throughout the United States, this was the first
to provoke such protest. Instead, he noted, in practically all instances, his
department heard protests when a camp was to be removed. In his four-day
investigation of the case, Hannon thoroughly studied the site, read relevant
correspondence, conducted interviews, and took photographs. His report was
the most comprehensive appraisal to date of the camp situation, and it contained a scathing indictment of Doolittle. In a letter to Washington, he wrote,
"Doolittle is responsible for all of the trouble and he ought to be removed as the
Park Supt., unless he is willing to behave himself. . . . Everybody whom I talked
with," he stated, "told me frankly, that Mr. Doolittle, Park Supt., was the one
man who was back of the efforts to have the camp taken out of the locality."

Addressing some of the charges in the petition, he said, "The statement (unsigned) that they have broken in to summer cottages that are vacant is a most
sinister attempt to influence sentiment against the camp." He noted that "the
unsigned resolution was sent to absentee [cottage] owners, and it was felt that
they would become alarmed . . . and ask that the camp be removed. There
is not a single case on record of any enrollee ever having broken in to any
dwelling or any other place." Hannon's statement about the enrollees (whom
the petition had described as "convicts") is of special interest because it reflects
his opinion of the general character and integrity of CCC enrollees. That de-
grading characterization, Hannon wrote, should

> cause the author . . . to hang his head in shame. These boys and the families
> they represent, are for the greater part citizens of Wisconsin, of good character
> and noted for their honesty and integrity. Because misfortune overtook them,
> and some proud Father or Fond Mother, was forced to go on relief, and gladly
> accepted the Government's offer to place their son in a CCC camp, it is most
> unfair and cruel to make a wholesale comparison of them with inmates of a
> Criminal Institution. I would say any man guilty of such an act, is unfit—in my
> humble judgment, to hold a position of public trust.

To Hannon, there was "no justifiable reason for the State of Wisconsin, or the U.S. Government, to move this camp out of here, until the work that has been started, and much additional work that is needed in this park, and in several county parks in Door County, has been . . . completed. In their hearts the people of Door County—with few exceptions—want this camp to remain in Door County."[25] To support his findings, he submitted signed statements from three reputable Fish Creek residents: Arthur Henry, Emil Krause, and William Pelke. Each questioned the methods used in developing the men's club petition and stated that charges in it were exaggerated and that they personally supported the work of the CCC camp. Some of the men were critical of Doolittle, charging that he not only urged people to complain about the camp but also used park equipment and material for the tourist cabins he operated at the park's Fish Creek entrance. The entire report was a stinging indictment of Doolittle and the Gibraltar Men's Club's petition. After Hannon's visit, state and federal officials again refused to disband the camp.

When it was first learned that the camp would be established in Door County, some local officials had hoped that the young men might also help at Potawatomi State Park and some of the county parks. Early in June, Ernald Viste, the respected elementary school teacher and town clerk at Baileys Harbor, asked Harrington whether the workers could be used at the new county park. It included a forty-acre tract that had been acquired from the U.S. Department of Commerce, and it contained the range lights that had been operated by the U.S. Lighthouse Service, as well as a portion of the sandy beach adjoining what is now the Ridges Sanctuary. Writing in his capacity as County Park Commission chairman, Holand too had requested CCC assistance "in putting the county parks into shape."[26]

Harrington's response to each was that initial consideration had been given to assigning crews to county parks, but, in view of the controversy, "we now feel that it would be unwise to attempt to continue this camp in operation any longer than was actually necessary." As soon as the work at Peninsula was done, he told Viste, "we would suggest that the camp be closed." In fact, he told Holand, "the Peninsula Park camp will be the first of Wisconsin's CCC camps to be closed."[27] The demise of Camp Peninsula was now imminent, possibly by April 1, 1937, when its designated work period would end.

The persistent Holand again asked Harrington for aid for the county parks, especially the two within nine miles of the camp. His letter also revealed more insights into the controversy and his concern about the actions of Doolittle. "You misapprehend the importance of the opposition to the CCC camp," he wrote. "There would be none whatsoever except for your own department as represented by Doolittle. Feeling sore at being temporarily shelved, he forgot his loyalty to you and the park and moved heaven and earth to get the camp out." Of the resolution passed by the county board, Holand said, "Its members, with a couple of exceptions, knew nothing about the camp but when Doolittle appeared before the board and dramatically told of the stinking sewage rolling down from the camp [at Nicolet Bay] . . . and of girls being corrupted (both charges 90 percent imaginary) the board, influenced by his talk, adopted his resolution." He also cited what had now become general acceptance of the camp by "the large majority of people" of Door County. Furthermore, the Ephraim Men's Club had unanimously adopted a resolution "praising CCC workers for their excellent work in eradicating poison ivy" and, he noted, "the ski slide which is now almost completed is also highly applauded."[28]

In September 1936, Congressman Schneider was asked to assist in convincing the CCC camp to undertake work on improvements at the Baileys Harbor park, where a small CCC "side camp" might be established. After looking into the situation, inspector Johnstone recommended that the work instead be carried out from Camp Peninsular. The most important work to be done there, according to Johnstone, was "further cleaning up of old slashings, which present a very serious fire hazard; although beach improvements, including the removal of the present bathhouse and the replacement of a more presentable building and the construction of trails and proposed planting[s], were next in order." Johnstone emphasized the fire hazard because "if a fire should start in this area . . . and the wind was blowing in the right direction, it may be impossible to save the buildings of the range light within the park, or those of the coast guard station adjacent to it."[29]

Subsequently, Harrington wrote to Schneider to clarify the Conservation Department's position against such involvement, for "we would not want anything to arise that would take the men from the Peninsula Park."[30] Replying nearly seven months later, Schneider indicated hope that arrangements could still be made for the work at Baileys Harbor. After reviewing the situation, however, both Conrad Wirth, assistant director of the National Park Service, and Paul V. Brown, regional officer of the National Park Service, recommended against it.

Had the controversy about Peninsula's CCC camp not arisen and caused so much concern and suspicion, the camp might have continued to provide invaluable service to Door County's young and growing park system and many of its young men.

～

CHAPTER 14

Winter Sports

Winter sports had long been popular with residents of Door County. When the bays froze over, "hundreds of people enjoyed skating, ice sail skating, ice boat sailing, playing hockey and in addition to this horse racing on a track laid out on the ice."[1] A resurgence of interest in organized winter sports occurred during the heart of the Great Depression when several Door County citizens began promoting winter sports in Peninsula Park.

H. R. Holand was an early advocate of such activities. In a letter to the *Door County Advocate* in 1935, he declared, with his usual flamboyant prose: "All people in good health like winter sports. Even if they are not able personally to take part in them, they like to see them for they abound in thrills which delight the eye. Ice boating is more delightful than dancing, tobogganing is more hilarious than the movies, and skiing—the greatest of all sports—is more amazingly thrilling than any amusement of man." Holand maintained that ideal conditions for winter sports, including plenty of snow, proper topography, and large expanses of frozen water, could be found "in good measure in Door County, particularly in and near Peninsula Park." There, he maintained, existed "big hills . . . for sliding and ski-in. . . . Nicolet Bay could be made into a splendid skating rink and Green bay [is] a grand field for ice boating." He believed this "would add a new glory to Wisconsin's most beautiful state park" and "would put thousands of dollars into the pockets of Door County's people."[2]

The *Advocate* quickly called for action on Holand's suggestion: "One of the first things should be the hiring of an expert to inspect the available lands and plan the ski slide. . . . Why not . . . turn Door county into a place that will draw as many people here in winter as come in the summer?" Doing so, it added, would "help every line of business . . . [and improve] the chances for labor to secure employment."[3] At a time when America's economy was in a deep depression with severe unemployment, these were words of hope for many local residents.

With the Ephraim Men's Club assuming leadership, a committee visited Oconomowoc and Milwaukee to examine ski slides. They located a hill for the ski slide in the park and invited Carl R. Haun of Milwaukee, a civil engineer and experienced ski slide designer, to look over the site. Haun was impressed with the location and estimated that the cost of erecting a steel structure for the slide would be approximately two thousand dollars. That summer, about thirty representative citizens of northern Door County met at the Anderson Hotel in Ephraim to discuss establishing a winter sports program. Holand chaired the meeting, reported on Haun's visit, and displayed a plan for a steel superstructure that would enable 140-foot jumps.[4]

Several days later, forty men and women from throughout the county met at Sturgeon Bay to organize the Door County Winter Sports Club. A. E. Doolittle stated optimistically that men from the soon-to-be-established CCC camp might build a ski slide. The new club elected a president, John Bertschinger of Egg Harbor, and three vice presidents, Anton Martinson of Liberty Grove, Dr. Dan Dorchester of Sturgeon Bay, and Harry Schuyler of Fish Creek. Sam Hogenson of Ephraim was designated secretary-treasurer. A committee was also appointed to formulate a plan for Doolittle to present to the Conservation Commission for consent to use the state park and obtain the commission's cooperation in carrying out the club's activities.[5]

Eager to prepare for the coming winter, the club met in September at the Alpine Resort in Egg Harbor. Antone A. Mauer of Algoma, a Swiss one-time ski jumping champion and former world record holder for jumping distance, was present. Mauer emphasized the advantages of building the jump at the Alpine, which, he maintained, had a suitable hill, plus close-at-hand lodging facilities. Several other sites for ski, toboggan, and bobsled slides were also discussed, including Burr's Hill between Fish Creek and Egg Harbor.[6]

In November, Holand reported to the group that, under the supervision of CCC authorities, a "ski slide, toboggan slide and skating rink would be built in the state park."[7] For the time being, however, a steel structure was not being planned. The club also discussed organizing contests with prizes for winners of various winter sports events. At a meeting at the Baileys Harbor School several days before Christmas, Bertschinger reported an enthusiastic response to the club's efforts throughout the county. Some communities had even formed committees to promote local winter sports programs.[8]

Early the next year landscape architect Kenneth Greaves completed plans for the proposed ski and toboggan slides between Skyline Trail and Hidden

Bluff Road. A Sturgeon Bay native working with the CCC camp's National
Park Service staff, Greaves pointed out that the slope for the ski and toboggan
runs "would be about 1,200 feet long and [would] permit ski jumps up to 130
feet in length if a large enough scaffold is built."⁹ In a resolution to the Conservation Commission at Madison, thirteen county organization requested
approval of the project. It would be located between Skyline Trail and Hidden Bluff Road near Sven's Tower, where a steep slope ran down to the flats
east of Nicolet Bay. Nearby campsites would be available to winter sports
enthusiasts, and existing roads made the site accessible on both the upper and
lower levels.

That spring CCC workers built the slide, but the next winter when a group
of jumpers tested it they found it dangerous and expressed their concerns to
the Winter Sports Club. As built, the jump was not positioned high enough
on the hill, so that skiers were landing at the bottom rather than on the slope.

Erected by CCC workers early in 1936, the popular ski slide was located between
Skyline Trail and Hidden Bluff Road near Sven's Tower. Here a steep slope ran down
to a flat landing area east of Nicolet Bay. This was probably one of the first jumping
contests held at the park, since stumps and felled trees can be seen to the right of
the jumper. Note the attentive observers lining the slide and landing area. (Courtesy
Peninsula State Park office)

They indicated that the slide needed to be extended back and upward to provide greater takeoff speed and longer jumps.

The necessary alterations were made, and the first ski tournament of the season was held in January 1937. A large crowd lined the runway to see five local jumpers make leaps as high as fifty-seven feet. Anton Martinson, captain of the Ellison Bay ski club, was the first to jump. Over the next two months further alterations were made to the slide and several more ski jumping meets were held. They attracted greater numbers of skiers who made jumps as long as seventy-eight and a half feet. Large crowds of spectators braved bitter northwest winds to cheer them on.

Early in 1938, at the urging of the Winter Sports Club, another level was added to the ski slide. It permitted longer jumps from the 145-foot runway to the landing of similar length. In a feature article about Door County, the *Green Bay Press Gazette* described the new slide: "Now the structure towers to a height of seventy feet. This height added to the height of the cliff on which it stands constitutes one of the finest ski slides in the state."[10]

Three ski meets were held at the park that year. At one event, members of the Racine Ski Club "put on the most daring and beautiful ski riding exhibition ever seen in Door County. The boys did single, double, triple and diamond box jumps and all without a fall. . . . The headwind prevented them from doing other jumping tricks they had planned." The "dizzy toboggan run" was also popular for those who dared. "Spills were numerous," the *Advocate* reported, "as the less experienced riders, after gaining breath-taking speed down the steep take-off, were unable to make the banked curve."[11]

A top-notch jumping program in March wound up the ski events for 1938. It included more Door County skiers since "the basketball season [was] over, releasing several of the better young jumpers."[12] Again, members of the Racine Ski Team were well represented and there was a contingent of skiers from Scandinavia, Wisconsin. After the final jump, not a single previous hill record remained. Attendance at the meet was estimated to be between three thousand and thirty-five hundred, and observers came from "every section of Northeastern Wisconsin, Milwaukee, the Fox River Valley and even Chicago."[13]

After the event Clarence Brodd, a Sister Bay businessman who by then was the club's president, announced that funds derived "from the sale of booster tags . . . were sufficient to clear up the deficit the organization had incurred in promoting [that] winter's program."[14] On behalf of the club, James C. Langemak, Gibraltar High School principal, acknowledged those who made the meets such a grand success, especially the newspaper sportswriters and photographers who gave the events generous publicity. As a result, the Associated

Press requested an account of the jumps and the United Press also sent out dispatches on the meet.

During the winter of 1938–39, Door County jumped into winter sports with both skis! Northeast Wisconsin Works Progress Administration leaders agreed to help sponsor and plan a three-day winter sports institute at the park. It would demonstrate winter sports ideas to recreation directors who could then teach the activities in various communities. In conjunction with this event, the Winter Sports Club planned a "three-day winter sports carnival . . . with a queen, pageant and all the trimmings," plus a ski jumping tournament.[15] Skiers would use the rebuilt 70-foot high jump with its 145-foot runway and landing hill of similar length. New were the twin toboggan slides over one-half mile long and cross-country ski trails. Smooth ice at Nicolet Bay and Eagle Harbor would also be used.

WPA officials helping with the event would include Charles Lutz of Madison, state director of physical education, to direct the skating races; Hans Schmidt of Madison, state director of dramatics, to write the pageant's "Winter Wonderland" production; and Terry Ryan of Milwaukee, to photograph and film the events.

With activities thrilling "a crowd of several thousand persons," the entire weekend program became the most spectacular ski and winter sports celebration ever held in Door County. A huge parking area at Nicolet Bay was cleared and roads were converted to one-way driving to accommodate the traffic. To avoid what could have been a terrific traffic jam, an ice road was plowed to Ephraim.

Ideal weather prevailed the first day. There was considerable merriment as skaters skimmed across the ice in a 220-yard oval that had been cleared of snow at Nicolet Bay. Scores of the county's best skaters competed in a series of races, with Sturgeon Bay skaters winning gold medals in two of the three boys' divisions. In the fastest group, for skaters sixteen and over, Bob Moore won first place, while Clyde Casperson of Sister Bay and Charles Tishler of Baileys Harbor, took second and third respectively. In the two races for girls, Eunice Krause of Fish Creek, Sylvia Seiler of Ephraim, and Peggy Newberry of Fish Creek were winners. Medals were awarded for first, second, and third places in each class. After the races, Ray Litton of Chicago, formerly of Sister Bay, performed a skating exhibition. Litton gracefully spun and swooped across the ice, receiving loud applause as he finished. In the next event, two Green Bay hockey teams whacked their way at opposing goals in an hour-long exhibition of a sport that was rapidly becoming popular on the Door Peninsula.

That night, the crowd stood in wide-eyed fascination as huge floodlights illuminated a veritable fairyland of evergreens that formed the setting for the pageant. Scores of spruces and cedars flanked the side entrances, background, and arch over the stage, which, the *Advocate* proclaimed, "for beauty" nothing "can ever rival its appearance." To begin the "Winter Wonderland" pageant, some fifty schoolchildren, directed by Raymond Slaby and Alice Woerfel of Gibraltar High School, danced and paraded across the stage to music by the high school band, conducted by Arthur Blahnik. The brilliantly costumed pageant characters appeared to be performing in a mythical forest kingdom.

Next came a parade of floats, up the ramp and directly in front of the stage where everyone could see them. As James Langemak announced the entries over a loudspeaker, the floats stopped in front of the stage in full glare of the spotlights to receive a full round of applause. First prize went to the Gibraltar Men's Club for its mock railroad engine and caboose. Second went to Adolph Roeser of Sister Bay for his Paul Bunyan entry, and third went to George Johnson and Co. of Ellison Bay for its net fishing float that featured George and Percy Johnson, assisted by Clarence Linn and Harry Olsen, pulling up real fish. Other floats included an immense load of logs (sponsored by men of the town of Gibraltar), the Baileys Harbor Men's Club's King Winter on a throne of lighted blue ice, a fancy skater performing on the ice-coated platform of a truck, an old-fashioned sail sleigh commonly used in the early days of ice fishing operated by Harold Wilson and Lloyd Olson from Ephraim, and several other colorful and clever floats.

After the pageant, hundreds of people left over the ice road to Ephraim, and for a time the line of cars "extended clear across Eagle Harbor, a spectacular sight . . . according to those who saw it from the bluff road." The following week, the *Advocate* reported that the audience would long remember the pageant "as one of the most outstanding outdoor, amateur dramatic events in the history of Door County." It acknowledged that "Northern Door County is noted for its Fourth of July parades, but nothing ever exceeded this winter carnival show."

Unfortunately heavy rain and sleet arrived on Sunday, making the ski events difficult. The conditions also precluded further viewing of the handsome floats, which were to have been shown a second time at the ski tournament. With the ski slide covered with icy snow, ski jumping had to start from the platform halfway up the structure. A strong wind and driving rain made jumping even more hazardous; only class B and C jumpers competed, and the junior jumping event was canceled. One skier from the Milwaukee-Oconomowoc club, caught by a strong puff of icy wind about halfway down the takeoff slide, took

an alarming tumble into the side railings, but came up smiling and continued to make more jumps. Other contestants competed from the Racine and
Kettle Moraine ski clubs. Ralph Payne from the latter group took top honors
with jumps of sixty-one and sixty-four feet. But holding the spotlight, said the
Advocate, was "a middle aged, lightly attired tourist. . . . The man, apparently
one who once knew ski jumping, was reported as having virtually dived off
the scaffold when he lost his balance at the take-off. Head first he went but
luckily leveled off to skid on his stomach to the bottom. Sitting up in a daze,
the man reached for a bottle, took a hasty nip, and was as good as new as he
tramped back for a second try."[16]

The day concluded with a skiers' banquet at the Mary Ann Cafe in Sister
Bay. Club President Everett Valentine served as master of ceremonies, and
Clarence Brodd, who had worked tirelessly for the county's winter sports pro-
gram, gave out the awards.

The season's final and most successful ski meet was held in March. Because
it did not conflict with other tournaments, "the largest field of skiers ever to
compete in Door County" was expected.[17] A large crowd of nearly three thousand attended and bonfires kept spectators warm. The ideal conditions resulted
in record jumps by the thirty-four contestants, the longest being 104 feet.
After the competitive jumping, several daring exhibition jumps were held, with
skiers going off in double, triple, and diamond-box formations. At breathtaking speeds, "the ease and grace of [these] daring feats would have been a credit
to a troupe of ballet dancers," reported the *Advocate.*[18] That evening skiers
were treated to a festive banquet at the Hotel Carmen in Sturgeon Bay. Before
the season ended, there was talk of building a "ski-tow" to eliminate "labori-
ously climbing the hill" after each jump.[19]

Early in 1940, another series of ski jumping tournaments was held at the
park. These were now being sanctioned by the Central U.S. Ski Association,
and once again new records were set. By now, park employees had made even
more improvements for winter activities. A new toboggan run was completed
and, at the foot of the ski run, the Winter Sports Club had drilled a well to
flood the new, large skating and hockey rink. Miles of cross-country ski trails
were in shape and a large new shelter house had been built at the foot of the
ski run. In addition, work on a bobsled run was underway. "Just about everything winter sports fans could ask for in the line of outdoor winter activities"
was now available in the park. Always supportive of winter recreation, the
Advocate editorialized, "There is no reason why Door County should not draw
thousands of pleasure seekers here in the winter as well as summer. . . . As winter sports develops it is probable that arrangements could be made with local

bus lines to conduct weekend tours." In addition, in a visionary statement, it
noted that as time goes by "Door County will be handicapped . . . without railroad passenger service."[20] Proceeds from that year's sale of "booster tags" were
donated to the Finnish relief fund. To better finance winter activities, the Door
County Sports Club was incorporated the following year, enabling the group
to charge admission for the tournaments: fifty cents for adults and fifteen cents
for children. A one-dollar club membership admitted the member to all of the
season's events. The money was used for prizes, advertising, and fees for having the ski meets sanctioned by the Central U.S. Ski Association.

Record jumps continued at the park into the 1940s, but attendance at the
meets began to dwindle. To encourage outdoor activities throughout the
county, the Winter Sports Club helped finance a new ski hill at Ellison Bay,
where tournaments for young skiers began early in 1941. The newly incorporated winter sports organization also began considering plans for developing
facilities at Potawatomi State Park. This effort was spearheaded by the Com-
modore Club, a Sturgeon Bay men's social group. Some years previously a
local group in which Gerhard Miller (later, a prominent watercolor artist) was
active had attempted to build a toboggan slide there.[21] By the end of 1941, a
separate Sturgeon Bay Winter Sports Club had been organized to promote the
use of Potawatomi Park's hill. By now, the Central Ski Association's wartime

View of the ski slide in summer. It was built in a wooded area that had been cleared
for the sport, along with a toboggan run to the immediate left of the jump landing
area. (Author's collection)

program was promoting winter sports close by for those who avoided distant travel because of gas rationing. Thus, the Vagabond Ski Club of Green Bay expressed considerable interest in the Potawatomi hill. In fact, demands for winter recreation at Sturgeon Bay were surging, not only from the greatly increased local population of defense workers but also from interest throughout northeastern Wisconsin.

In January 1942, the sixth annual ski meet was staged at the Peninsula Park's ski hill, but poor conditions required hauling snow to the scaffold and landing hill. Baileys Harbor, Egg Harbor, and Gibraltar furnished the trucks, and volunteers groomed the hill under the direction of Anton Martinson of Sister Bay, the "Father of ski jumping in Door County."[22] The contest had a record number of fifty-two entrants, and jumpers from Michigan carried off the lion's share of honors. Late in February, the season concluded with the annual Cherryland Winter Carnival at the park. With the nation focused on the war and in observance of George Washington's birthday and National Cherry Week, patriotic pageantry was blended into the program. An avenue of flags and bunting lined the slide and landing hill, said the *Advocate,* which went on to describe the spectacle:

> Thrills galore, and color with a capital "C" ruled the day's events. At the opening of the program, the bugler sounded assembly; then the Gibraltar High School band, George and Martha Washington (in costumes), and the young skiers all went sliding down the hill to fan out into a large "V" at the moment K. O. Jacobson, Door County's expert jumper who represents the club at the big time meets all over the Middle-West, came flying through the air, to land and ride out through the big "V" for Victory. The band struck-up the "Star Spangled Banner." It was a scene of sheer beauty, and especially inspiring at this particular time.[23]

Mrs. Joseph Kwaterski of Liberty Grove and her crew of bakers had made plenty of pies from the peninsula's famous cherries provided by the Fruit Growers Co-op. Charming young ladies from Gibraltar High School served it in "suitable costumes" as the band played patriotic and popular music. It was another of the grand winter extravaganzas of the park.

By this time, the club had financed an addition to the Ellison Bay jump, making it suitable for tournaments. The first of a series of ski meets during the 1943 season was held there. Nearly all of the contestants were local jumpers. "Due to belief that gas rationing would cut down entries," and because many of the park staff had gone off to war, the "Big Slide" at Peninsula Park was not going to be opened.[24] However, since the Smith shipyard had recently employed several ski jumpers, and members of the Coast Guard at Sturgeon Bay had offered to pack the snow on the long run, it was decided to have just one meet at the park. Unfortunately, the landing hill had frozen so hard for the event that skiers could not start from the top of the scaffold to take a crack at the hill record of 119 feet set by Carl Sorenson of Racine in 1941. Sadly, it would be the last ski meet at the Big Slide, where so many grand jumping events had taken place. Because of safety concerns, shortly after the war the long slide was condemned and dismantled, and the sport began to decline in Door County.[25]

During the war years, work continued on the Potawatomi Park hill, as stumps were pulled out, rocky ledges blasted, and the surface graded and planted with grass. Progress was slow because the area's heavy equipment was busy with housing projects, and the hill had to be reshaped with considerable fill.[26] The lack of funds and unfavorable weather also complicated development. But by 1944, sixteen acres of hillside and parking areas had been cleared and smoothed. The following year the ski tow and a double-track steel rail toboggan run were completed. Finally, after a foot of snow fell on Christmas Day of 1945, the hill was ready for the public. A ski jump was never built there.

After the Peninsula Park jump was dismantled, ski jumping continued at Ellison Bay, and a new area for ski meets was built at Lone Pine Hill south of Fish Creek. With backing from the Winter Sports Club, contests were held there that attracted some of the county's best skiers, including Sister Bay's legendary Harold "Winky" Larson. Larson organized the county's last ski jumping meet at Lone Pine Hill (later renamed Nor-Ski Ridge) in 1966. After three decades, this exciting sport was no longer part of winter activities in Door County. Now, where crowds of thousands were once thrilled by skiers flying gracefully through the air, the swish of cross-country skis and the roar of distant snowmobiles echo near what once was the Big Slide.

CHAPTER 15

World War II and Beyond
at the Park

Several months after A. E. Doolittle retired in 1942, Ralph Halvorsen arrived at the park as a conservation aide. Later, after serving at several other state parks, Halvorsen would return to become superintendent at Peninsula.

Early in 1943, the Conservation Department announced the appointment of Peninsula's new superintendent: Paul A. Lawrence. A man with considerable experience as a park custodian, Lawrence had been in charge of developing Wyalusing and managing Nelson Dewey and First Capitol state parks. His tenure at Peninsula Park was astonishingly brief, however, and he served only three months before returning to his former park assignments in southwestern Wisconsin.

A short time later, William H. Beckstrom was appointed superintendent. A native of Ashland, Wisconsin, Beckstrom had a deep love of plants and was a skilled botanist. He began his career in Chicago doing landscape work with several architects from that city. Continuing to apply his vast knowledge of plants, he was then employed by a well-established Chicago nursery, and he worked on the horticultural building at the Chicago World's Fair in 1933. Presumably it was in Chicago that he met Jens Jensen, with whom he maintained a lifelong friendship. In 1935, Beckstrom returned to Wisconsin to take charge of First Capitol State Park at Belmont. Later, he was transferred to state parks at Devils Lake and Copper Falls. When Point Beach State Forest was designated in 1938, Beckstrom took charge of its development. Thus, he came to Peninsula with a wealth of knowledge and experience.[1] Beckstrom soon became active at The Clearing, served as a trustee of the Ridges Sanctuary, and was involved with other conservation efforts on the Door Peninsula.

Under Beckstrom's tenure as superintendent at Peninsula, important issues arose that required his considerable tact and diplomacy. These included placing a limit on the number of campers and dealing with such camping-related issues as trailers brought to the park from "April 15 to the end of October, and using them only on weekends."[2] The latter practice outraged some campers because it denied them the use of choice locations. Complications resulting from leasing park buildings became another sensitive problem, as was implementing the policy of buying out the "islands" of private property within the park.

The new superintendent also had to deal with an unusual request by an Ohio couple to operate a "fun camp" emphasizing outdoor activities in the park. It would cater to the children of parents who wanted supervised recreation for their children while vacationing in the park. Writing to C. L. Harrington about the proposal, its promoters suggested locating the project at the site of the former Camp Meenahga. Opposing this location, Beckstrom suggested using Horseshoe Island instead since it was no longer occupied. Harrington ultimately denied the project because it was "against the over-all policy of the conservation commission" to permit such use of state parkland.[3]

Beckstrom left as superintendent in 1954 and began operating a plant farm at the Red Barn on the north edge of Ephraim, where he also crafted fine furniture. His design for street signs is still used at Ephraim and in other areas of northern Door County. Beckstrom also had expertise in log building, having restored several such structures in Door County. The author recalls Beckstrom once telling him of developing a technique for waterproofing the sod roof on Al Johnson's Swedish Restaurant at Sister Bay. The traditional Scandinavian method used large overlapping sheets of birchbark as a leak-proof membrane under the turf, but Beckstrom's used fiberglass panels under the sod for a longer lasting and relatively permanent solution. Johnson's popular restaurant is probably the most photographed spot in Door County, with its sod roof kept trimmed by nimble goats that relish the green grass.

Ever since Jens Jensen had settled into his new abode at The Clearing, he'd been sending frequent letters to the editor of the *Advocate* and several other state newspapers about an array of environmental and conservation issues. He also wrote sharply worded letters to staff and commission members of the Conservation Department and even the governor.

William T. Evjue, editor of the *Capital Times* in Madison, met Jensen in Door County where he often vacationed at Gordon Lodge in Baileys Harbor. They soon became close friends. While on vacation, Evjue continued to write his front-page column of opinion, "Good Morning Everybody," sometimes referring to local people, places, and conditions. During the summer of 1936, he related an afternoon "when we went deep into the woods and sought out the sylvan retreat of the modern Thoreau, Jens Jensen, on the majestic headland at Ellison Bay. It was inspiring to sit at the feet of this naturalist of national reputation and listen to his explosive fulminations against those who despoil the beauties of nature's handiwork."[4] Both men were of Scandinavian ancestry, and they shared similar views about conservation and politics. Over the years, they frequently corresponded.

In what was probably Jensen's first letter to Evjue, he expressed concerns about the scarcity of deer in the area and his fierce opposition to illegal hunting. "By the way," he stated, "I heard this morning that the hunters shot five deer in the state park in spite of a CCC camp, a park Supt., and his staff. . . . I wrote the conservation commission about this today." Evjue reported the shooting to his readers, commenting, "How silly it is for the state of Wisconsin to appropriate hundreds of thousands of dollars to the conservation commission to carry on game and wild life protection and then to permit such slaughter."[5] Jensen's outspoken views impressed Evjue. That same day he wrote to Jensen: "Mrs. Evjue and I frequently recall the pleasant hours that we have spent under your hospitable roof and how we enjoyed your thunderous maledictions upon those who wantonly despoil the beauties of the great outdoors. More power to you."[6]

Their close relationship and mutual respect for the environment led to Jensen's occasionally writing a column for the editorial page of the *Capital Times*. Under the byline "Jens Jensen, Noted Landscape Architect, Ellison Bay, Wis.," some thirty-five columns appeared from 1940 to early in 1949, two years before his death. Accompanied by a photo of the handsome, smiling author, they were eloquently written with thoughtful insights into Jensen's concerns about conservation and the environment. They focused on such topics as the growing tide of commercialism engulfing the peninsula, the management of state parks, illegal deer hunting, the introduction of nonnative game species, the influence of the Wisconsin Conservation League (an organization primarily of hunters), and campgrounds that he called "slums."

Several columns referred to conditions at Peninsula Park. In "The State Parks of Wisconsin," he wrote, "Our state parks do not serve their true purpose and their responsibility to humanity. Our parks have no leadership, no guiding hand to lead the people into enlightenment and understanding." He charged that tourist money was being "used to destroy our parks and sanctuaries with roads and more roads and camping places which are cheap imitation of the slums of our great cities."[7] In "The Door County Summer Slums," he wrote critically of conditions at Peninsula: "In Door county the unthinking individual is allowed to come into our state park, a shrine of Nature's mighty forces, where beauty and the oneness of all speak most forcefully, and alongside

Nature's giants create another slum, perhaps far worse than the one he left at home. All this is tolerated so we might boast that thousands visited our state park during the year."[8]

It was clear that Jensen kept a watchful eye on what was happening at Peninsula Park. In "Our Parks Will Become Sanctuaries," he referred to another problem at Peninsula:

> Years ago the eagle was quite common in these parts, but so-called progress has taken its toll. Until recently, he was an inhabitant of the Peninsula state park. High in the pines on Swens [sic] Cliff he built his nest. But more important to our park officials was the motor car and a means of it reaching every corner of the park.
>
> In a world built for the tourist who considers nothing worth seeing unless the motor car leisurely takes him there, the King of the Sky has no place.[9]

Yet, his writings still expressed cautious notes of optimism for the future of human relationships with the land. For example, despite the prospect of a disastrous world war, he wrote hopefully on August 21, 1941:

> Someday there will be beautiful roadsides. Someday there will be no roadside advertising. Someday our parks will come into their own. But this will not come about by helping the careless indifferent attitude to grow and develop and expand. Tomorrow is a new day, a new day when the voice of the grandeur and the magnificence of our mighty land have awakened our people to their great heritage.
>
> This tomorrow will break with a rosy dawn on the horizon that will expand into pure sunlight. The small percentage of our people who have an understanding of the necessity of beauty to daily living, of gracious living, the graciousness our forefathers fought and struggled for, that those who followed them might always have a benevolent life will usher forth that rosy dawn. These few, a small minority, who in spite of our present deteriorating influences has set their goal high and are keeping the torch burning.

The article concluded with a poetic paragraph:

> They shall clean and purify the American home, the American mind, so we as a people shall be fit and ready to inherit our God given American soil in all its grandeur, loveliness, and graciousness. Then we shall be a one people worthy of a mighty land.

Jensen was keenly aware of the destiny of Door County. In one of his last letters on the subject, to William Longenecker, then secretary for the Friends of Our Native Landscape, he stated prophetically, "Door County is slowly being ruined by the stupid money crazed fools. This tourist business is destroying the little bit of culture that was."[10]

During World War II, a camp for German war prisoners was established on Evergreen Road adjoining the park. The prisoners slept in a large building and picked cherries in nearby orchards. The author still has vivid memories of seeing large open-air trucks with prisoners standing in the back. Many still wore shirts and caps of their uniforms. The camp was one of many in Wisconsin where the prisoners provided the scarce labor necessary to harvest crops or work in the forests.

One year after the war ended, the Wisconsin Legislature was considering three more state parks in Door County. They were to be at Cave Point, in the Mink River forest, and at Europe Lake. The Door County Park Commission, with Jensen its most outspoken member, endorsed the recommendation. He had advocated setting aside these areas for some time. In an article in the State Planning Board's *Lands for State Parks,* Jensen wrote:

> Much of that part of Wisconsin nearest to its principal centers of population has more and more developed into a summer vacationland. Year by year those areas unfit for agriculture, and which represent the only wilderness left in that part of our State, are fast disappearing under the hand of the vacationist who comes because of these wilderness areas, not realizing that the very wilderness that brought him here is being destroyed by him.

In a typically visionary statements he said:

> The day is close at hand when the last remnant of primitive America along the shore of Lake Michigan will be a memory, and the thing that attracted the tourist and the vacationist be gone forever unless something is done, and done now, to prevent such a calamity. . . .
>
> Of remaining tracts along the Lake Michigan shore, the dunes country south of Jacksonport, and the Mink River country and adjacent lands, including Europe Lake and the low cliffs along the shores of Lake Michigan where are found evidence of pre-historic times in the fossils imbedded in the rocks . . . are the most important wilderness areas to be preserved from destruction. . . .
>
> May our love for all creation, for its infinite beauty and true purpose, guide us into a right reverence for this world not of our making so we will see to it that unborn generations will have the right to drink at this fount.

Jensen's dream would ultimately become a reality. All of these areas either became state parks or have been protected, thanks to the diligent efforts of the Nature Conservancy, the Door County Land Trust, the Department of Natural Resources, and other environmental organizations.

By the mid-1950s, Wisconsin's outstanding state park system was facing serious problems because of insufficient funding. An informative and well-illustrated brochure entitled "Wisconsin State Parks Going Downhill, Why?" highlighted the dilemma.[11] By this time, Wisconsin had thirty state parks encompassing eighteen thousand acres in twenty-five counties. They included significant historical sites and some of the Midwest's best scenic places with outstanding inspirational and recreational values. Yet, like city, state, and national parks throughout the nation, Wisconsin's state parks were struggling with pressures from increasing attendance. Visitor numbers tripled during the decade after World War II. At Peninsula, the Nicolet Bay camping area, which was designed for two hundred tents or trailers, sometimes had to accommodate up to four hundred such units. "This adds up to two thousand people," the brochure claimed—essentially a small town. "Slum conditions are the result of such overcrowding," it stated, noting that projected growth rates and the corresponding numbers of visitors would simply overwhelm the system in the future. It was clear from available studies that Wisconsin did not stack up with other states in funding its parks. The report concluded by pointing out the specific needs of the park system: better maintenance, new facilities, and more new parks. The real need, it stated was "for a sound financing program—adequate—flexible—and capable of growing with the needs of the state."

By 1954, Lowell Hansen had become Peninsula's superintendent. A botany major from the University of Wisconsin–Madison, he had taken courses in landscape architecture and was skilled at designing changes needed at the park. Hansen supervised modifications at the golf course, campsites, and the extension of electric power along Highland Road to the heavily used Nicolet Bay area. During his first year, work at the park also included removing many of the park's estimated one thousand abandoned apple trees to comply with state statutes on deserted orchards.

Insufficient funding and other problems remained to be dealt with. In 1957 an article in *Wisconsin Conservation Bulletin* said, "Our largest state park has unique features, but is typical of others in that demands exceed facilities." It went on to note that Peninsula's "camp spots are far too small, as are the picnic places and their highway boundary makes further expansion difficult. Serious crowding has resulted." This meant that often "a family had its tent mere inches from the next." Thus, instead of "having a sense of being in the great out-doors, people felt they had fled the city only to find themselves in a noisy, crowded little settlement which, if things got much worse, might well be called a slum."[12]

With the deadline for their termination drawing near, the leased properties in the park became a sore spot throughout the 1950s. When the Marshall cabin on Shore Road near Weborg Point was to be vacated by its leaseholder, Margaret Dyer, the fate of the building attracted considerable attention. Built circa 1847–49, it was thought to be the oldest standing home in Door County still in its original condition. (The Thorp cabin in Fish Creek, which had been modified over the years, was determined to be the oldest.) Park policy normally required that when leases expired, buildings would be sold for removal, razed, or otherwise disposed of. However, because of the Marshall cabin's historical significance, several individuals and groups wanted to preserve the building. The Colonial Dames of America expressed interest in it as early as 1950. Four years later, the State Historical Society indicated that the

The Marshall cabin on Shore Road near Weborg Point. After unsuccessful attempts to feature the building as a historic structure, it was finally dismantled and moved to the Ridges Sanctuary. In 1983 the venerable dwelling was dedicated as the Ridges nature center. (Photo by Lowell G. Hansen, courtesy Peninsula State Park office)

cabin did indeed have "historical significance as an example of an excellent pioneer cabin," and urged its preservation.[13] In 1955, both the Dames and Ms. Dyer suggested operating the cabin as a historical site. Dyer's will provided that certain furnishings would go to the Dames for use in the cabin, along with some funds to manage it. After financial support for the project grew, the matter was brought to Harrington's attention, but he did not act on it, perhaps because of a prickly controversy over the fate of another cabin. In a letter to Roman Koenings, superintendent of the Parks and Forests Division of the Conservation Department, Hansen explained the issue:

> In the period of 1955 thru 1958 there was a running "rhubarb" and considerable pressure was applied by local organizations for the State to preserve as an historical attraction . . . the Ole Larson cabin (often referred to as the old Game Farm house). . . . During that encounter, we often pointed out that the Ole Larson cabin was much younger, was in poorer condition, had been considerably revamped and altered and that it generally had much less historical significance than the Marshall cabin. We expressed the opinion that we should not divide our interests and try to preserve two (or more) cabins but rather we should concentrate on the best of several old cabins in the Park which was certainly the Marshall cabin. This opinion finally prevailed and the Ole Larson cabin (as well as several others) was razed in 1956 and the site marked by a monument furnished by the Larson family and the Ephraim Men's Club. At the time . . . there were many others who also thought the Marshall cabin was worthy of preservation and the principal group indicating such interest was the Colonial Dames of America.

To preserve the cabin, Hansen suggested an arrangement whereby the conservation department would retain ownership of the building but operated it as a historical site in conjunction with the State Historical Society. "We have been floundering on this since 1950 and we need to face up to a positive decision." He added: "Will we go down the 'historical rabbit trail' with the Dames or not? We strongly recommend that we do. We believe that this cabin is a worthwhile historical attraction and that when it is furnished and operated it will be another dignified and interesting point of interest for visitors in Peninsula Park." A skilled photographer, Hansen sent two supporting eight-by-ten photographs of the cabin with his letter.

Another matter complicated preservation of the Marshall cabin: its well water was too contaminated to drink. For years, Dyer had been carrying her drinking water from the park office. Hansen and conservation department

officials in Madison did not want to provide the funds necessary to rehabili-
tate the well or drill a new one.

Establishing the Marshall cabin as a historic site never became a reality, and
for several years its future remained uncertain. Eventually it was offered to the
Ridges Sanctuary near Baileys Harbor. For some time, the Ridges had hoped
to expand its educational programs with the addition of a classroom, and the
Marshall cabin could meet this need. The logs of the cabin were stored in a
nearby barn until funds became available, and by August of 1981 the Ridges
announced that work on erecting and restoring the cabin was nearly complete.
A special appeal was made for funds to complete the project and, as in the
past, loyal members and friends of the sanctuary raised the necessary money.
On July 16, 1983, the cabin was formally dedicated as a nature center at the
Ridges, where it continues to be used for that purpose.

In 1968, the affable Hansen left Peninsula to take a position at the Department of Natural Resources' Madison office. That year Ralph Halvorsen
returned to Peninsula to become its superintendent (1968–74). A conservation department employee with considerable experience, Halvorsen began his
career during the Great Depression, when the department was still headquartered in the west wing of the State Capitol. At a salary of sixty-five dollars per
month, his first assignment was at the Poynette Game Farm. In an address to
the Door County Historical Society in 1973, he recalled some humorous experiences. One of them occurred after an exhibit of the game farm's birds and
animals at the University Field House in Madison. Halvorsen had not brought
along enough milk for the bottle-fed cubs and he was unable to purchase
more because it was Sunday and grocery stores were closed. To solve the problem he placed them in a cardboard box for the return trip to Poynette, where
his wife, Dorothy, had milk in their refrigerator. By the time he was five miles
out of Madison, as he put it, "I had one bear on each shoulder sucking my
ear. And that can be a distraction when you are driving along . . . it's not like
wearing earrings."[14]

After serving in the military during World War II, Halvorsen worked at several state parks before his retirement from a distinguished career of managing
some of Wisconsin's prime natural features.

Meanwhile, the nature of camping at Peninsula was changing. Campers
could experience all of the many delights of the park's natural setting but,
because of their increasing numbers, the camping experience became more
regimented. Until 1950, virtually anyone who came could find room to camp.
After that, limits were placed on their numbers. Eventually individual campsites were established and the old days of pitching one's tent almost anywhere

The author during one of the delightful summers he spent living at Nicolet Bay while working as the park's camp master, August 1958. (Author's collection)

in a campground area ended. To cope with the growing demands for campsites, many of the campgrounds were revamped. A reservation system was
instituted at Peninsula and five other popular state parks in 1974. Initially, the
procedure applied only to the Tennison Bay campground, and that year over
sixteen hundred campers reserved campsites there.

Gary Patzke became the park superintendent in 1974, when visitor numbers
were ever increasing. By the end of the 1976 season, the number went over the
million mark, surpassing the previous year's record of 982,000. More changes
occurred under Patzke's supervision, and visitor numbers continued to spiral
upward. In 1983 Patzke left to serve in the Peace Corps.

Patzke's successor was Tom Blackwood, the sixth person to hold the position (not counting Paul Lawrence's brief stint). At this writing, Blackwood
is still supervisor—he considers it a "dream job"—and he exudes the joy that
comes from loving his work. The job now involves overseeing the park's four
programs: visitor services; the rangers or law enforcement; the maintenance
and repair of close to one hundred buildings, twenty-five miles of road, and
forty miles of trails; and the educational naturalist program, which includes
the White Cedar Nature Center. At the peak of the season in the park, he is
in charge of what is essentially the second largest community in the county.
As of the summer of 2003, he supervised a staff of eleven permanent employees and an additional thirty-two summer workers.

In an interview for the *Advocate*, Blackwood revealed some of his inner-
most feelings about Peninsula, stating, "I find it hard to comprehend that
in 1909, people had the incredible foresight to buy up all this land. I'm totally
sold on natural land and natural heritage for our grandchildren."[15] In the best
tradition of the legendary A. E. Doolittle and the other superintendents and
park workers before him, Blackwood's dedication continues to protect the
magnificent resources of the park, while making them available to growing
demands of the public.

For nearly a century the abundant natural and cultural features of Peninsula
State Park have enriched the human spirit of millions throughout the Midwest and beyond. The park's traditional attractions—its breathtaking scenic
beauty, abundant opportunities to commune with nature, delightful pleasure
drives, extensive hiking trails, camp grounds, Eagle Tower, the golf course,
scenic overlooks, boating amenities, and a host of other features—continue
to be popular. In recent years new features have been developed to reflect
changing recreational needs. These include the construction of bike trails, the
White Cedar Nature Center, tours of Eagle Bluff Lighthouse sponsored by the
Door County Historical Society, nature programs, playground equipment, an

exercise circuit, and, most impressive of all, the popular American Folklore Theatre (AFT). This critically acclaimed professional group presents original musical and dramatic shows in an eight-hundred-seat outdoor theater under a canopy of stars and towering pines. Many of their productions capture humorous aspects of Wisconsin's and Door County's traditions and culture. AFT has become a highly successful summer attraction with tens of thousands of visitors enjoying their presentations each season. Now a Door County icon, the theater has become known nationwide

Changing social, economic, and natural conditions have traditionally brought new challenges and threats to America's beloved parks. Such has been the case throughout the history of Peninsula State Park, and these forces will continue to confront it, perhaps to an even greater degree, in the future. Countless individuals with a deep love for the park can only hope that these changes will be met with visitors who have an abiding respect for nature, enlightened park management, favorable political backing, and sympathetic support from the public for generations far into the future.

NOTES
BIBLIOGRAPHY
INDEX

Notes

Preface

1. Nolen to Raymond H. Torrey, field secretary of the National Conference on State Parks, May 11, 1926, Nolen Papers.

Chapter 1. Patterns of the Park's Landscape

1. Wisconsin Department of Natural Resources, "Wisconsin State Natural Areas Program," Madison, 2003. Report on file at Wisconsin Department of Natural Resources Library, Madison.

2. Wisconsin Department of Natural Resources, Bureau of Endangered Resources, "Peninsula Park Beech Forest State Natural Area," Madison, 2003. Report on file at Wisconsin Department of Natural Resources Library, Madison.

3. Wisconsin Department of Natural Resources, Bureau of Endangered Resources, "Peninsula Park White Cedar Forest State Natural Area," Madison, 2003. Report on file at Wisconsin Department of Natural Resources Library, Madison.

4. Curtis, *Vegetation of Wisconsin,* 184.

5. Holand, "Glimpses of Door County," 9, 10.

6. U.S. Government Public Land Survey, Exterior Lines, 1835, Series 701, vol. 32. Microfilm at Wisconsin Historical Society.

7. U.S. Government Public Land Survey, Interior Lines, 1836, Series 701, vol. 219. Microfilm at Wisconsin Historical Society. Spelling and syntax are Sibley's.

8. U.S. Government Public Land Survey Map, T 31N, R 27E, 4th Mer. 1836, Series 701, 25. Microfilm at Wisconsin Historical Society.

9. *Milwaukee Sentinel,* June 20, 1860.

10. *Milwaukee Sentinel,* March 3, 1865.

11. Petterson, "Ephraim Is My Home," 208.

12. *Evening News,* January 25, 1908.

13. Nolen, *State Parks for Wisconsin,* 32.

14. Dee, "A Yacht Ride," 18.

15. Map, "Peninsula State Park," Wisconsin Conservation Department (hereafter WCD) Files, box 63.

16. *Wisconsin Blue Book* (Madison: State Printing Board, 1923), 55.

17. Wisconsin Department of Agriculture, "Door County, Wisconsin Land Cover Maps," 24. For an overview of this mapping project, see John S. Bordner, "The Use of Wisconsin Land," *Wisconsin Blue Book* (1935), 59–70.

18. *Milwaukee Journal,* July 23, 1931.

19. Reprinted in *Door County Advocate,* September 8, 1932.

20. U.S. Department of Interior, National Park Service, and Wisconsin Conservation Department, Division of Forests and Parks, "Peninsula State Park No. 10 Master Plan," 1936, WCD Files, box 439, folder 4.

21. Retzer, "Peninsula Park—and Its Problems," 3.

22. *Milwaukee Journal,* April 23, 1967.

Chapter 2. The Native Americans

1. Storrow, "The Northwest in 1817," 165; Brown, "Record of Wisconsin Antiquities," 319; Brown and Chipman, "Indian Mounds," 8; Ritzenthaler, "Wisconsin Petroglyphs and Pictographs," 97.

2. Schumacher, "Indian Remains in Door County."

3. Kuhm, "Indian Place Names in Wisconsin," 4–5, 36, 38, 50–51, 125–26.

4. Dirst, *Shanty Bay,* 53.

5. Ibid., 19, 54, 55.

6. Ibid., 32.

7. *Door County Advocate,* December 17, 1937.

8. *Door County Advocate,* July 3, 1925.

9. Ibid., and Holand, "Ceremonies Attending the Funeral of Simon Kahquados."

10. *Door County Advocate,* April 30, 1926, and *Forest County Republican,* November 28, 1985.

11. *Door County Advocate,* September 27, 1935.

12. *Door County Advocate,* August 19, 1927.

13. *Door County News,* August 18, 1927.

14. *Door County News,* August 11, 1927.

15. *Door County Advocate,* August 19, 1927.

16. *Sheboygan Press,* June 1, 1931. This article provides comprehensive coverage of this important event. The editor of the *Press,* C. E. Broughton, was a member of the advisory council of the Conservation Commission and a curator of the State Historical Society. C. L. Harrington asked him to "take full charge of the ceremonies attending the burial." See Paul D. Kelletor to Broughton, March 26, 1931, WCD Files, box 897, folder 5. Another excellent article appears in the *Advocate,* March 22, 1962.

17. Writers' Program of the Work Projects Administration in the State of Wisconsin, *Wisconsin: A Guide to the Badger State,* 464.

18. *Door County Advocate,* February 6, 1931.

19. *Forest County Republican,* November 28, 1985.

20. *Door County Advocate,* May 28, 2002.

Chapter 3. Early Residents

1. Hjalmar Holand, *Old Peninsula Days,* 64.

2. Tract book records for Gibraltar Township, Door County, Wisconsin, U.S. General Land Office, Wisconsin local office tract books, 1835–1909, series 1673, Green Bay office, vol. 73, Wisconsin Historical Society Archives, Madison.

3. Dirst, *Archaeological Survey for a New Septic System,* 14. This report contains details of land ownership in the area and corrects prior information provided by Holand about nearby Scandinavian settlement.

4. Hansen to Koenings, November 24, 1959, WCD Files, box 128, folder 14.

5. Treichel, "Door County Cemetery Index," 12.

6. Stevens, "Ole Larson of Door County," 3.

7. Hansen to Koenings.

8. U.S. Census Office, *Eighth Census of the United States, Taken in the Year 1860* (Washington, DC: U.S. Census Office, 1860), Town of Gibraltar, vol. 2, reel 1402, 13–22. Microfilm at the Wisconsin Historical Society, Madison.

9. Paul and Frances Burton. *Ephraim's Founding Father,* 98.

10. *Door County Democrat,* September 5, 1908.

11. Wisconsin State Census, "Population Schedules" (1875), Door County, unpaged. Microfilm at the Wisconsin Historical Society, Madison. U.S. Census Office, *Tenth Census of the United States, Taken in the Year 1880* (Washington, DC: U.S. Census Office, 1880), Town of Gibraltar, reel 1424, 69. Microfilm at the Wisconsin Historical Society, Madison.

12. *Door County Advocate,* October 20, 1964.

13. U.S. Census Office, *Eighth Census of the United States, Taken in the Year 1860,* Town of Gibraltar, vol. 2, reel 1402, 973–82.

14. U.S. Census Office, *Ninth Census of the United States, Taken in the Year 1870* (Washington, DC: U.S. Census Office, 1870), Town of Gibraltar, reel 1712, 1–12. Microfilm at the Wisconsin Historical Society, Madison.

15. U.S. Census Office, *Tenth Census of the United States, Taken in the Year 1880,* Town of Gibraltar, reel 1424.

16. U.S. Census Office, *Twelfth Census of the United States, Taken in the Year 1900* (Washington, DC: U.S. Census Office, 1900), Town of Gibraltar, vol. 15, reel 1785, 54–71. Microfilm at the Wisconsin Historical Society, Madison.

17. *Door County Democrat,* March 7, 1913.

18. Sigurd Erixon's "North-European Technique of Corner Timbering" provides an excellent discussion of Nordic log construction. This ancient building system incorporated tightly fitted logs hewn flat on their inner and outer surfaces and fastened together at the corners, probably with dovetail notches.

19. For a good overview of historic preservation in the National Park Service, see Ahern, *Cultural Landscape Bibliography.*

Chapter 4. Weborg Point

1. *Sturgeon Bay Advocate,* August 14, 1913, and *Door County Democrat,* August 15, 1913.

2. *Sturgeon Bay Advocate,* August 14, 1913.

3. Vida Weborg to C. L. Harrington, February 5, 1940, WCD Files, box 128, folder 5.

4. *Door County News,* August 18, 1927.

5. Weborg to Davidson, November 22, 1908, Davidson Papers, box 27.

6. Davidson to Weborg, December 23, 1908, Davidson Papers, box 27.

7. WCD Files, box 17, folder 13.

8. Weborg to Davidson, March 29, 1910, WCD Files, box 30.

9. *Door County Democrat,* November 18, 1910.

10. Johanna Weborg to Governor Emanuel L. Philipp, October 26, 1934, WCD Files, box 27.

11. *Sturgeon Bay Advocate,* August 14, 1913.

12. Gilson to Kelleter, October 1, 1930, WCD Files, box 897, folder 5.

13. Harrington to Kelleter, December 22, 1930, WCD Files, box 897, folder 5.

14. Holand to Kelleter, April 10, 1932, WCD Files, box 897, folder 5.

15. Doolittle to Kelleter, April 14, 1932, WCD Files, box 897, folder 5.

16. Kelleter to Doolittle, May 3, 1932, WCD Files, box 897, folder 5.

Chapter 5. Eagle Bluff Lighthouse

1. *Door County Advocate,* January 4, 1902.

2. Cetin, "Lighthouses: Sentinels of the Inland Seas."

3. *Encyclopedia Americana* (1995), s.v. "Lighthouse."

4. *Milwaukee Sentinel,* June 16, 1868.

5. Karges, *Keepers of the Lights,* 227.

6. *Milwaukee Sentinel,* October 16, 1868.

7. *Annual Report of the Light-House Board of the United States* (Washington, DC: Government Printing Office, 1900), 144.

8. Badtke, *Eagle Lighthouse,* 23.

9. *Door County Advocate,* November 5, 1893.

10. *Door County News,* September 9, 1926, and *Door County Advocate,* September 10, 1926.

11. *Door County Advocate,* October 27, 1964.

12. *Annual Report of the Light-House Board of the United States* (Washington, DC: Government Printing Office, 1893), 131; *Annual Report of the Light-House Board of the United States* (Washington, DC: Government Printing Office, 1898), 150.

13. *Door County Advocate,* October 13, 1964.

14. Avery, *The Mystery Ship from Nineteen Fathoms.*

15. *Door County Democrat,* January 30, 1909.

16. *Door County Advocate,* February 4, 1909.

17. *Door County Advocate,* November 13, 1913, and January 29, 2004.

18. Jack Matthews, "Our Hike to the Government Lighthouse Tower," *Pack and Paddle,* 1925, 69.

19. Frances Jane Farson, "The Light House," *Pack and Paddle,* 1925, 55.

20. *Door County News,* September 9, 1926.

21. *Door County Advocate,* August 30, 1929.

22. Fred S. Bishop to A. E. Doolittle, June 15, 1936, WCD Files, box 128, folder 4.

23. Peterson to A. E. Doolittle, June 23, 1936, WCD Files, box 128, folder 4.

24. *Door County Advocate,* April 19, 1961, and *Milwaukee Sentinel,* September 4, 1983. Numerous articles appeared in the *Advocate* beginning in 1963. The most detailed are those by Frances Badtke, November 3 and November 10, 1964.

25. J. A. Alger Jr., "Amendment to Revocable License Furnished Senator Nelson by U.S. Coast Guard Commandant Admiral E. J. Roland," March 16, 1964, WCD Files, box 122, folder 20.

26. Badtke, "Oak Leaf Anchor at Eagle Light."

27. D. N. Anderson, "Eagle Lighthouse National Register of Historic Places Nomination Form," 1970, at Preservation Division, Wisconsin Historical Society.

28. *Door County Advocate,* October 18–19, 2003.

Chapter 6. Thomas Reynolds, John Nolen, and Legislation to Establish the Park

1. *Racine Daily Times,* February 10, 1897.

2. Wisconsin Department of Natural Resources, Parks and Recreation Program, "Wisconsin State Parks for the Year 2000," 1987. Report on file at Wisconsin Department of Natural Resources Library, Madison.

3. *Wisconsin Blue Book* (Madison: Democratic Printing Company, 1917), 446.

4. Warren Manning, "Dalles of the St. Croix," *Wisconsin Blue Book* (Madison: Democrat Printing Company, 1905), 979.

5. Chapter 232, 1903 Wis. Laws.

6. Chapter 169, 1905 Wis. Laws.

7. See also W. H. McFetridge, "The Proposed Devil's Lake State Park," *Wisconsin Arbor and Bird-Day Annual* (1908).

8. Chapter 495, 1907 Wis. Laws.

9. *Wisconsin Blue Book* (Madison: Democratic Printing Company, 1909), 1115.

10. Chapter 560, 1907 Wis. Laws.

11. Wisconsin State Park Board, Minutes, July 23, 1909, 1.

12. Mollenhoff, *Madison,* 338.

13. Nolen to Olin, March 11, 1908, Nolen Papers.

14. Nolen to Olin, March 17, 1908, box 7, folder 105, Van Hise Papers, University of Wisconsin Archives, Madison.

15. Miscellaneous correspondence and reports in Nolen Papers.

16. Nolen Papers, 1908.

17. *Door County Democrat,* April 25, 1908.

18. *Door County Democrat,* May 2, 1908.

19. *Door County Democrat,* May 16, 1908.

20. Olin to Nolen, July 11, 1908, Nolen Papers.

21. Brittingham to Senator H. R. Bird, July 27, 1908, Davidson Papers, box 24.

22. *Door County Advocate,* August 6, 1908.

23. Nolen, *State Parks for Wisconsin,* 30.

24. *Daily Eagle-Star,* August 8, 1908.

25. Ibid.

26. *Door County Democrat,* August 8, 1908.

27. *Daily Eagle-Star,* August 6, 1908.

28. *Door County Democrat,* August, 8, 1908.

29. *Madison Democrat,* August 8, August 9, and August 13, 1908.

30. *Madison Democrat,* August 9, 1908.

31. *Milwaukee Sentinel,* August 16, 1908.

32. Nolen Papers.

33. Ibid.

34. Gruber, *Diamond Anniversary.*

35. Nolen Papers.

36. *Madison Democrat,* August 8, 1908

37. Nolen, *State Parks for Wisconsin,* 35.

38. Ibid., 9, 12, 13, 24, 30–32.

39. Ibid., 30–32.

40. Ibid., 38.

41. Governor's Address, January 14, 1909, *Journal of the Proceedings of the Forty-Ninth Session of the Wisconsin Legislature,* 41.

42. 106, S, 1909 Wis. Laws.

43. 147, A, 1909 Wis. Laws.

44. 147, A, 1909 Wis. Laws, amendment no. 1A.

45. Bill 180, A, 1909.

46. Bill 150, S 1909.

47. Chapter 327, 1909 Wis. Laws.

48. Reynolds, "Plea for the Door County Park," *Assembly Journal* 2 (1909): 1065–67.

49. H. P. Bird letter to editor of the *Door County Democrat* (June 9, 1909), in Wisconsin State Park Board, Minutes, 8.

50. Olin to Nolen, 1908, Nolen Papers.

51. *Door County News,* January 16, 1919.

Chapter 7. Naming the Park and Purchasing the Land

1. Brittingham to Bird, July 27, 1908, Davidson Papers, box 24; Wisconsin State Park Board, Minutes, April 13, 1910, 16.

2. *Door County Advocate,* December 24, 1908.

3. *Door County Advocate,* March 18, 1909.

4. Stevenson to Davidson, August 11, 1909, Davidson Papers, box 28.

5. Wisconsin State Park Board, Minutes, June 24, 1910, 7.

6. *Door County Democrat,* June 23, 1911.

7. *Door County Democrat,* February 17, 1911.

8. *Algoma Herald,* February 2, 1911.

9. *Milwaukee Daily News,* June 19, 1911.

10. *Door County Democrat,* July 8, 1908.

11. Van Hise to Alice R. Van Hise, July 16, 1910, box 4, Van Hise Papers, University of Wisconsin Archives, Madison.

12. *Door County Democrat,* July 28, 1911.

13. *Door County Advocate,* January 28, 1909.

14. *Door County Advocate,* February 4, 1909.

15. *Door County Democrat,* February 13, 1909.

16. *Door County Advocate,* February 18, 1909.

17. *Door County Advocate,* February 25, 1909.

18. *Door County Democrat,* March 6, 1909.

19. *Door County Advocate,* March 4, 1909.

20. *Door County Advocate,* March 6, 1909.

21. Ibid.

22. *Door County Advocate,* February 18, 1909.

23. *Door County Democrat,* March 20, 1909.

24. *Door County Advocate,* April 1, 1909.

25. Quoted in *Door County Democrat,* March 27, 1909.

26. *Milwaukee Free Press,* March 14, 1909.

27. Wisconsin State Park Board, Minutes, July 23, 1909.

28. *Door County Democrat,* August 21, 1909.

29. Sholem, *Horseshoe Island,* 28.

30. *Door County Advocate,* January 12, 1911.

31. Wisconsin State Park Board, Minutes, February 16, 1914.

32. *Door County News,* November 7, 1912.

33. *Door County Democrat,* March 24, 1916.

34. *Door County Advocate,* November 12, 1943.

Chapter 8. The Doolittle Years

1. *Door County Democrat,* July 24, 1913.

2. *Door County Democrat,* August 8, 1913.

3. Doolittle, *Boulder Junction.*

4. Wisconsin State Park Board, Minutes, September 4, 1913, 39.

5. *Door County Democrat,* December 25, 1914.

6. *Door County News,* November 13, 1913.

7. *Door County Democrat,* January 9, 1914.

8. *Door County Democrat,* January 16, 1914.

9. *Door County Advocate,* November 13, 1914.

10. Wisconsin State Park Board, Minutes, February 16, 1914, 40.

11. *Minneapolis Journal,* April 5, 1914.

12. *Door County Democrat,* April 1, 1914.

13. *Door County Democrat,* July 2, 1914.

14. *Door County Democrat,* December 24, 1914.

15. Several early picture postcards in the author's possession show this flagpole.

16. Clarise (Erickson) Berns to Tom Blackwood, July 27, 1993. On file at Peninsula State Park office.

17. A. E. Doolittle, "Park Superintendent's Notebook," 103. On file at Peninsula State Park Office.

18. "Biennial Report of Wisconsin Conservation Department, 1915–16."

19. *Door County Democrat,* January 8, 1915.

20. *Door County News,* March 1, 1916.

21. *Door County Democrat,* September 10, 1915.

22. *Door County Democrat,* April 21, 1916.

23. *Door County Democrat,* June 23, 1916.

24. *Door County Democrat,* July 14, 1916.

25. *Door County Advocate,* August 3, 1916, quoted from *Post Crescent.*

26. *Door County Advocate,* August 24, 1916.

27. *Door County News,* February 7, 1917.

28. *Door County Democrat,* May 4, 1917.

29. *Door County News,* ovember 29, 1917.

30. "Biennial Report of Wisconsin Conservation Commission, 1917–18," 84–87. Five thousand seems to be an exaggeration, since the *Door County News* stated that the largest crowd was at the Peace Day Celebration in 1919, where Doolittle estimated that one thousand automobiles came.

31. *Door County Democrat,* March 8, 1918.

32. *Door County News,* September 26, 1918.

33. *Door County Democrat,* May 10, 1919.

34. *Door County News,* August 14, 1919.

35. *Door County News,* August 5, 1920.

36. *Door County News,* September 7, 1922.

37. *Door County Advocate,* December 5, 1930.

38. *Door County Advocate,* May 18, 1932.

39. *Door County Advocate,* February 27, 1925.

40. *Door County News,* March 26, 1925.

41. *Door County Advocate,* August 20, 1926.

42. *Door County News,* November 25, 1926.

43. *Door County Advocate,* November 26, 1926.

44. *Door County News,* July 21, 1927.

45. *Door County News,* February 2, 1928.

46. W. B. Grange to Harry Johnson, November 12, 1929, WCD Files, box 374, folder 12.

47. *Door County Advocate,* July 5, 1929.

48. *Door County Advocate,* September 12, 1941.

49. Memo to Conservation Commission, November 30, 1954, WCD Files, box 122, folder 3.

50. Harrington to Otto A. Vogel, September 27, 1940, WCD Files, box 128, folder 5.

51. Harrington to David Sigman, January 10, 1936, WCD Files, box 128, folder 4.

52. *Chicago Tribune,* December 22, 1929.

53. *Door County Advocate,* May 4, 1934.

54. *Door County Advocate,* March 7, 1930.

55. *Door County Advocate,* June 13, 1930.

56. *Door County Advocate,* November 14, 1930.

57. *Door County Advocate,* February 11, 1921.

58. *Milwaukee Journal,* September 18, 1925.

59. Quoted in *Door County Advocate,* August 22, 1934.

60. *Door County Advocate,* February 13, 1931.

61. *Green Bay Press Gazette,* September 8, 1932.

62. *Door County Advocate,* July 20, 1939.

63. *Door County Advocate,* July 14, 1933.

64. *Door County Advocate,* September 6, 1935.

65. George F. Ingalls to M. W. Torkelson, August 5, 1937, WCD Files, box 901, folder 3.

66. Wisconsin State Planning Board, *Attendance and Use of the State Parks.*

Chapter 9. Camp Meenahga

1. In 1933 Mrs. Clark married Laurence Sturgis Day, who died in 1950; she subsequently married James B. Peddle in 1955. Alice Clark Peddle, Clark's daughter, later wrote several accounts of how the camp began and of spending her early summers in Fish Creek. One of her essays was included in a two-volume report, "Fish Creek, the Summertime," edited by Betsy Guenzel in 1991. The author is indebted to Carol Krug and John Notz for this manuscript. Peddle's essay was later published in *Fish Creek Echoes,* ed. Kinsey and Schreiber. She also gave an informative summary of her recollections about the camp in an address to the Door County Historical Society in 1976.

2. Alice Clark Peddle, manuscript of address given to the Door County Historical Society, 2. On file at the Nolen Room, Sturgeon Bay Library.

3. Alice Clark Day, *Pack and Paddle* (St. Louis: privately published, 1940), 26.

4. Alice Clark, "Camp Meenahga," 4. Typewritten paper on file at Peninsula State Park office.

5. Ibid., 3.

6. *Door County Democrat,* July 14, 1916.

7. *Door County News,* September 6, 1916.

8. Peddle, "Fish Creek and Camp Meenahga Summers," 58.

9. F. W. Mabley and A. O. Clark, "Camp Peninsular State Park, Fish Creek, Wisconsin" (1919). Brochure on file at Wisconsin Historical Society.

10. *Door County News,* July 6, 1920.

11. *Pack and Paddle,* 1942, 23.

12. *Pack and Paddle,* 1927, 28.

13. *Pack and Paddle,* 1917, 8–9.

14. *Pack and Paddle,* 1920, 27; 1921, 23.

15. *Pack and Paddle,* 1919, 10; 1920, 9; 1922, 43.

16. *Pack and Paddle,* 1917, 13.

17. *Pack and Paddle,* 1923, 12.

18. *Pack and Paddle,* 1923, 22.

19. *Pack and Paddle,* 1918, 5.

20. *Pack and Paddle,* 1923, 8.

21. *Pack and Paddle,* 1930, 29–30.

22. *Pack and Paddle,* 1918, 6.

23. *Door County Advocate,* August 15, 1919.

24. *Pack and Paddle,* 1921, 27.

25. *Pack and Paddle,* 1940, 26.

26. *Pack and Paddle,* 1938, 4.

27. *Pack and Paddle,* 1922, 63.

28. *Pack and Paddle,* 1921, 1.

29. *Pack and Paddle,* 1918, 24.

30. *Pack and Paddle,* 1940, 27.

31. C. L. Harrington to Paul D. Kelleter, director, Wisconsin Conservation Department, February 27, 1931, WCD Files, box 102.

32. For example, see the 1920 issue of *Pack and Paddle.*

33. 1916 expense list attached to Alice Clark and Fanny Mabley letter to Wisconsin Conservation Commission, March 2, 1931, WCD Files, box 897, folder 5. This detailed list indicates all camp buildings and major camp equipment items.

34. Edmunds, *The Loving Spice of Life,* 235.

35. *Pack and Paddle,* 1923, 14.

36. *Pack and Paddle,* 1920, 36.

37. *Pack and Paddle,* 1921, 6.

38. *Pack and Paddle,* 1922, 20.

39. Lucia Woods Lindley to author, July 5, 2001.

40. Mary Ellen (Jensen) Dietz to Laurence C. Day, February 21, 2001, in Day's possession.

Chapter 10. The Golf Course

1. Wisconsin State Park Board, Minutes, February 16, 1914, 40.

2. A. E. Doolittle, Park Superintendent's Notebook, "Fish Creek Golf Links, No. 4 Summer 1914," and "Cost, Ephraim Golf Links No. 6," 106. On file at Peninsula State Park office.

3. *Door County Democrat,* December 25, 1914.

4. *Door County Democrat,* February 20, 1914.

5. *Door County Democrat,* June 12, 1914.

6. *Door County Democrat,* July 24, 1914.

7. *Door County Democrat,* October 1, 1915.

8. Wisconsin Conservation Department, "Memorandum for State Conservation Commission," July 1, 1915, Misc. Subject File, box 5, C. L. Harrington Papers, Wisconsin Historical Society, Madison.

9. *Door County News,* April 12, 1916.

10. *Door County Democrat,* June 23, 1916.

11. *Door County Democrat,* April 21, 1916.

12. *Door County Democrat,* March 23, 1917.

13. *Door County News,* December 28, 1916.

14. *Door County Democrat,* August 3, 1917.

15. *Door County Advocate,* June 3, 1921.

16. *Door County Advocate,* May 28, 1993.

17. *Door County Advocate,* March 14, 1924.

18. *Door County Advocate,* January 16, 1925.

19. *Door County Advocate,* September 18, 1925.

20. *Door County News,* October 28, 1926.

21. *Door County Advocate,* August 22, 1930.

22. *Door County Advocate,* July 30, 1991.

23. Jack Notabaart, "Peninsula Park Golf Course, Some Recollections of the Golf Pro Jack Notabaart: 1941 through 1954," undated, unpaged report on file in Peninsula State Park office.

24. *Door County Advocate,* September 19, 1941.

25. Lowell Hansen, undated, typewritten report, on file in Peninsula State Park office.

26. Dennis McCann, "Peninsula Park Course Designed by Nature," *Milwaukee Journal,* September 1, 1996.

Chapter 11. Potawatomi

1. *Door County Advocate,* November 3, 1944.

2. *Door County Advocate,* March 22, 1962.

3. Dennis East, "Conservation Reminiscences of Frank N. Graass," January 28, 1965, Frank N. Graas Papers, Wisconsin Historical Society, Madison.

4. U.S. Army Corps of Engineers, *Chart of Sturgeon Bay.*

5. Holand, *History of Door County,* 167.

6. Ibid., 438.

7. *Door County Advocate,* January 16, 1904.

8. *Door County Advocate,* February 18, 1909.

9. East, "Reminiscences of Graass."

10. *Green Bay Press Gazette,* July 20, 1923; *Door County News,* July 12, 1923.

11. *Green Bay Press Gazette,* July 20, 1923; *Manitowoc Herald News,* July 27, 1923. Portions of these articles were reprinted in the *Door County Advocate,* August 3, 1923.

12. *Door County Advocate,* September 28, 1923.

13. *Door County Advocate,* January 28, 1924.

14. *Door County Advocate,* December 20, 1923.

15. *Door County News,* September 26, 1924.

16. *Door County News,* January 19, 1928.

17. *Door County Advocate,* March 23, 1928; *Door County News,* April 12, 1928.

18. *Door County Advocate,* May 4, 1928.

19. *Door County News,* September 6, 1928.

20. Quoted in *Door County Advocate,* April 20, 1928.

21. *Door County Advocate,* April 20, 1928.

22. *Door County News,* May 9, 1929.

23. *Door County Advocate,* August 30, 1929.

24. *Door County Advocate,* October 25, 1929.

25. *Door County Advocate,* August 21, 1931, and September 24, 1931.

26. *Door County Advocate,* October 9, 1931.

Chapter 12. Camp Peninsular and the CCC

1. *Door County News,* October 12, 1933.

2. Ermentrout, *Forgotten Men,* 76.

3. Fechner, "Civilian Conservation Corps."

4. Ibid.

5. Dennis McCann, "Outdoors Lovers of Today Can Thank CCC of Yesterday for Parks, Trees," *Milwaukee Journal Sentinel,* August 11, 1998.

6. Carr, *Wilderness by Design,* 257.

7. McCann, "Outdoor Lovers"; CCC, *Sparta Civilian Conservation Corps Sixth Corps Area Annual,* 25.

8. Pager, "Civilian Conservation Corps Program," 11.

9. CCC, *Sparta Annual* 25.

10. McCann, "Outdoors Lovers."

11. Newton, *Design on the Land,* 576.

12. Ermentrout, *Forgotten Men,* 77.

13. Ibid., 88.

14. Ibid., 82.

15. Salmond, *Civilian Conservation Corps,* 137–39.

16. Ibid., 141.

17. Ermentrout, *Forgotten Men,* 84, 87.

18. *Door County Advocate,* February 1, 1935.

19. *Door County News,* February 7, 1935.

20. *Door County Advocate,* February 15, 1935.

21. *Door County Advocate,* March 8, 1935.

22. *Camp Peninsular Breeze,* January 1937. Microfiche at Wisconsin Historical Society.

23. *Door County Advocate,* August 9, 1935.

24. *Door County News,* August 15, 1935.

25. *Door County Advocate,* October 4, 1935.

26. *Camp Peninsular Breeze,* February 1937.

27. CCC, *Sparta Annual,* 189.

28. *Door County Advocate,* March 12, 1936.

29. *Camp Peninsular Breeze,* October 29, 1936.

30. *Camp Peninsular Breeze,* March 1937.

31. Albert H. Good, *Park and Recreation Structures* (Washington, DC: Government Printing Office, 1938), 5, 6.

32. *Door County News,* August 22, 1935.

33. *Door County Advocate,* September 27, 1935.

34. G. H. Nickell, "Narrative Report for October and November," 1935, record group 79, box 140, National Archives.

35. Burnett to Hannon, May 12, 1936, record group 79, box 242, National Archives.

36. *Door County Advocate,* December 27, 1935.

37. *Door County Advocate,* September 27, 1935.

38. *Door County Advocate,* February 21, 1936.

39. *Camp Peninsular Breeze,* October 29, 1936.

40. *Camp Peninsular Breeze,* July 25, 1936.

41. *Door County Advocate,* October 2, 1936.

42. *Camp Peninsular Breeze,* January 1937.

43. Wisconsin Bureau of Engineering, Architectural Drawings for Wisconsin Parks in the WPA Period, series 2424, box 3, December 9, 1936. On file at Archives Division, Wisconsin Historical Society, Madison.

44. *Door County Advocate,* June 11 and June 18, 1937.

45. *Door County News,* November 5, 1936.

46. *Door County Advocate,* April 9, 1937.

47. *Door County Advocate,* June 25, 1937.

48. *Door County Advocate,* July 2, 1930.

49. *Door County News,* September 23, 1937.

50. Sanderson to Harrington, January 1, 1938, WCD Files, box 899.

51. *Door County Advocate,* March 18, 1938.

52. *Door County Advocate,* May 21, 1937.

53. *Door County Advocate,* April 9, 1937.

54. *Camp Peninsular Breeze,* October 29, 1936.

Chapter 13. The CCC Controversy

1. *Saturday Evening Post,* December 18, 1934, 2.

2. *Door County Advocate,* May 9, 1935.

3. Jensen to La Follette, July 25, 1935, box 9, Jens Jensen Papers, Morton Arboretum, Lisle, IL.

4. *Door County Advocate,* August 16, 1935.

5. *Door County Advocate,* September 6, 1935.

6. *Door County News,* March 12, 1936.

7. Abramson and Erickson to W. H. MacKenzie, March 24, 1936, WCD Files, box 901, folder 8. The resolution was signed by Walter M. Abramson, the organization's secretary, and August W. Erickson.

8. *Door County Advocate,* March 20, 1936.

9. Grafton to District Commander, Sparta CCC District, March 20, 1936, box 149, RG 79, National Archives.

10. Hollister to Fifth Regional Office, National Park Service, March 21, 1936, WCD Files, box 901, folder 8.

11. Ibid.

12. Ibid.

13. Ibid.

14. Burnett to Harrington, March 27, 1936, WCD Files, box 901, folder 8.

15. Jensen to Malcolm Dill, April 2, 1936, WCD Files, box 901, folder 8.

16. Harrington to Abramson, April 3, 1936, WCD Files, box 901, folder 8.

17. Holand to Harrington, April 6, 1936, WCD Files, box 901, folder 8.

18. *Milwaukee Journal,* May 7, 1936.

19. *Door County News,* April 7, 1936.

20. Fred Bishop to McKenzie, March 24, 1936, WCD Filese, box 901, folder 8; H. "Skipper" Noyes to MacKenzie, July 2, 1936, WCD Files, box 901, folder 8.

21. *Door County Advocate,* July 6, 1936.

22. Paul Bertschinger to Door County Board of Supervisors, May 6, 1936, WCD Files, box 901, folder 8.

23. Johnstone to Fifth Regional Office, National Park Service, May 11, 1936, box 247, RG 79, National Archives.

24. LaPlant to Harrington, May 8, 1936, WCD Files, box 901, folder 8.

25. Hannon to J. J. McEntee, May 14, 1936, box 242, RG 79, National Archives.

26. Holand to Harrington, June 16, 1936, WCD Files, box 901, folder 8.

27. Harrington to Viste, June 15, 1936, WCD Files, box 901, folder 8; Harrington to Holand, June 22, 1936, WCD Files, box 901, folder 8.

28. Holand to Harrington, June 24, 1936, WCD Files, box 901, folder 8.

29. Johnston to Regional Office, Region Two, National Park Service, November 21, 1936, WCD Files, box 490.

30. Harrington to Schneider, November 25, 1936, WCD Files, box 901, folder 1.

Chapter 14. Winter Sports

1. *Door County Advocate,* January 11, 1946.
2. *Door County Advocate,* March 22, 1935.
3. *Door County Advocate,* April 5, 1935.
4. *Door County Advocate,* July 5, 1935.
5. *Door County Advocate,* July 12, 1935.
6. *Door County Advocate,* September 19, 1935.
7. *Door County Advocate,* November 29, 1935.
8. *Door County Advocate,* December 20, 1935.
9. *Door County Advocate,* January 31, 1936.
10. *Green Bay Press Gazette,* June 15, 1938.
11. *Door County Advocate,* March 4, 1938.
12. *Door County Advocate,* March 11, 1938.
13. *Door County Advocate,* March 18, 1938.
14. Ibid.
15. *Door County Advocate,* December 16, 1938.
16. *Door County Advocate,* February 24, 1939.
17. *Door County Advocate,* March 3, 1939.
18. *Door County Advocate,* March 10, 1939.
19. *Door County News,* March 9, 1939.
20. *Door County Advocate,* February 2, 1940.
21. *Door County Advocate,* September 19, 1941.
22. *Door County Advocate,* March 29, 1984.
23. *Door County Advocate,* February 27, 1942.
24. *Door County Advocate,* February 26, 1943.
25. *Door County Advocate,* March 29, 1984.
26. *Door County Advocate,* December 12, 1942.

Chapter 15. World War II and Beyond at the Park

1. *Door County Advocate,* July 12, 1944, and July 27, 1977.
2. Beckstrom to Harrington, March 20, 1948, WCD Files, box 21.
3. Harrington to C. R. Corbett, September 19, 1952, WCD Files, box 122.
4. *Capital Times,* September 13, 1936.
5. Jensen to Evjue, November 24, 1936, Jens Jensen Papers, Morton Arboretum, Lisle, IL.
6. Evjue to Jensen, November 24, 1936, Jens Jensen Papers, Morton Arboretum, Lisle, IL.
7. *Capital Times,* July 31, 1941.

8. *Capital Times,* August 21, 1941.

9. *Capital Times,* January 6, 1943.

10. Jensen to Longenecker, February 27, 1944, Friends of Our Native Landscape papers, in author's possession.

11. Wisconsin Conservation Department publication, undated, in author's possession.

12. Retzer, "Peninsula Park—and Its Problems."

13. Hansen to Koenings, November 24, 1959, WCD Files, box 128.

14. Halvorson, "Thirty-Seven Years."

15. *Door County Advocate,* March 7, 2003.

Bibliography

Ahern, Katherine. *Cultural Landscape Bibliography: An Annotated Bibliography on Resources in the National Park System*. Washington, DC: Government Printing Office, 1992.

Ahlgren, Carol Ann. "A Human and Landscape Architectural Legacy: The Influence of the Civilian Conservation Corps on Wisconsin State Park Development." Master's thesis, University of Wisconsin–Madison, 1987.

———. "The Civilian Conservation Corps and Wisconsin State Park Development." *Wisconsin Magazine of History* 71 (Spring 1988): 184–204.

Aust, F. A. "General Park System for Wisconsin." Typewritten manuscript in the author's possession, 1922.

Avery, Thomas. *The Mystery Ship from Nineteen Fathoms*. Au Train, MI: Avery Color Studies, 1974.

Badtke, Frances. *Eagle Lighthouse*. Sturgeon Bay, WI: Door County Publishing Co., 1964.

———. "Oak Leaf Anchor at Eagle Light." *Peninsula* 8 (Summer 1969): 31–33.

Bassford, George Ainslee. "The Economic Influence of Lake Michigan in the Development of Marinette, Oconto, Door and Kewaunee Counties." Bachelor of philosophy thesis, University of Wisconsin, 1917.

Borke, Judith Joy. "Wisconsin's State Park System, 1878–1994: An Oral History." Master's thesis, University of Wisconsin–Madison, 1987.

Bosman, Peter. *Lighthouses and Range Lights of Door County, Wisconsin*. Ellison Bay, WI: Wm. Caxton, 2000.

Brown, Charles E. "A Record of Wisconsin Antiquities." *Wisconsin Archeologist* 5, nos. 3–4 (April to October 1906): 289–429.

Brown, Charles E., and Karyl Chipman. "Indian Mounds in Wisconsin State Parks." *Wisconsin Archeologist*, n.s., 15, no. 1 (July 1935): 1–9.

Burton, Paul, and Frances Burton. *Door County Stories*. Ephraim, WI: Stonehill, 2003.

———. *Ephraim's Founding Father: The Story of Reverend A. M. Inverson.* Ephraim, WI: Stonehill, 1996.

———. *Ephraim Stories.* Ephraim, WI: Stonehill, 1999.

Carr, Ethan. *Wilderness by Design: Landscape Architecture and the National Park Service.* Lincoln: University of Nebraska Press, 1998.

Cetin, Frank. "Lighthouses: Sentinels of the Inland Seas." *Wisconsin Tales and Trails* (Autumn 1966): 22–27.

Civilian Conservation Corps. *Sparta Civilian Conservation Corps Sixth Corps Area Annual, 1937.* Baton Rouge, LA: Direct Advertising, 1937.

Cohen, Stan. *The Tree Army: A Pictorial History of the Civilian Conservation Corps, 1933–1942.* Missoula, MT: Pictorial Histories, 1980.

Curtis, John T. *The Vegetation of Wisconsin: An Ordination of Plant Communities.* Madison: University of Wisconsin Press, 1959.

Damm, James J. "Development of Wisconsin's Park and Forest Recreation System, 1867–1967." Master's thesis, University of Wisconsin, 1968.

Davidson, James O., Papers. On file at the Wisconsin Historical Society Archives, Madison.

Dee, Harry. "A Yacht Ride and What Came of It." *Our Young People* (September 1913): 18.

Department of Landscape Architecture and Wisconsin Conservation Department. Park Management Seminar, University of Wisconsin–Madison, 1965. Report on file at Steenbock Library, Madison.

Dirst, Victoria. *An Archaeological Survey at the Shanty Bay Site in Peninsula State Park, Door County, Wisconsin.* Madison: Wisconsin Department of Natural Resources, 1987.

———. *An Archaeological Survey for a New Septic System in Peninsula State Park, Door County, Wisconsin.* Madison: Wisconsin Department of Natural Resources, 1990.

———. *Shanty Bay: A Great Place to Camp in Door County, Wisconsin.* Madison: Wisconsin Department of Natural Resources, 1995.

Doolittle, Shirley. *Boulder Junction: The Early Years, 1880s to 1950s.* Boulder Junction, WI: Friends of the Library, 1996.

Edmunds, Adeline. *The Loving Spice of Life.* Sturgeon Bay, WI: A. Edmunds, 1980.

Erixon, Sigurd. "The North-European Technique of Corner Timbering." *Folkliv* 1 (1937): 13–63.

Ermentrout, Robert. *Forgotten Men: The Civilian Conservation Corps.* Smithtown, NY: Exposition Press, 1982.

Fapso, Richard J. *Norwegians in Wisconsin.* Madison: State Historical Society of Wisconsin, 1977.

Fechner, Robert. "The Civilian Conservation Corps." *Annals of the American Academy of Political and Social Sciences* 194 (November 1937): 129–40.

Geib, W. J., Carl Thompson, and H. V. Geib. *Soil Survey of Door County, Wisconsin.* Washington, DC: Government Printing Office, 1918.

Gould's St. Louis Directory for 1915. St. Louis: Gould Directory Company, 1915.

Gruber, Bonnie. *The Diamond Anniversary: Seventy-five Years of Devil's Lake State Park.* Ed. Kendra Nelson. Madison: Wisconsin Department of Natural Resources, 1986.

Hagene, Margaret Fitzgerald. "Peninsula State Park in the 1920s." Address, meeting of the Door County Historical Society, September 20, 1976. Typewritten manuscript on file at the Laurie Room of the Door County Library, Sturgeon Bay, Wisconsin.

Hale, James B. *Going for the Mail: A History of Door County Post Offices.* Green Bay, WI: Brown County Historical Society, 1996.

Halvorsen, Ralph. "Thirty-seven Years with the State of Wisconsin Department of Natural Resources." Address, meeting of the Door County Historical Society, November 19, 1973. Typewritten manuscript on file at the Peninsula State Park office.

Harrington, C. L. "The Needs of a More Comprehensive State Park System." In Wisconsin State Planning Board, *Lands for State Parks,* 79–84.

Hershbell, Kristin E., ed. *Door County and the Niagara Escarpment: Foundations for the Future.* Madison: Wisconsin Academy of Sciences, Arts and Letters, 1989.

Historical Atlas of Wisconsin. Milwaukee: Snyder, Van Vechten, 1878.

Holand, Hjalmar R. "Ceremonies Attending the Funeral of Simon Kahguados." Sponsored by the Door County Historical Society and the State Conservation Commission, May 30, 1931.

———. "Glimpses of Door County by Early Travelers." *Peninsula Historical Review* 6 (April 1932): 1–22.

———. *History of Door County, Wisconsin.* Chicago: S. J. Clark, 1917.

———. *Old Peninsula Days: Tales and Sketches of the Door County Peninsula.* Ephraim, WI: Pioneer Press, 1925.

Hubbard, Nancy J. *1991 State Facilities Survey: Reconnaissance Survey Report.* Milwaukee: University of Wisconsin–Milwaukee, 1991.

Hyde, Charles K. *The Northern Lights: Lighthouses of the Upper Great Lakes.* Lansing, MI: TwoPeninsula Press, 1986.

Illustrated Atlas of Door County, Wisconsin. Oshkosh, WI: Randall and Williams, 1899.

Jensen, Jens. "The 'Why' of Parks and Wilderness Areas." In Wisconsin State Planning Board, *Lands for State Parks,* 3–4.

Kahlert, John. *Pioneer Cemeteries, Door County, Wisconsin.* Baileys Harbor, WI: Meadow Lane, 1981.

Karges, Steven. *Keepers of the Lights.* Ellison Bay, WI: Wm. Caxton, 2000.

Kuhm, Herbert W. "Indian Place Names in Wisconsin." *Wisconsin Archeologist* 33 (1952): 1–157.

Lange, Kenneth I. *Ancient Rocks and Vanished Glaciers: A Natural History of Devil's Lake State Park, Wisconsin.* Madison: Wisconsin Department of Natural Resources, 1989.

Lange, Kenneth I., and D. Debra Berndt. "Devil's Lake State Park: The History of Its Establishment." *Transactions* 68 (1980): 149–66.

Lange, Kenneth I., and Ralph T. Tuttle. *A Lake Where Spirits Live: A Human History of the Midwest's Most Popular Park.* Madison: Wisconsin Department of Natural Resources, 1975.

Lapham, I. A., J. G. Knapp, and H. Crocker. *Report on the Disastrous Effects of the Destruction of Forest Trees, Now Going On So Rapidly in the State of Wisconsin.* Madison: Atwood and Rublee, 1867.

Link, Ernest G., Steven L. Elmer, and Sidney A. Vanderveen. *Soil Survey of Door County, Wisconsin.* Washington, DC: U.S. Department of Agriculture and University of Wisconsin, 1978.

Lotz, Marvin. *Discovering Door County's Past.* Fish Creek, WI: Holly House Press, 1994.

Lukes, Roy. *The Ridges Sanctuary: Its History, Geology, Plants, and Animals.* Baileys Harbor, WI: Ridges Sanctuary, 1988.

Martin, Chas. I. *History of Door County, Wisconsin: Together with Biographies of Nearly Seven Hundred Families, and Mention of Four Thousand Persons.* Sturgeon Bay, WI: Expositor Job Print, 1881.

Martin, Lawrence. *The Physical Geography of Wisconsin.* Madison: University of Wisconsin Press, 1963.

McFetridge, William H. *An Appeal for the Preservation of the Devils Lake Region.* Baraboo, WI: privately printed, 1906.

Mollenhoff, David V. *Madison: A History of the Formative Years.* Dubuque, IA: Kendall Hunt, 1984.

Mueller, A. "The Geology and Physiography of Wisconsin State Parks." Master's thesis, University of Wisconsin, 1927.

Newton, Norman T. *Design on the Land: The Development of Landscape Architecture.* Cambridge, MA: Harvard University Press, 1971.

Nolen, John. Papers. Rare and Manuscript Collections. On file at the Carl A. Kroch Library, Cornell University Library, Ithaca, New York.

———. *State Parks for Wisconsin.* Madison, WI: State Park Board, 1909.

Nolte, M. Chester, ed. *The Civilian Conservation Corps: The Way We Remember It, 1933–1942.* Paducah, KY: Turner, 1990.

Pager, John. "The Civilian Conservation Corps Program with Emphasis on Wisconsin." *Proceedings of the 8th Annual Meeting of the Forest History Association of Wisconsin* (1983): 11.

Paige, John C. *The Civilian Conservation Corps and the National Park Service, 1933–1942: An Administrative History.* Washington, DC: Government Printing Office, 1985.

Peddle, Alice Clark. "Fish Creek and Camp Meenahga Summers." In *Fish Creek Echoes: A Century of Life in a Door County Village,* ed. Virginia Kinsey and Edward Schreiber. Fish Creek, WI: John and Nancy Sargent, 2000.

Petterson, Lucille, trans. and ed. "Ephraim Is My Home Now: Letters of Anna and Anders Petterson, 1884–1889 (Part 1)." *Wisconsin Magazine of History* 69 (Spring 1986): 187–210.

Raney, William F. *Wisconsin, a Story of Progress.* New York: Prentice-Hall, 1940.

Retzer, F. H. "Peninsula Park—and Its Problems." *Wisconsin Conservation Bulletin* (May 1957): 3–6.

Ritzenthaler, Robert E. "Wisconsin Petroglyphs and Pictographs." *Wisconsin Archeologist*, n.s., 31, no. 4 (December 1950): 83–129.

Salmond, John A. *The Civilian Conservation Corps, 1933–1942: A New Deal Case Study.* Durham, NC: Duke University Press, 1967.

Schumacher, J. P. "Indian Remains in Door County." *Wisconsin Archaeologist* 16, no. 4 (January 1918): 134–42.

Sholem, Stanford H. *Horseshoe Island: The Folda Years.* Ephraim, WI: Ephraim Foundation, 1998.

Stapleton, Grover. "Tom Reynolds and the Peninsula State Park." *Peninsula Historical Review* 3 (June 1958): 1–6.

State Conservation Commission. *State Parks of Wisconsin.* Bulletin, no. 6. Madison, 1922.

Stevens, David. "Ole Larson of Door County." *Peninsula* 4 (May 1959): 2.

Storrow, Samuel A. "The Northwest in 1817." *Wisconsin Historical Collections* 6 (1872).

Tishler, William H. "John Nolen and the New Era of American Planning." *Historic Madison* 12 (1995).

Tishler, William H., and Erik Ghenoiu. "Conservation Pioneers: Jens Jensen and the Friends of Our Native Landscape." *Wisconsin Magazine of History* 86, no. 4 (Summer 2003): 2–15.

Treichel, Sally. "Door County Cemetery Index, Vol. I." Manuscript on file in the Door County Library, Sturgeon Bay, n.d.

U.S. Army Corps of Engineers. *Chart of Sturgeon Bay, Canal and Harbor of Refuge, Lake Michigan.* Washington, DC: Headquarters Corps of Engineers, U.S. Army, 1901.

U.S. Department of Agriculture. *Soil Survey of Door County, Wisconsin.* Washington, DC: Government Printing Office, 1918.

U.S. Department of Commerce. *United States Lighthouse Service Annual Report, 1915.* Washington, DC: Government Printing Office, 1915.

Vanderwall, E. J. "Historical Background of the Wisconsin State Park System." 1953. Typewritten manuscript on file at the Wisconsin Historical Society, Madison.

Wardius, Ken, and Barb Wardius. *Wisconsin Lighthouses: A Photographic and Historical Guide.* Madison, WI: Prairie Oak Press, 2000.

Weiss, George. *The Lighthouse Service: Its History, Activities, and Organization.* Baltimore: Johns Hopkins Press, 1926.

Wisconsin Conservation Department. Files. 1917–67. On file at the Wisconsin Historical Society, Madison.

———. "Wisconsin State Parks." Madison, 1933. On file at the Wisconsin Department of Natural Resources Library, Madison.

Wisconsin Department of Agriculture, Land Use Section. "Door County, Wisconsin Land Cover Maps." Series 1955. On file at the Wisconsin Historical Society Archives, Madison.

Wisconsin Department of Natural Resources. "A Century of Wisconsin State Parks History." Madison, 2000. Report on file at the Wisconsin Department of Natural Resources Library, Madison.

———. "Potawatomi State Park Master Plan Concept Element." Madison, 1987. Report on file at the Wisconsin Department of Natural Resources Library, Madison.

Wisconsin State Park Board. "Minutes of Meetings, July 23, 1909, to July 13, 1912, by L. C. Colman, secretary; September 16, 1913, to November 5, 1915 (?), by E. M. Griffith, acting secretary." On file at the Wisconsin Historical Society Archives, Madison.

Wisconsin State Planning Board. *Attendance and Use of the State Parks, 1938 Season.* Madison, 1939.

———. *Lands for State Parks.* Bulletin, no. 17. Madison, 1946.

Writers' Program of the Work Projects Administration in the State of Wisconsin. *Wisconsin: A Guide to the Badger State.* New York: Duell, Sloan and Pearce, 1941.

Index

Abramson, Walter, 175
Ackley, Arnold, *158,* 159, 160
Adams, Jas., 47
administration of park: Beckstrom as
   superintendent, 190; Blackwood as
   superintendent, 200; conflicts
   with CCC administration, 155;
   Conservation Commission policies,
   94, 121–22; Conservation Department policies, 40–41, 110; Doolittle
   as superintendent, 40–41, 83–84, 89,
   108, 109–11, 174–79; federal control
   of park, 175; Halvorsen as superintendent, 25, 139, 190, 198–99; Hansen
   as superintendent, *xiii–xiv,* 53, 140,
   195, 196–98; Jensen as critic of park
   policies, 104–5, 192–95; Lawrence
   as superintendent, 190; Patzke as
   superintendent, 200; resource
   management issues, 94; as State
   Natural Area, 5–6; State Park Board
   policies, 85–86; wildlife management
   issues, 100–101
agriculture: Door County Farm Bureau
   programs, 97; early settlement and,
   32–34; experiment station in park, 85,
   89, 95, 96; Native American, 8;

orchards, 85, 95, 97, 120, 195;
   threshing crew pictured at farm, *33;*
   Wisconsin Land Economic Inventory
   (Bordner Survey), 12–13
airports, 40, 102, 148
Al Doolittle's Cottages souvenir map
   (c. 1930s), *xii*
Algoma Herald (newspaper), 75
Al Johnson's Swedish Restaurant (Sister
   Bay), 191
Alpine Resort (Egg Harbor), 181
Alvin Clark (shipwreck), 50
American Association of Park
   Superintendents, 66
American Folklore Theater (AFT), 201
American Park and Outdoor Art
   Association, 57
amphitheater, 108
Amundson, Anton, 50
Anderson, A., 5
Anderson, Adolph, 133
Anderson, Elmer, 127, *158,* 159
Anderson, Leslie, 127
Anderson, Lester, 99
Anderson, "Swen," 28–29
arboretum, 106
archeology, 16–18, 25, 51, 141–42

WISCONSIN LAND AND LIFE

ARNOLD ALANEN
Series Editor

A Thousand Pieces of Paradise: Landscape and Property in the Kickapoo Valley
LYNNE HEASLEY

A Mind of Her Own: Helen Connor Laird and Family, 1888–1982
HELEN L. LAIRD

Buried Indians: Digging Up the Past in a Midwestern Town
LAURIE HOVELL MCMILLIN

Wisconsin Land and Life: A Portrait of the State
EDITED BY ROBERT C. OSTERGREN AND THOMAS R. VALE

Door County's Emerald Treasure: A History of Peninsula State Park
WILLIAM H. TISHLER